ISBN 978-0-265-20650-8
PIBN 10211234

A JOURNAL

OF THE

LIFE, TRAVELS, AND CHRISTIAN EXPERIENCES

OF

THOMAS CHALKLEY,

WRITTEN BY HIMSELF.

A New Edition, detached from his Works.

"Seeing we have this ministry, as we have received mercy, we faint not;—by manifestation of the truth commending ourselves to every man's conscience in the sight of God."—2 Cor. iv. 1, 2.

LONDON:
EDWARD MARSH, FRIENDS' BOOK & TRACT DEPOSITORY,
84, HOUNDSDITCH.

1850.

LONDON:
RICHARD BARRETT, JUN., PRINTER,
MARK LANE.

CONTENTS.

CHAPTER VIII.

CHAPTER IX.

CHAPTER X.

CHAPTER XI.

THE TESTIMONY

Of the Monthly Meeting of Friends in Philadelphia, concerning our ancient and worthy Friend, Thomas Chalkley, *deceased.*

The Christian experiences of the faithful being useful to direct such as are desirous of following them in the paths of true religion and virtue, and their good examples shining with the greatest clearness, when they have, with the flesh, put off all human infirmities; justice to their memory, and a concern for the benefit of their survivors, demand our grateful remembrance of them, and the contributing our endeavours to render their labours useful to posterity.

These considerations engage us to preface the writings of this our esteemed friend and elder in the truth, with this testimony concerning him.

He was a member of our Monthly Meeting above forty years, so that some of us had opportunities of being intimately acquainted with him, and of knowing his fidelity and diligence in promoting the cause of truth, and the edification of the church of Christ; this having been the principal engagement and concern of his mind, and which he preferred to any other consideration; as will evidently appear to those, who, with an honest and unprejudiced intention, peruse his Journal of his Life and Travels.

By this it will appear, that he was, in the early part of his life, sensibly affected with the visitation of Divine life and grace, and, by adhering thereunto, was preserved from the vanities and follies, which often divert and alienate the minds of youth from the due remembrance and awful regard of their Creator; so that he was enabled to bear a testimony of Christian patience and self-denial in his youthful days, and, by keeping under that exercise, as be advanced in years, attained to further knowledge and experience in the work of religion, in which he had a sight of the necessity of keeping in a state of humility, and of bearing the cross of Christ, which mortified him to the world; so that the loss many sustain by the anxious pursuit of the lawful things thereof appearing to him, he was concerned to avoid it, and in obedience to the precept of Christ, to "seek first the kingdom of God, and his righteousness," having faith in his promise, that "all these things," necessary for him, "should be added."

Thus the love of God influencing his mind, and opening his understanding, he became concerned for the general good of mankind, and received a gift of the ministry of the gospel of Christ, before he had attained the age of twenty-one years; in the public exercise of which, he soon after travelled through many parts of England, and into Scotland, and the next year, being 1697, he came to visit Friends in this and the adjacent provinces of America, where his ministry and conversation were to the comfort and edification of the faithful; (as some of us can with satisfaction declare, from our knowledge and remembrance of him at that time;) and the near fellowship and union he then had with Friends here, we believe, contributed to his more speedy determination of settling among us, which he afterwards thought it his duty to do, though the leaving his parents and relations (as he afterwards expressed) was no small cross to him; being of a dutiful and affectionate disposition.

After fixing his residence amongst us, he persevered in his concern and labour for the edification of the churches, and gathering people to faith and dependence on the inward teachings of Christ, and for that purpose only he travelled many long journeys and voyages through the several English colonies on this continent, and most of the islands in the West Indies, and in Europe, through England, Wales, Scotland, Ireland, Holland, Friesland, and several parts of Germany, and the adjacent northern kingdoms; and in many of these places his ministry and religious labours were blessed with the desired success, of which there are yet some witnesses living, and others who were convinced of the principles of truth by his means, became serviceable members of the church, and continued therein to the end of their lives.

But as the wise king Solomon formerly observed, that "One event cometh to the righteous, and to the wicked," so it happened to this good man, who met with various losses and disappointments in his temporal estate; after which, the circumstances of his affairs engaged him to undertake some business, in the management of which he was obliged to cross the seas frequently: this, however did not abate his zeal and religious care to make use of all opportunities of visiting the meetings of Friends when among them, and of calling at other times, to such who might be accounted as the outcast of Israel, and the dispersed of Judah, or as sheep not yet of the fold of Christ; and his services of that kind are worthy to be commemorated, having been often productive of good effects.

His patience was remarkable in disappointments and afflictions, of which he had a large share; and his meekness, humility, and circumspection, in the general course of his life and conversation, were conspicuous and exemplary; and as he frequently exhorted and admonished others to the observation and practice of the many excellent precepts and rules of Christ, our Lord and lawgiver; and more especially those expressed in his Sermon on the Mount, (which contains the sum of our moral and religious duties,) so he manifested himself to be one of that number, whom Christ compared to the wise builder, who laid a sure foundation; so that his building stood unshaken by the various floods and winds of tribulations and temptations he met with, both from within and without.

He was a lover of unity amongst brethren, and careful to promote and maintain it, shewing the example of a meek, courteous, and loving deportment, not only to Friends, but to all others, with whom he had conversation or dealings; so that it may be truly said, that few have lived so universally beloved and respected among us: and it was manifest this did not proceed from a desire of being popular, or to be seen of man: for his love and regard to peace did not divert him from the discharge of his duty in a faithful testimony to those that professed the truth, that they ought to be careful to maintain good works; and he was often concerned zealously to incite and press Friends to the exercise of the good order and discipline established in the wisdom of truth, by admonishing, warning, and timely treating with such as fell short of their duty therein, and by testifying against those who, after loving and brotherly care and endeavours, could not be brought to a sense and practice of their duty; and thereby he sometimes shared the ill-will and resentment of such persons.

The several essays he wrote on religious subjects at sea, are further proofs that his mind was principally engaged in the great business and concern of religion; and as he continued under the same engagement to the end, we are fully persuaded the words, with which he concluded his last public testimony on the island of Tortola, may be truly and properly applied to him, that he had "fought a good fight, and had kept the faith," and, we doubt not, he now enjoys a "crown of righteousness."

Much more might be truly said of his integrity,

faithfulness and worth, but we do not think it necessary; our chief intention being to express our respectful remembrance of him, and our unity with his labours and services, and in order to assure those, to whom he was not personally known, of the truth of what he has himself wrote of his life and travels; for we believe, as he was a man signally influenced with the spirit of universal love and good-will to mankind, this was his chief motive for writing; and we are sincerely desirous that his good design may be answered, and that the glory of every good and perfect work may be attributed to that Divine power alone, which can qualify others to supply the places of those faithful ministers and servants of Christ, who have been of late years removed from among us, and are of that number, of whom it is written, "Blessed are the dead, which die in the Lord, from henceforth, yea, saith the Spirit, that they may rest from their labours, and their works do follow them."

Signed on behalf, and by appointment of the Monthly Meeting of Friend sin Philadelphia, the twenty-eighth day of the Second Month, 1749, by

ISRAEL PEMBERTON.

A JOURNAL, &c.

CHAPTER I.

1675–1699.

BIRTH—EDUCATION—EARLY RELIGIOUS IMPRESSIONS—CALL TO THE MINISTRY—VISIT TO FRIENDS IN SOME PARTS OF GREAT BRITAIN—AND TO FRIENDS IN AMERICA—RETURN TO ENGLAND.

Having great cause to acknowledge the regard and protection of Divine Providence in the several stages of my life, I think it may be of service to others, to leave behind me the following account of my life and travels:

I WAS born on the third day of the Third Month, 1675, in Southwark, and descended of honest and religions parents, who were very careful of me, and brought me up in the fear of the Lord; and oftentimes counselled me to sobriety, and reproved me for wantonness; and that light spirit, which is incident to youth, they were careful to nip in the bud: so that I have cause to bless God, through Christ, on the behalf of my tender parents.

And I may not forget the dealings of God with me in my very tender years. When between eight and ten years of age, my father and mother sent me near two miles to school, to Richard Scoryer, in the suburbs of London. I went mostly by myself to the school; and many and various were the exercises I went through, by beatings and stonings along the streets, being distinguished to the people, (by the badge of plainness which my parents put upon me,) of what profession I was; divers telling me, it was no more sin to kill me, than it was to kill a dog.

About this time the Lord began to work strongly on my mind by his grace, insomuch that I could not forbear reproving those lads who would take the name of the Lord God in their mouths in vain; reminding them of the third commandment, "Thou shalt not take the name of the Lord thy God in vain; for the Lord will not hold him guiltless that taketh his name in vain;" and of Christ's saying, "Every idle word that men shall speak, they shall give account thereof in the day of judgment;" for which I was mocked and derided by some, and others would sometimes refrain from such bad words when I reproved them.

One time I remember I was amongst some men, one of whom I had reproved, and he told the rest of it, and turned to me, and said, that I was no Christian, and asked me when I said the Lord's prayer; I asked him, if he said it; he said, yes. I then asked him how he could call God Father, and be so wicked as to swear and take God's name in vain, which I had heard him often do; and I told him what Christ said to the Jews, "You are of your father the devil, because his works ye do;" and that those that did the devil's work, could not truly call God Father, according to Christ's doctrine. So being convicted in their consciences that what I said was true, they were all silent, and wondered that I, being so young, should speak in such a manner; in which I remember I had great peace and good satisfaction: and from thenceforth these men let me alone.

Notwithstanding I hated to hear wicked words, I loved play exceedingly, being persuaded that there was no harm in that, if we used no bad words. One time I was at play at a neighbour's house with the children, and in the midst of my sport I was reached to with strong convictions, insomuch that I could not forbear weeping. The children's mother observing that I wept, said, "Why do you weep, Tommy?" I told her I could not tell, except it was because I was a naughty boy. "Oh!" said she, "do not believe him, for that is the devil tells you so, for you are the best boy in all our street." But I knew I was told the truth by conviction, and that she was mistaken: for I plainly understood by clear conviction, and by the Holy Scriptures, (which I had been trained up in the reading of,) that I was too vain and wanton; for I loved music, dancing, and playing at cards, and too much delighted therein betimes, and was followed with the judgments of God therefore in the secret of my soul.

What I did in those sports and games, I always took care to do out of the sight, and without the knowledge of my tender parents; for I was afraid of their reproofs and correction, the which I was sure to have, if they had any intelligence of it.

I remember that, unknown to my parents, I had

bought a pack of cards, with intent to make use of them when I went to see my relations in the country, where there was liberty in the family so to do, at a place called Woodford, about seven miles from London, where I got leave sometimes to go; and at the time called Christmas I went to see them, and five miles on my way went to a meeting, at a town called Wanstead; at which meeting a minister of Christ declared against the evil of gaming, and particularly of cards; and that the time which people pretend to keep holy for Christ's sake, many of them spend mostly in wickedness, sports, and games; even some pretending to be religious: and, generally speaking, more sin and evil is committed in this time than in the like space of time in all the year besides; so that the devil is served instead of honouring Christ. From this meeting at Wanstead, I went to the house of my relations, where the parson of the next parish lodged that night, who used to play at cards with them sometimes; and the time drawing near that we were to go to our games, my uncle called to the doctor, (as he called him,) to me, and to my cousin, to come and take a game at cards; at which motion I had strong convictions upon me not to do it, as being evil, and I secretly cried to the Lord to keep me faithful to him; and lifting up my eyes, I saw a bible lie in the window, at the sight of which I was glad. I took it, and sat down and read to myself, greatly rejoicing that I was preserved out of the snare. Then my uncle called again, and said, "Come doctor, you and I and my wife and daughter will have a game at cards, for I see my cousin is better disposed." Then he looked upon me, and said he was better disposed also. So their sport for that time was spoiled, and mine in that practice for ever; for I never (as I remember) played with them more, but as soon as I came home, offered my new and untouched pack of cards to the fire; and of this I am certain, the use of them is of evil consequence, and draws away the mind from heaven and heavenly things; for which reason all Christians ought to shun them as engines of Satan: and music and dancing having generally the same tendency, ought therefore to be refrained from. The sentiments of the Waldenses, a people in great esteem among Protestants, are worthy the consideration of all true Protestants and Christians; which were, "That as many paces or steps, as the man or woman takes in the dance, so many paces or steps they take towards hell."

I very well remember the work of God upon my soul, when I was about ten years of age, and particularly at a certain time when I had been rebelling against God and my parents, in vanity and lightness: and as I offended both, so I was corrected by both: for I had not only the anger of my parents, but the Lord frowned upon me, insomuch that I trembled exceedingly, and was as though I heard a vocal voice say to me, "What will become of thee this night if I should take thy life from thee?" at which I was amazed and in great fear. Then I covenanted with God, that if he would be pleased to spare my life, (for I thought God would have taken my life from me that very moment,) I would be more sober, and mind his fear more than I had done before.

Nevertheless I broke covenant with God my maker, my adversary tempting me so to do, telling me I was but a child, and that it was natural for children to be brisk and to play, and that God would wink at my childhood and youth, and it was time enough for me when a man, to become religious. But still God followed me with his chastising rod, and often put me in mind of my covenant that I made with him in my distress; and that he had granted my request which I then made to him; and unless I would take up a cross to my own corrupt will and inclinations, he should take me out of the world. Then, oh then! I cried "Lord, help, or I die! save me, or I perish for ever! I cannot keep thy covenant nor do thy will, without thy help and assistance!" and indeed if the Lord had not helped, I had been undone for ever.

So I continued bowed down in my mind, calling on the Lord; thinking and meditating on heaven and heavenly things; but, as I am sensible, I had an inward enemy that always sought my hurt and overthrow, I have cause to bless God, who by his grace (as mine eye was turned to it) helped me to do his will, as he was pleased to manifest it to me, so that thereby some change was wrought on me, both inwardly and outwardly.

And I then began to delight in reading and sobriety, which before were irksome to me: and when I read the Holy Scriptures, I desired that God would open them to my understanding, which he did to my edification many times. I also begged earnestly of the Lord, that he would be pleased to be with me, and make me like to those his children and servants, of whom I read in the Holy Scriptures, who faithfully served him all their days. And when I read of the crucifixion of our blessed Lord and Saviour Jesus Christ, it would break my soul into tenderness. I thought it was enough to awaken and humble any soul that was well-meaning, and had any sense of the power, love, and grace of Christ. Thus I went on for several years, feeling that peace which passeth natural understanding, which many times accompanied my poor and needy soul: and being advanced to about fourteen or fifteen years of age, I remember that I used to shun the cross of speaking in the plain language (which I always read in the Holy Scriptures) to those whom I conversed with, except my father and mother, who would not allow me to speak otherwise. I was convicted in my conscience that it was not right to play the hypocrite after that manner; and on a certain time I had occasion to speak with an officer, a great man in our neighbourhood, and my heart moved within me for fear I should shun the cross of Christ; (for it was Christ's language to all, as we may read in the New Testament; and the Scriptures, from Genesis to the Revelations, speak thee and thou, to a single person in a general way.) So I took up the cross, and said "thee" to him; and he was much affronted, and said, "Thee! what dost thou thee me for?" I soberly asked him, if he did not say thee to his Maker in prayers? and whether he was too good, or too great, to be spoken to in the same language in which he addressed the Almighty? unto which he made no reply, but seemed to fall from his passion into admiration, as one smitten in himself; and he bore me respect ever after; and I greatly rejoiced that I was preserved faithful. Though it may look like a little thing to some, yet I found it good (as the Scripture saith) not to despise the day of small things.

About the twentieth year of my age, I was pressed and carried on board a vessel belonging to a man of war. I was put down into the hold in the dark, not having any thing to lie upon but casks; and what made it worse to me, I was among wicked, debauched men; and as we were shut up in darkness, so was their conversation dark and hellish. In the morning, (for which I longed more than the watchmen,) the lieutenant called us up on deck, and examined us, whether we were willing to serve the king; he called me to him, and asked me if I were willing to serve his majesty; I answered, that I was willing to serve him in any business, and according to my conscience; but as for war or fighting, Christ had forbid it in his excellent sermon on the mount, and for that reason I could not bear arms, nor be instrumental to destroy or kill men. The lieutenant looked on me and on the people, and said, "Gentlemen, what shall we do with this fellow? he swears he will not fight." The commander of the vessel made answer, "No, no, he will neither swear nor fight." Upon which they turned me on shore. I was thankful that I was delivered out of their hands; and my tender parents were glad to see me again.

Now as I grew in years, the world began to take too much root in me, and my unwearied enemy would tell me that it was lawful enough, (and indeed I see that he hurts many with lawful things, with whom he knoweth the unlawful things will not take;) and here I had been lost if God had not been gracious to me. But he, in whose presence I delighted, withdrew, and deprived me of that enjoyment which was comfortable above all things to my soul. Then did I pray, with tears, O that it might be with me, as it was at other times before! and I was willing to let the world go, rather than grace and God's glory.

The Psalmist saith, "No good thing will he withhold from them that walk uprightly." Psalm lxxxiv. 11.

About this time there was a great concern on my mind, rightly to distinguish between the voice of Christ, and the whisperings of Satan; and thus it opened to me: that Christ, the Truth, always speaketh good, and for a good end, and that there is Divine life to the soul in this speaking; but the devil never speaks good, unless sometimes for a bad end, and then not good in reality, only coloured with a good or fair shew.

And keeping under this exercise, the Lord appeared to me again, and many times refreshed my heart with his goodness. And when I was in my business amongst men, I did witness the Holy Ghost, the Comforter, to be near me; which was more to me than all the world, or the riches, glory, and beauty of it; the love of God being so sweet to my soul and spirit, my breathings, prayers, and supplications, were to the Lord, that my neighbours, acquaintance, and relations, might also partake of the like precious faith and love which I enjoyed; and that the children of men might answer that great and good end for which the Lord did create them; which is, that glory, honour, and praise, might ascend and be given to him.

I had such a sense and fear of dishonouring God, that I often, with tears, cried, "Never let me live to dishonour thee. Oh! it had been better for me that I had never been born, or my mother's womb had been my grave, than that I should live to dishonour thee, or wilfully reproach the name of Christ, who, with the Father, is only worthy of Divine honour."

In this concern I felt the gospel power of our Lord Jesus Christ to work upon my soul, and the word of God was as a seed in my heart, growing and opening in me, speaking to me, and making my understanding fruitful in the things of his kingdom; and in that ability which was given me of God, through his grace and Holy Spirit, I exhorted people to repentance and amendment of life; and I always humbly desired the help and divine influence of God's eternal Word therein. Oh! I did fervently pray, that I might minister the gospel in the power of Jesus; for I clearly discerned, in the light of the Son of God, that all ministering out of Christ's power, was neither edifying nor efficacious unto souls: therefore I did earnestly beseech God for the continuance of the gift of his Spirit, that I might be enabled to preach the gospel in the power of Christ Jesus. The concern that was upon me on this account at that time, is hard to be expressed in words.

The latter end of the year 1695, my father sent me into Essex on some business, which, when I had accomplished, I visited some meetings of Friends there, and my mind being much affected with the apprehension of an impending storm, (the nation being about this time threatened with an invasion from France, in favour of the late king James, so that there was expectation of much bloodshed and confusion in the land,) I wrote a letter to my parents, and another to Friends of the evening meeting, (kept weekly at my father's house,) expressing my great thankfulness to the Almighty, in remembrance of the many precious visitations of Divine love and favour we had been made partakers of, to the uniting our hearts to him, and to one another; and my earnest prayers and supplications, that we might be preserved in true love, and the unity of the Spirit, which is the bond of everlasting peace; and that the world might be made sensible of this true peace, which abounds in those who love and fear the Lord, and truly believe in the name of Jesus. Oh! surely they would then depart from sin, and abandon iniquity, by which they incur the wrath of the Lord, and provoke the Just One to anger; so that the line of confusion seems to be stretched over the city and nation, and the eye of the faithful seeth it to the grief of their souls. Yet the mercy of the Lord, even of the just God (who will render a just reward to every one according to his deeds done in the body) is still handed forth to the land. Oh! that the inhabitants thereof would consider their ways, and be wise, and turn to the Lord with unfeigned repentance, while the day of mercy lasteth, before it be said, "Now it is hid from thine eyes," for the Lord, even the God and Father of spirits, hath said, "My Spirit shall not always strive with man, for that he also is flesh." Gen. vi. 3.

On the expiration of my apprenticeship, having served my father faithfully seven years, I entered more strongly into covenant with my heavenly Father and Master, to serve him all my days, through his assistance: and was soon after drawn forth, in the Spirit and love of Christ, to visit the meetings of Friends westward from London, viz. through Surrey, Sussex, Hampshire, Wiltshire, Devonshire, and Cornwall, to the Land's End; in which journey I was accompanied by William Hernould. At one of our meetings at Falmouth, in Cornwall, two men (called gentlemen) came from the inn to hear the strangers;

and after meeting, they said they could take their oaths that I was a Jesuit, and that they had heard me preach in a Romish chapel in France; which was utterly false, for I never was in France in my life. Besides, had I been a Papist, or popishly inclined, (which I was not,) I was too young to be a Jesuit.

Indeed I thought I was mean for the work of the ministry, but the good Remembrancer brought those truths to my remembrance, which strengthened me in the work and service of God. The spirit breatheth where it listeth. Out of the mouths of babes and sucklings thou hast perfected praise, &c. We having great peace in our labours in this journey, and being edified therewith, returned to London, after about four months' absence from home.

And after I had been two weeks at home, my dear mother departed this life, in a sweet frame of spirit, praising the Lord. She was one who lived the life of the righteous, and whose latter end was like theirs, and left a good report behind her, being well beloved (I think I may safely say) by all our neighbours; not only by those of our own society, but others also, to whom she was often very helpful.

So I went to my calling, and got a little money, (a little being enough,) which I was made willing to spend freely, in the work and service of my great Master Christ Jesus. And about this time I was concerned to travel into the north of England, and part of Scotland, which I did in that ability God gave me; and that dispensation which I had freely received, I freely handed forth to the people, devoting my strength and time to serve Him, (that had done so much for me,) and I had the satisfaction to find divers confessing the truth, as it is in Jesus. In this journey I was from home about four months, being mostly alone as to any yoke-fellow in that work, travelling many hundreds of miles, being as far as Edinburgh in Scotland, where our meeting was in the street, we being locked out of our meeting-house by the then power, and great numbers of people were there. This news being carried to the Provost of the city, he said, "The Quakers would do more hurt out of doors, than within," and he ordered Friends their key. Since which I have understood that Friends in that city have enjoyed their meetings in the meeting-house; and sometimes when the rabble have disturbed Friends, the magistrates have sent officers to disperse them.

Now after I had visited the churches of Christ in divers parts of England, and had many sweet seasons of God's love, and good opportunities with my friends and others in this nation; (the word of life being declared in the simplicity of the gospel—in several places people were very open-hearted, and received the testimony of it with gladness;) and after I had been at my father's, and at my calling, a little after this north-country journey, I found myself engaged in the love of the gospel to visit Friends in America; and having acquainted my friends and relations with my mind, they being willing to give me up in order for the voyage, Friends of the Monthly Meeting gave me a certificate, and I had another from the meeting of ministers in London.

My father, and several other friends with me, took boat from London, and accompanied me to Gravesend, on the 21st of the Tenth Month, 1697, and I went on board the ship *Josiah*, Thomas Lurting master, and sailed that day from Gravesend, and got to the Downs the next day, where we tarried some days for a fair wind; in which time several others, that were concerned in the same gospel-labour, came on board, viz. Thomas Turner, William Ellis, and Aaron Atkinson. In about four days' time the wind was fair for us, and we set sail, and in a little time we got out of sight of the land; soon after which the wind was contrary, and we proceeded but a small distance for several weeks; the weather was rough and the sea boisterous, so that with the motion thereof, most of the passengers were sick. In this time we lost a lad, that fell into the sea, as he was drawing a bucket of water, and was drowned; the ship running swiftly, he could not be saved, although it was speedily endeavoured. Several others died before we got over; but for the most part we were healthful. The Lord be praised! he was, is, and will be with those that faithfully serve him to the end.

We were three ships in company, but by distress of weather, soon after we came out, we parted. After we had been at sea about eight weeks, on the 25th of the Twelfth Month we saw two vessels astern of us One of them came up with us, and the people hailed us, and told us they came from Bristol, and had been out ten weeks. The other came up with us next day. The people informed us they had been at sea seven weeks, and that they had a dreadful time of it. She had lost part of her topmast, and her spritsail topmast was gone. She was a new ship, and never at sea before, belonging to London, and bound for Virginia, as near as we could understand. Our ship lost none of her tackling, through the great mercy of God to us, though the wind and sea was wonderfully high at times: the mate told me, I might go to sea all my life, and not see the like; he said he had been at, or used the sea twenty years, and never saw it so rough and high before. We had meetings twice a week, several of which were comfortable and refreshing meetings, to which most of the passengers, being in all about sixty in number, sometimes came; and several of them were affected with the sense of truth, and the Lord strengthened our faith and hope in him.

Oh! for ever blessed be the living and eternal God, who kept my soul above the fear of death, hell, and the grave; for my trust was in him, and he did bear up my spirit above the waves of the sea; and in the times of tossing with tempests, I was comforted and cheerful, praising the Lord in my heart, both in the day time, and in the night season.

I was much concerned in my mind for many of the passengers, who, with the second mate, and several of the seamen, were very sick, (by some it was thought near unto death:) I cried to the Lord to heal them, in the name of his dear Son, and that it might be a means to convince them of the efficacy of love to, and faith in Christ Jesus, the physician of value; and the Lord was pleased to heal them. The mate of the ship desired that I would come and pray by him. I went to him, and prayed in the power and name of the Lord Jesus Christ, and the Lord helped him, that he said he was fine and easy, and thanked me for my love; and in a little time he recovered. Several others of the seamen and passengers I was instrumental to help in their sickness. The Lord blessed my endeavours in supplicating him on their behalf, and administering what I had to them. One of the seamen said, he was bound to pray for me as long as he lived, and that the Lord would bless me. Another of the passengers said, that I was the blessed doctor, (for there was not a surgeon or doctor in the ship.) I was very free to communicate of what I had to any sick person in the ship, and several blessed the Lord on my behalf. Indeed I thought I could scarce do enough for any that were in distress. I write not thus, that I might seem popular, but with my mind bowed before the Lord. Many times in this voyage there were consultations in my mind, whether I had best write a memorandum hereof; but at last conceiving in my spirit that it might strengthen and excite love to God, and faith in his beloved Son, in true believers, I wrote as aforesaid; and then I was satisfied, and gave the glory to God.

Before we came to the land, we saw a ketch which had saved the lives of some that belonged to a ship that was a little before foundered in the sea; who said also, that a fleet of New-England ships which had been upon that coast, by stormy weather were forced to Barbadoes; and within a few days after he saw the land of Virginia, and also a New-England ship, which sailed or came from England three weeks before us. We arrived within the Capes of Virginia the 31st of the First Month, 1698, and overtook the *John and Margaret*, a ship that came out of the English channel with us, (the master, Thomas Salmon, being dead,) and the next day we anchored our ship at the mouth of Patuxent River in Maryland, where our boats were hoisted out, and we were rowed up Patuxent River twelve miles, to Arthur Young's house, where we lodged that night; and for our preservation and safe arrival, we bless the Lord our God, and my spirit praised him who lives for ever and ever. Our voyage was about twelve weeks, it being then winter time, and for the most part the winds so high, that the ships could carry but little sail, which made our voyage the longer.

About four days after we landed, we had a meeting near Patuxent River, and a blessed one it was. When it was ended, we went to Daniel Rawling's, and from thence to the Clifts, to Richard John's, a friend that came with us from England, at whose house we had a meeting, wherein God's presence was powerfully felt. We had several meetings on that side the bay called the Western Shore, and then we sailed over to the east side of Chesapeak Bay, with Thomas Everden, in his sloop; went to his house, and had a meeting, where many people came. Here we met with our friends Jonathan Tyler, Henry Payton, and Henry Payton's sister. While I was at this Friend's house, there was one Robert Cathing, who being very ill, sent for Thomas Everden, and he (not being very well) desired me to visit the sick person. So I went, and the man was near to death. Howbeit he said he was comforted much with the visit, and that he never had received so much benefit by the parish priest in his life: "Although," said he, "it cost me dear for what I had; and if ever I live to get over it, by the assistance of God I shall have nothing to do with them more." But, he said, he should not live three days. And before the end of three days he expired. He desired, if I were not gone, I would be at his funeral. On notice hereof, about ten Friends went; and there was a great many people, among whom we had a good opportunity, and many weighty truths were opened to them in the love of God; and some of them were tender and wept; and the most, if not all (I think I may say) were solid and weighty.

From Thomas Everden's house we went to George Truit's, at whose house we had a meeting: this Friend and I went to an Indian town not far from his house, because I had a desire to see these people, having never seen any of them before. When we came to the town they were kind to us, spoke well of Friends, and said they would not cheat them (as some others did.)

From George Truit's, in Maryland, we went down to Virginia; and in Accomack and Northampton counties we had large meetings, and I hope they were effectual to many: I think my hope is not without ground. In those parts we had several meetings, where we were informed Friends had not had any before. And really I cannot but bless the Lord for the opportunities we had with the people; for the goodness of God, through Christ our Lord, was great, both to us and them, and with tears they did acknowledge the truth. Now Thomas Turner who had hitherto accompanied me, went by the sea-side the nearest way to Philadelphia; and afterwards I had a meeting at George Truit's brother's, and on the First-day, another near the court-house, and went to Thomas Everden's, and so to Levin Denwood's, and thence to Nanticoke River, and visited Friends up the bay until I came to the river Choptank, about which there is a pretty many Friends. So I went on, and took the meetings till I came to Philadelphia, in and about which place, and in other parts of the province of Pennsylvania, I had many large and precious meetings, the power of the Eternal Son of God being wonderful; in which power we many times blessed his name together. It was in my heart much to exhort Friends to love to God, and to unity one with another, without which there is no fulfilling the law or gospel. There are many Friends in that province, and many sober young people, which greatly rejoiced my spirit; so that for their encouragement, the Lord opened my mouth in a prophetic manner to declare unto them the blessings which he had in store for them, on condition of their walking in the truth. Glory to God on high! untruth decays, and the branches of it mightily wither; the darkness is much past, and the true light shineth gloriously in many souls. O! powerful praises be given to God, who is light for ever.

From Philadelphia I went to Burlington, and so to Croswicks, where we had a large meeting under the trees, where some were convinced of the truth. From hence I went to Shrewsbury, and had meetings there. From Shrewsbury we went, mostly by water, to Woodbridge and Staten-Island, from thence to Long-Island, being accompanied by several Friends. On Long-Island we had several large and good meetings, wherein Christ was preached freely; and after we had been two weeks there, we went on board a sloop bound for Rhode-Island, and by the way we touched at Fisher's and Block Islands, and on the First-day morning we set sail from Block-Island to Rhode-Island, the Yearly Meeting being just over when we got there. That evening we sailed over to Connanicut-Island. On the Third-day of the week had a meeting there, and from thence we went over to Narraganset, and had a meeting, and so over to Rhode-Island again; where Ruth Fry, a sober young woman, was convinced, and remained a Friend till her death. Here I met with several travelling Friends.

From the island we went over to the main, and had a large meeting on First-day, at a place called Greenwich. It was thought there were about five hundred people, and many of them were tender. We went over the same night to the island, and after several open times with Friends and others on Rhode-Island, about twelve Friends of that island went with me to Warwick and Providence Yearly Meetings, in our friend Borden's boat. We set sail about noon, and having but little wind, it was late in the night before we got there, and very dark, insomuch that we could neither see nor know one another, but only by our speech, and the darkness occasioned us to run our vessel against the rocks; but at last we got on shore (with our horses) and after going over a very dirty slough, we entered a dismal wilderness, so that these difficulties occasioned our not getting to the Friend's house until the next day, on which, being the last in the week, we had a meeting; and on the First-day we had a large and satisfactory meeting. Many of us were so united in the love of God, that it was hard for us to part one from another.

From Providence I went to Boston and Salem, where I had meetings, and from thence to Hampton. In those parts God Almighty hath shortened the power of persecutors, and hath brought his righteous judgments upon them for their unrighteousness. Oh! that New England's professors might live in the sense of the same, and repent. I being a stranger and traveller, could not but observe the barbarous and unchristianlike welcome I had into Boston, the metropolis of New England. "Oh! what pity," said one, "it was that all of your society were not hanged with the other four."* In the eastern part of New England, God hath a seed left of his people.

From thence I returned in order to get a passage to the isle of Nantucket; and from a place called Cushnet, we sailed over to the said island in about ten hours, where we tarried several days, and had five meetings. The people did generally acknowledge to the truth, and many of them were tender-hearted. Some of the ancient people said, that it was never known that so many people were together on the island at once. After the first meeting was over, one asked the minister (so called) whether we might have a meeting at his house; he said, with a good will, we might. This minister had some discourse with me, and asked what induced me to come thither, being such a young man. I told him that I had no other view in coming there, than the good of souls, and that I could say with the apostle, that a necessity was laid upon me, and woe would be to me if I did not preach the gospel. "Then," said he, "I wish you would preach at my house in God's name." So next day we had a meeting at his house; and on the First-day we had the largest meeting that we had on the island. It was thought there were about two hundred people. The Lord in his power did make his truth known to the praise of his name. Oh! how was my soul concerned for that people! the Lord Jesus did open my heart to them, and theirs to him: they were also loving and kind to us. The chief magistrate of the island desired that I would have a meeting at his house, there being no settled

* Marmaduke Stephenson, William Robinson, Mary Dyer, and William Leddra, who were put to death in 1659 and 1660.

meeting of Friends before I came; and after meeting he disputed about religion with me. I thought we were both but poor disputants; and I cannot remember all that passed between us, but that, in the close of our dispute, he said, "I disputed with your Friends in Barbadoes, and they told me, That we must eat the spiritual flesh, and drink the spiritual blood of Christ: and," said the governor, "Did ever any one hear of such flesh and blood; for is it not a contradiction in nature, that flesh and blood should be spiritual?" "O, surely," said I, "the governor hath forgot himself; for what flesh and blood was that which Christ said, 'Except ye eat my flesh, and drink my blood, ye have no life in you.'" "Why," said he, "I do not think they were to gnaw it from his arms and shoulders." Then I told him he had answered himself. Thus our dispute ended. And from that time forward they have continued a meeting, and there is now a meeting house, and a Yearly Meeting for worship; it is a growing meeting to this day, and several public Friends are raised up among them, who preach the gospel of Christ freely.

At this time a Friend was convinced, whose name was Starbuck, who became very serviceable, and lived and died an eminent minister of Christ on that island. Several scores of them came and accompanied us to the water-side; and when we embarked on board our sloop, they desired that I would come and visit them again. So I recommended them to the grace of our Lord Jesus, and we parted in great love and tenderness. In the evening of the next day we got to the main land, where we were gladly received. Now it was in my heart again to visit the eastern parts of New-England before I left America; therefore I went to Boston Yearly Meeting, thence to Lynn and Salem, where we had a sweet comfortable time; likewise to the Yearly Meeting at Dover, and so to Piscataway, where we had several meetings, which were profitable opportunities to many. From Piscataway, James Goodbridge and I went over to the Isle of Shoals; we had with us a church member of the Presbyterians, whose brother invited her over with us to the said island, to the meeting which was at his house; and while he was talking with her in the yard or garden, I saw a bible, and took it, and read therein. When she came into the house she asked me what I did with that book; I told her if she was offended I would lay it down. "No, no,' saids he, "do not think to come off so, for you disown or deny that book." I told her she was mistaken, and asked, Who told her so. "Why," said she, "our minister in his pulpit." I replied, that it was a great abuse upon us, for I had been trained up from my childhood in the reading and belief of the scriptures, and my father and mother were Friends (that is Quakers). She willing to try me further, said, "Did your father and mother suffer you to read the bible when you were a little boy?" "Yes," said I, 'and gave me correction when I was not so willing to read therein as they would have me." "Then," said she, "our minister has belied you; and since you say so, if it please God, I will go and hear you." She went with us to meeting, and after it was over, going home, one asked her, how she would answer it to their minister, for going to meeting; she replied, it was truth she had heard, and she would stand by it through the grace of Christ, and need not be ashamed of it (though we are of ourselves but poor weak creatures.) This woman was sober and religious, and one of good report. By the foregoing we may see how slanders flow from some pulpits; the more is the shame and pity. We went on and preached the gospel of our Lord Jesus Christ in that ability he gave us, with which the people were affected, and would have had us tarry longer, but we could not, (although they much importuned us,) because we had appointed a meeting at Oyster River. After we had had several meetings about Piscataway and Dover, we went to Hampton, where we had meetings; and at Salisbury we had a large open meeting, as it was supposed, of about three hundred people, (which was at this time accounted a great concourse of people thereabouts;) also at Jamaica and Haverill we had meetings, and from thence went to Salem and Lynn again, where we had good service for truth; and then to Boston, and had a meeting at the meeting-house, and another at a Friend's house in the evening, at which there were many people. From Boston I went to visit Friends about Cape Cod, till I came again to Rhode Island. By the way I met with Aaron Atkinson, who was on a visit to Friends in New England. I had several good opportunities, and powerful meetings, in those parts, and truth wrought a tenderness in divers at Rhode Island. The presence of Him who said, "Where two or three are gathered together in my name, there am I in the midst of them," being sensibly witnessed by many; for he was with us of a truth. From thence I went round the Narraganset country, and had meetings at several places, and was accompanied by John Rodman and William Beackley, through Connecticut to Long Island, which is accounted two hundred miles. We had one meeting by the way, in which Christ was preached to them, as he is the light of the world, at a place where we were told there never was a Friends' meeting before. I came to Long Island about two weeks before the general meeting, and visited Friends in several places on this island, as at Hampstead, Jerusalem, Jericho and Bethphage, where there were large meetings, and much openness among the people, and some were convinced. We had a meeting at a place called Matinicock, where I met with some of the people called Ranters, who disturbed our meeting. I may say as the apostle Paul (only altering Ephesus to Matinicock) that I fought with beasts there; and thence I travelled to New York, where we had two meetings; from thence we went to the Jerseys, and there we had several serviceable meetings that were large; and so to Pennsylvania, where there are many very large meetings of Friends, and the Lord is with his people there, and prospereth them spiritually and temporally. Here I met with my dear friend, William Ellis. From Philadelphia, Richard Gove (of that city) and I travelled to Maryland, and visited Friends on the western shore, and from thence to Virginia. In Virginia, near James river, I met with an aged Friend whose name was William Porter. He was ninety-two years of age; and had then a daughter two years old.* We had several meetings there amongst Friends and

* Some years after I saw him, and he was weeding Indian corn with a hoe. He was then about 106 years of age, and had upwards of seventy children, grand-children, and great grand-children. We went divers friends of us to see him, and he preached to us a short, but very affecting sermon, which was (as near as I remember) verbatim thus, "Friends, you are come to se .

others, many being well satisfied concerning the truth, and spoke well of it.

And after we had had several good and open meetings in Virginia, we found ourselves clear of America, and in order for our passage, we agreed with our friend F. Johnson, on board the *Elizabeth and Mary*, to carry us for England.

On the 11th of the First Month 1698-9, we were accompanied on board by several Friends, who abode with us all night; and the next day, being the first day of the week, we had a little comfortable meeting, and then parted in much love, having the evidence of the power of the Almighty with us. We waited for a fair wind until the 20th of the aforesaid month, and left the Capes of Virginia that day, and at night we got our ship into a sailing posture; and I was glad in my spirit, that I was setting my face towards my native land; and more glad, that I was returning with peace in my bosom. Oh! the power and presence of Him who said, "Go, teach all nations," was sweet to my soul at that time, and now in some measure I enjoyed the fruits of my having laboured in that ability God had given me. Glory to God, through Christ, who is worthy for ever! the presence of God was with us on the great ocean, and we were strengthened through his goodness wonderfully. We had several good meetings on board our ship, and were opened in the love of God to the poor seamen very largely.

When we launched forth into the deep, we were

me in the love of God. God is love, and those that dwell in God dwell in love. I thank God, I feel his divine life every day and every night." He lived to see his above mentioned daughter married, and died, aged 107 years.

several ships in company; but we had been but a little time at sea, before we lost sight of them all. Several ships passed by us about a week after we sailed; and about this time we saw a very large whale, who lifted himself part out of the water with his mouth open, which looked like the entrance of a large cave. We likewise saw several other large sea-fish, such as grampusses, sharks, &c. All which shew forth the wondrous works of the Great Creator of all things. Elizabeth Webb and Elizabeth Lloyd went over with us in this vessel, both virtuous women. About two weeks the winds were mostly fair for us, in which time we got finely on our way; but for above a week afterwards the winds were mostly contrary, and the ship had a great motion, which caused some of us to be sea-sick, especially Elizabeth Lloyd,* who was but weakly. One night our sailors thought that an enemy or pirate was near us, who fired two guns, and so passed by us; but it being night, we could not certainly know what she was. I rather judged it might be some ship in distress, for we saw one of the ships that evening that came out with us, and the next morning we could see none at all, and there was hardly any wind that night, so I feared that our companions had sprung a leak and foundered; and when I told our master my opinion, he said, he feared the same likewise. Now for two weeks time, or thereabouts, we beat about

* She was the daughter of Thomas Lloyd, late deputy governor of Pennsylvania. She lived and died a virtuous woman; and, I think, generally beloved by all who were acquainted with her. When she died she was the wife of Daniel Zachary, a merchant at Boston, New England, well known, and much beloved there for his piety and virtue.

the sea, and made little progress. Howbeit we had several good meetings, wherein we gave glory to God our Saviour; and for ever let it ascend, saith my soul, to him over all! After 'contrary winds about two weeks, the wind sprung up westerly, and was fair for several days; in which time we got finely on our way again, and left the Western Islands about two days sail behind us; and then the wind was contrary again. Contrary winds are commonly tedious at sea, (especially to those that know not where to stay their minds,) but we being several Friends of us on board that were passengers, had oftentimes good meetings several times a week; and if any of our ship's company came to meeting, they always were sober, and sometimes tender; and truly, God's love was extended towards them. And when it was not our meeting days, we spent not our time idly, but for the most part in reading the Holy Scriptures, and writing, &c. in which we were at sundry seasons greatly refreshed, strengthened, and comforted. O my soul! glorify God thy Maker, and Christ thy Saviour for ever, in the sense of his goodness and mercy, both by sea and land, by night and by day! After we had been almost seven weeks at sea, we thought that we were near the land, but we sounded several days, and found no bottom, although we let out abundance of line, I think above 300 yards.

About this time our doctor dreamed a dream, which was to this effect, himself relating it to me: He said, he dreamed that he went on shore at a great and spacious town, the buildings whereof were high, and the streets broad; and as he went up the street he saw a large sign, on which was written in great golden letters SHAME. At the door of the house (to which the sign belonged) stood a woman with a can in her hand, who said unto him, "Doctor, will you drink?" he replied, "With all my heart, I have not drank any thing but water a great while," (our wine and cyder being all spent, having had a long passage,) and he drank a hearty draught, which he said, made him merry; so went up the street reeling to and fro, when a grim fellow coming behind him, clapped him on the shoulder, and told him, that he arrested him in the name of the governor of the place. He asked him for what, and said, "What have I done?" he answered, "For stealing the woman's can." The can he had indeed, and so he was had before the governor, which was a mighty black dog, the biggest and grimmest that ever he saw in his life; and witness was brought in against him by an old companion of his, and he was found guilty, and his sentence was to go to prison, and there to lie for ever.

He told me this dream so punctually, and with such an emphasis, that it affected me with serious sadness, and caused my heart to move within me, for to me the dream seemed true, and the interpretation sure. I then told him he was an ingenious man, and might clearly see the interpretation of that dream, which exactly answered to his state and condition, which I thus interpreted to him: "This great and spacious place, wherein the buildings were high and the streets broad, is thy great and high profession: the sign, on which was wrote SHAME, which thou sawest, and the woman at the door, with the can in her hand, truly represents that great, crying, and shameful sin of drunkenness, which thou knowest to be thy great weakness; which the woman with the can did truly represent to thee: the grim fellow which arrested thee in the devil's territories, is death, who will assuredly arrest all mortals: the governor which thou sawest, representing a great black dog, is certainly the devil, who, after his servants have served him to the full, will torment them eternally in hell." So he got up, as it were in haste, and said, "God forbid! it is nothing but a dream." But I told him it was a very significant one, and a warning to him from the Almighty, who sometimes speaks to men in dreams.

In seven weeks after we left sight of the land of America, we saw the Scilly Islands, and next day we saw the land of England, which was a comfortable sight to us; in that God Almighty had preserved us hitherto, and that we were so far got on our way. We drove about the channel's mouth for several days for want of wind; after which, for two days, the wind came up, and we got as far up the channel as Lime-bay, and then an easterly wind blew fresh for several days, and we turned to windward, but rather lost than got on our way, which was tiresome and tedious to some of us.

Now about this time (being some days after the doctor's dream) a grievous accident happened to us. We met with a Dutch vessel in Lime-bay, a little above the Start, hailed her, and she us. They said they came from Lisbon, and were bound for Holland. She was loaded with wine, brandy, fruit, and such like commodities; and we having little but water to drink, (by reason our passage was longer than we expected,) therefore we sent our boat on board, in order to buy us a little wine to drink with our water. Our doctor, and a merchant that was a passenger, and one sailor, went on board, where they staid so long until some of them were overcome with wine, although they were desired to beware thereof; so that when they came back, a rope being handed to them, they (being filled with wine unto excess) were not capable of using it dexterously, insomuch that they overset the boat, and she turned bottom upwards, having the doctor under her. The merchant caught hold of a rope called the main sheet, whereby his life was saved. The sailor not getting so much drink as the other two, got nimbly on the bottom of the boat, and floated on the water till such time as our other boat was hoisted out, which was done with great speed, and we took him in; but the doctor was drowned before the boat came. The seaman that sat upon the boat saw him sink, but could not help him. This was the greatest exercise that we met with in all our voyage; and much the more so, as the doctor was of an evil life and conversation, and much given to excess of drinking. When he got on board the aforesaid ship, the master sent for a can of wine, and said, "Doctor, will you drink?" he replied, "Yes, with all my heart, for I have drank no wine a great while." Upon which he drank a hearty draught, that made him merry (as he said in his dream;*) and notwithstanding the admonition which was so clearly manifested to him but three days before, and the many promises he had made to Almighty God, some of which I was a witness of, when strong convictions were upon him, yet now he was unhappily overcome, and in drink when he was

* This relation about the doctor's dream, when I was at Barbadoes, I had occasion to write to a friend in Ireland, which he got printed, and is the same with this in substance, only that is somewhat fuller and larger.

drowned. This is, I think, a lively representation of the tender mercy, and just judgment of the Almighty to poor mortals; and I thought it was worthy to be recorded to posterity, as a warning to all great lovers of wine and strong liquors. This exercise was so great to me, that I could not for several days get over it; and one day while I was musing in my mind on those things relating to the doctor, it was opened to me, that God and his servants were clear, and his blood was on his own head; for he had been faithfully warned of his evil ways.

We were obliged by contrary winds to put into Plymouth harbour, and from Plymouth I went by coach to London, where I was gladly received by my relations and friends. In this journey I travelled about 2000 miles by land, and 6000 by water. I got to the Yearly Meeting of Friends in London, in the year 1699, which was large, and was at divers public meetings for the worship of Almighty God. I may truly say, the Holy Ghost was amongst us, blessed be God our Saviour for evermore.

CHAPTER II.

1699–1707.

THE AUTHOR'S FIRST MARRIAGE—REMOVES WITH HIS WIFE TO AMERICA, AND SETTLES IN PHILADELPHIA—VISIT TO BARBADOES AND BERMUDAS—ACCOUNT OF HIS TRAVELS IN VARIOUS PARTS OF NORTH AMERICA.

In this year [1699] I thought it my place to enter into a married state, and I acquainted my father of my design, and that I inclined to make choice of Martha Betterton, a religious young woman, whom I entirely loved for that piety, virtue, and modesty, which I beheld in her; (I was in the twenty-fourth year of my age, and she in her twenty-first.) I likewise acquainted her father and mother with my intentions, to which both our parents consented; her father saying (when I spoke to him) "Go together, and the Lord bless you together." And my father said, "If I was worth my weight in gold, she deserved me." The heartiness of both our fathers in this matter, was more to me than a portion of silver or gold, of which we had but very little; but our love to each other was very great, and being well and honourably grounded, it was not easily shaken. So after consent of parents, we proposed our intentions of marriage to the Monthly Meeting unto which we belonged; and because I had been travelling in America, I had certificates from my brethren there, not only of my industry and labour in the ministry, with the good effects thereof; but also of my clearness in relation to marriage; and after having twice published our intentions, we had liberty of the said meeting to proceed to the solemnization of our marriage, which was accomplished at Devonshire-house in London, at a meeting appointed for that end, on the 28th day of the Seventh Month, in the aforesaid year, in the presence of many hundreds of people, and many worthy brethren and elders. A day of days it was to my soul! wherein I was made sensible of the love and goodness of God in a particular manner, which to me was an earnest of our future well-doing. My dear wife was one who truly loved and feared God, and had an excellent gift of the ministry given to her, and was serviceable therein. A paper coming to my hands of her own hand writing and composing, I transcribe it here. She calls it an account of the exercise of Martha Betterton, viz. "As I was walking in the city of London, with a concern on my mind, in beholding the abominable pride of the people, it opened upon my mind in this wise: Wo, wo! to the crown of pride! and then I was deeply bowed in my spirit before the Lord, and it was said to me, I will yet spare a little longer; I have sheep which I will gather home to me, and there shall be one Shepherd and one sheepfold. Then I said in my heart, Oh Lord! shall I be one of thy sheep belonging to thy sheepfold of eternal rest? And again it was answered me, My sheep hear my voice, and they follow me. Then a cry was raised in me, Cause me to hear thy voice; and not only so, but enable me to obey the same. And then this charge was returned to me, Be thou faithful."

Soon after I was married, I had a concern to visit Friends in the counties of Surrey, Sussex, and Kent, which I performed in about two weeks time, and came home and followed my calling, and was industrious therein; and when I had gotten something to bear my expenses, and settle my wife in some little business, I found an exercise on my spirit to go over to Ireland, to visit our Friends and brethren on that island, in which William Townshend accompanied me, and Friends in that nation were generally satisfied with our service among them. When we had been from home about ten weeks, and had visited most parts of that nation, having had many meetings among Friends and others, we found freedom in our minds to return home, which we did, being comforted in our service, and blessed the name of the Lord.

After some few months I acquainted my wife and my father, with her father and mother, that I thought it my duty to go over and live in America. To which proposal my father consented, though with tenderness of heart, considering that I must be so far separated from him. I also laid it before the Monthly Meeting of Friends at Horslydown in Southwark, of which meeting I was a member, who consented to it, though somewhat unwilling to part with us; and gave us their certificate, to let our brethren know that we were in love and unity with them, and walked according to our profession. And when we were ready, and in order for going, we agreed for the freight of our goods and servants, with John Snowden, and shipped them on board the *Josiah*, bound for Maryland. When the ship was at Gravesend, and ready to sail, several of our dear relations and friends accompanied us to the ship, on board of which we had a good meeting, and took our solemn leave of one another, as never expecting to see each other any more in this world. It was a solemn time indeed! we prayed for one another, and so parted, our ship sailing that evening, and we got to Margate Road, where we anchored, and the wind sprung up very fresh, and blew tempestuously, so that we broke our cable, and lost our best bower anchor, and drove violently towards the Goodwin Sands. We let go our sheet anchor, and three more, which were all we had, but they did not stop her; upon which the master ordered the carpenters to stand by the main-mast, with their axes upon their shoulders, and when he gave the word, then they were to cut the mast. The people in the ship (there being divers passengers) were in great consternation, expecting nothing but death: but for my part, being exceedingly sea-sick, and having been in many storms, I was not so much surprised with this, the sailors sometimes making a great noise when there is but little danger; but there was more danger than I was aware of, as appeared afterwards. One of the passengers came weeping, and said, our case was very bad. The doctor also came in the same manner, and cried, "Oh! Mr. Chalkley, we are all dead men!" then I thought with myself, I would go out on deck, and see what the matter was; and when on deck, I went to the pilot, who had the lead in his hand, and he sounded, and cried out, "Lord have mercy upon us! she is gone, she is gone, she is gone!" by which I perceived that we were very near the Goodwin Sands, on which many ships have been lost with all their crews. In this sense of danger I sent for the passengers into the cabin, and told them that I thought it would be well for us to sit still together, and look unto, and wait upon God, to see what he would please to do for us; that, if death came, we might meet him in as good a frame of mind as we could, and that we might not be surprised beyond measure: and as we were thus composed in our minds, a concern came upon my dear wife, and she prayed to God the Father, in the living power and sense of his Son, and he heard from his holy habitation, and answered the prayer; for immediately after the wind abated, and our anchors held us. This was a great deliverance, which is not to be forgotten. When we saw the longed for morning, we were very near the Sands, and the sea ran prodigiously high, and broke upon them mightily, so that we were forced to leave our cables and anchors, and make the best of our way to Deal, as well as we could. One of the owners being on shore, and seeing us in distress, sent off a cable and anchor to us; and we anchored before Deal with our new cable and anchor, and sent a boat for our other anchors and cables, when it was calm, which brought them to us. And after we had supplied ourselves with what we wanted, we put to sea again, and had fair winds till we got as far as the Western Islands, where Captain Cant being in company with us, he spoke to our captain in the evening, and the two captains concluded it would be stormy that night, which happened accordingly. They took in their sails, and we all but our mainsail; notwithstanding which, the storm was such, that we lost our main-mast, sprung the head of our fore-mast, and broke our cross-jack-yard, and thus lay rolling upon the sea for about two weeks: the ship *Bristol-Merchant* coming by in that time, lent us a spare top-mast, of which we made a main-mast, and a top-mast of our topgallant-mast, and so refitted out as well as we could, and had a pretty good passage afterwards. We were about eight weeks from the Land's-End to the Capes of Virginia; had meetings twice a week on board, and they helped to stay our minds on our Maker, though our bodies were tossed to and again on the mighty waters. We went on shore at Patuxent River, and went by land to Herring Bay, where I, my wife, and family, tarried that winter; and I, with my three servants, followed my calling. In the spring 1701, we transported ourselves, our goods, and servants, from Maryland to Pennsylvania, where we intended to settle when we came from our native country. At Philadelphia I bought a lot of ground upon the river Delaware, and there I followed my calling that summer, and in the fall I had an inward call to visit Friends in Barbadoes, which I proposed to our Monthly Meeting, and they certified on my behalf, that they had unity with me in my proposal, conversation and ministry: so I took ship at Philadelphia, about the 20th of the Seventh Month, 1701, on board the *Abraham*, —— Street, commander, and was about a month on our voyage; Josiah Langdale was with me. We had several good meetings in the ship to our satisfaction; and were well received, and had many meetings at Barbadoes, which were often very large and open, and some of the people loving and tender. We had several meetings at Bridge-Town, Speights-Town, the Spring, and the Thickets, and at Pumpkin-Hill; and after being there about six weeks, we went in a sloop to Bermudas, where we found but very few Friends, yet had meetings in several places, and at the houses of some people who were not of our profession; and the longer we tarried the larger our meetings were; and many began to be affected, and spoke well of us and our devotion; but some were disturbed, and spoke to the governor to break up our meeting, which at the desire of one of the inhabitants we had appointed at his house, upon which he sent orders by one of his colonels to break up our meeting, which troubled divers sober people. After this I met with the governor at the house of one judge Stafford; and he being a moderate man, we had the following discourse:—

Gov. How do you like our country? We are but a little spot in the sea.

T. C. I like it well for its moderate climate. If the people were moderate also, it would be well.

Gov. Doth it answer your end in coming?

T. C. My end in coming, was to visit the people in Christian love.

Gov. Do you think the people will be brought over?

T. C. If they are brought to truth and righteousness, it will be well with them. That is the end of our coming.

Gov. If you had acquainted me with your design, when first you came, you had done well. It was your duty.

T. C. If we had known the governor's will herein, or that thou wouldst have spoken with us, we should readily have answered it: but knowing nothing of it, we could not tell but that it might be taken for rudeness in us, considering our homely way and manner of addressing such men.

Gov. Then your design in coming here was to preach. Had you no other end.

T. C. Yes. As we found a concern upon us to preach, and a desire in the people to hear.

Gov. Why do not you tarry with them? That looks strange. Here the people are affected with you, and you go away and leave them: upon my word I blame you for that.

T. C. We do not direct them to man, but to the Lord Jesus Christ, their Teacher and Bishop of their souls. And why should our leaving them look strange to the governor? for it was the practice of the apostles of our Lord Jesus Christ, and his own practice and command to his followers. And further the apostles (which word signifies ambassadors or messengers) say, follow us, as we are followers of Christ. And they travelled up and down the world preaching the gospel; and our great Lord himself had not whereon to lay his head.

Gov. The apostles were inspired men: inspired by the Holy Spirit to preach the gospel. I suppose you do not pretend to be inspired.

T. C. Every true Christian ought to pray for the pouring out of the Holy Spirit, or Holy Ghost upon him. The church of England* also, prays for it, the receiving of which is inspiration.

Gov. Your reasons being grounded on Scripture, you are well grounded; for no man can deny the Scriptures. Then you say you are inspired.

T. C. I hope I am. I pray for it with great earnestness.

Gov. Then it is but ask, and have, you think.

T. C. If we ask in faith, without wavering, we shall receive; according to the doctrine of Christ and his apostles in the New Testament.

* Of which church the Governor was a member.

Gov. Well, if any have a desire to hear you, you may preach and welcome.

After I had this discourse with the governor, it was reported on the island, that the governor had given us license to preach, which report was not true, further than the aforesaid discourse; and then we had larger meetings than before. We had a meeting at judge Stafford's house, and one at a house not far from his.

It is observable, that this island had formerly been a very healthful and fruitful place. Red cedar, or sweet wood, is all the timber they have in the island, with which they build their houses, make their household goods, build their ships and sloops, and make their fires; so that there is continually a fragrant and pleasant smell, which we could smell at sea some time before we saw the land; and it is yet a pretty healthy and fruitful island, but not so healthy and fruitful as formerly. In one of the meetings I was concerned to let them know, that it was the evil of their ways and doings, that had caused the Almighty to withhold from them the fruits of the earth, and to make their island more unhealthful than formerly it was. After meeting, the judge told me, I had said truly, for that was the cause; and if I had spoke more to that matter, or on that subject, I had done well. Several were convinced at this time on this island.

Soon after an opportunity offered, in a sloop belonging to this island, that was bound for Philadelphia, in which we, being clear, embarked, and on our voyage had indifferent good weather, only one hard gale of wind, which caused us to hand our jib. A Mulatto man, named Stavo, being the master's servant, went out upon the bowsprit to hand the sail, and there came a sea and washed him off, and the vessel ran over him; and, in all probability, he had certainly been drowned, had he not been a good swimmer; for he swam, as we judged, three-quarters of a mile, before he got to the sloop, it not coming into any one's mind to lower the sails, until I sharply ordered it to be done, which they then did readily; and the course of the vessel being stopped, he soon got on board, having stripped himself of his clothes in the sea, and brought them in his mouth. I was very thankful for the poor fellow's life, and praised the Lord in the secret of my soul, for his preservation. In about two weeks' time we arrived at Philadelphia, and I had great peace in my labours in this visit, in which I was from home about five months. The Friends of Barbadoes were so well satisfied with this labour of love, that they certified the same by way of certificate, more than is proper for me to mention. But though they thought so well of me, yet I had occasion to think very meanly of myself, for I was emptied to exceeding great spiritual poverty at times.

After I came home from Barbadoes and Bermudas, I followed my calling, and kept to meetings diligently; for I was not easy to be idle, either in my spiritual or temporal callings; and at times travelled in the work of the ministry in our own province, in which there are many large meetings of Friends, and they increase and multiply from time to time. Since my settling in this province, which is now about a year, some hundreds of people are come here to settle, and divers meeting-houses are built; and I do certainly know from above, that this province of Pennsylvania, and city of Philadelphia, will flourish both spiritually and temporally, if the inhabitants will love, and live in, righteousness, and in the fear of God; otherwise the hand that planted them can soon pluck them up. After some time I was drawn forth to visit Friends in Maryland, Virginia, and North Carolina, and went with the unity of Friends, having their certificate; according to the good order established among us. So about the 26th of the First Month, 1703, I went through Maryland, and visited Friends in Virginia and North Carolina, to the river Pamphlico, where no travelling public Friends, that ever I heard of, were before; and we had several meetings there on each side of the river. One day going out of our canoe through a marsh, I trod on a rattle-snake, (which is accounted one of the most poisonous snakes,) but it only hissed at me, and did no harm. This was one deliverance, among many, the Lord by his providence wrought for me; and I bless his holy name for all his mercies. In going to, and coming from this place, we lay two nights in the woods, and I think I never slept better in my life. It was the eighth hour in the evening when I laid down on the ground one night (my saddle being my pillow) at the root of a tree, and it was four o'clock in the morning when they called me. When I awoke, I thought of good Jacob's lodging he had on his way to Padanaram, when he saw the holy vision of angels, with the ladder, whose top reached to heaven. Very sweet was the love of God to my soul that morning, and the dew of the everlasting hills refreshed me; and I went on my way praising the Lord, and magnifying the God of my salvation. In this journey I met with another remarkable deliverance: going over a river eight miles broad, we put our horses, we being eight men and seven horses, into two canoes tied together, and our horses stood with their fore-feet in one, and their hind-feet in the other. It was calm when we set out, but when we were about the middle of the river the wind arose, and the seas ran high, and split one of our canoes, so that with our hats we were obliged to cast out the water; and with much difficulty, at last, all of us, with our horses, got safe on shore, through the good providence of God. And on return through North Carolina, we had several large meetings, and an open time it was; as also at Nansimund and Chuckatue, and several other places in Virginia; and when my service was over in those two provinces, I went back to Maryland, and visited meetings there, and then went home. As near as I can compute it, I rode about a thousand miles on this journey. After which I staid at home, following my business, in order to the maintenance of my family, being blessed with wife, children, and servants, and with other things; for which I am truly thankful.

While I was at home, I visited the neighbouring meetings as I found a concern on my mind; and on the 6th day of the Third Month, 1704, I laid before our Quarterly Meeting of ministers and elders an exercise that was upon my mind, to visit our Friends' meetings on Long Island, Rhode Island, and in New England, and the places adjacent; from which Quarterly Meeting I had a good certificate, which I thought it my duty to endeavour to live up unto; and being accompanied with several Friends to Burlington and Croswicks, Joseph Glaster being my fellow-labourer in the work of the gospel; at the two aforesaid places we had meetings, and then we travelled to New York and Long Island, where we had divers meetings; as at Flushing, Westbury, Jerusalem, Jericho, Bethphage, Matinicock, and also at West Chester, on the main; and from thence we travelled to Rhode Island Yearly Meeting, which was large and serviceable to many. From hence Joseph Glaster went towards Boston, the inland way, and I went by the sea-side, and we met together, after I had been at meetings at divers places, viz. Dartmouth and Nantucket Island, at which island there are large meetings, people there being mostly Friends, and a sober growing people in the best things; though not of our Society when they first received the truth, yet they received it with gladness; and although divers of the people called Presbyterians were very cruel in their expressions, and bitter in their spirits against us, yet there were some who went under that name, who were more open and charitable towards us, and received us gladly with tenderness; and at some places we had meetings at their houses to our mutual satisfaction. We likewise had meetings at Suckanuset, Scituate and Sandwich. About this time the Indians were very barbarous in the destruction of the English inhabitants, scalping some, and knocking out the brains of others, men, women and children, by which the country was greatly alarmed both by night and day; but the great Lord of all was pleased wonderfully to preserve our Friends, especially those who kept faithful to their peaceable principle, according to the doctrine of Christ in the holy scriptures, as recorded in his excellent sermon which he preached on the mount, in the 5th, 6th and 7th chapters of Matthew, which is quite opposite to killing, revenge and destruction, even of our enemies: and because our Friends could not join with those of fighting principles and prao-tices, some of them were put into prison; divers people railing and speaking very bitterly against their peaceable neighbours, and wishing the Quakers might be cut off. Some of the New England priests and professors were so bitter against Friends, that instead of being humbled under the mighty hand of God upon them, in suffering the Indians to destroy them, they expressed their enmity against the poor Quakers, on a day appointed for humiliation and a fast; and particularly in a sermon preached by one of their priests, which he divided into three heads, viz. First, That the judgments of God were upon them, in letting loose the savage Indians to destroy them. Secondly, In that he withheld the fruits of the earth from them (for there was great scarcity). Thirdly, That the Quakers prevailed, and were suffered to increase so much among them; which, he said, was worse than the Indians destroying of them, and gave this absurd reason for it, the Indians destroy our bodies, but the Quakers destroy the soul.* This is an abominable falsehood; for it is sin that destroys the soul, and such as those that preach to the people that there is no freedom from it in this world, contradict Christ's doctrine, "Be ye perfect," &c. And that of the apostles, He that is born of God cannot sin. And thus their blind guides mistake light for darkness, and darkness for light. Among the many hundreds that were slain, I heard

* This priest was soon after killed by the Indians, as I was told by a minister.

but of three of our Friends being killed, whose destruction was very remarkable, as I was informed; the one was a woman, the other two were men. The men used to go to their labour without any weapons, and trusted to the Almighty, and depended on his providence to protect them, (it being their principle not to use weapons of war, to offend others, or defend themselves,) but a spirit of distrust taking place in their minds, they took weapons of war to defend themselves; and the Indians, who had seen them several times without them, and let them alone, saying, They were peaceable men and hurt nobody, therefore they would not hurt them; now seeing them have guns, and supposing they designed to kill the Indians, they therefore shot the men dead. The woman had remained in her habitation, and could not be free to go to a fortified place for preservation, neither she, her son, nor daughter, nor to take thither the little ones; but the poor woman after some time began to let in a slavish fear, and did advise her children to go with her to a fort not far from their dwelling. Her daughter being one that trusted in the name of the Lord, the mighty tower, to which the righteous flee and find safety, could not consent to go with her; and having left a particular account, in a letter to her children, of her and their preservation, I think it worthy to be inserted here in her own words.

"When the cruel Indians were suffered to kill and destroy, it was shewed me, that I must stand in a testimony for truth, and trust in the name of the Lord that was a strong tower, and we should wait upon him. And I often desired my mother and husband to sit down, and wait upon the Lord, and he would shew us what we should do: but I could not prevail with him, but he would say it was too late now, and was in great haste to be gone; but I could not go with him, because I was afraid of offending the Lord: but still he would say I was deluded by the devil, so that my mother would often say, a house divided could not stand; and she could not tell what to do. Although she had most peace in staying, yet she had thoughts of moving, and said to me, 'Child, can thee certainly say it is revealed to thee that we should stay? if it be, I would willingly stay, if I was sure it was the mind of God.' But I being young, was afraid to speak so high, said, 'Mother, I can say that it is so with me, that when I think of staying and trusting in the name of the Lord, I find great peace and comfort, more than I can utter, with a belief we shall be preserved; but when I think of going, oh, the trouble and heaviness I feel, with a fear some of us should fall by them!' And my dear mother sighed, and said, she could not tell what to do. But I said to them, if they would go, I would be willing to stay alone; if they found freedom, I was very willing, for I was afraid of offending the Lord. But still my poor husband would say, I took a wrong spirit for the right. And he would say, how I should know; for if I was right I would be willing to condescend to him. And then I said, in condescension to him, I would move; but I hope the Lord will not lay it to my charge, for was it not to condescend to him, I would not move for the world; and after I had given away my strength, in a little time there came men from the garrison, with their guns, and told us, they came for us, and told us the Indians they thought, might be near; and then away we went; and my mother went in with my brother-in-law, although I persuaded her not to do it. But she said, 'Why, my child is there: and why may not I be with him as well as thee?' and so we went along to Hampton, to my husband's brother's. But O the fear and trouble that I felt! and told my husband, it seemed as if we were going into the mouth of the Indians. And the next day was the First-day of the week; and our dear friend, Lydia Norton, came with my dear mother; and in her testimony she said, there was there that was very near to her life that was very near death. O then I was ready to think it would be I, because I believed we had done amiss in moving, and great trouble was I in, and told dear Lydia of it; but she comforted me as much as she could, and said she did not think it would be I. And my dear mother went to my sister's again, to the garrison, where she found herself not easy; but, as she often said to many, that she felt herself in a beclouded condition, and more shut from counsel than ever she had been since she knew the truth; and being uneasy, went to move to a friend's house that lived in the neighbourhood; and as she was moving, the bloody cruel Indians lay by the way and killed her! O then how did I lament moving. And promised, if the Lord would be pleased to spare my life, and husband, and children, and carry us home again, I would never do so more. But O the fear, and trouble, and darkness, that fell upon me and many more at that time! And three or four of us kept our meeting, but although we sat and waited as well as we could, yet we sat under a poor beclouded condition, till we returned home again; then did the Lord please to lift up the light of his love upon our poor souls. O then I told my husband, although he had built a little house by the garrison, I could not move again. So he was willing to stay while the winter season lasted, but told me he could not stay when summer came, for then the Indians would be about; and so told me, that if I could not go to the garrison, I might go to a friend's house that was near it. And I was willing to please him, if the Lord was willing; and then applied my heart to know the mind of truth, and it was shewed me, that if I moved again, I should lose the sense of truth, and I should never hold up my head again. O then I told my husband he must never ask me to move again, for I durst not do it. Still he would say it was a notion, till our dear friend Thomas Story came and told him, he did not see that I could have a greater revelation than I had. And satisfied my husband so well, that he never asked me more to go, but was very well contented to stay all the wars; and then things were made more easy, and we saw abundance of the wonderful works, and of the mighty power of the Lord, in keeping and preserving of us, when the Indians were at our doors and windows, and at other times; and how the Lord put courage in you, my dear children; do not you forget it, and do not think that as you were young, and because you knew little, so you feared nothing; but often consider how you staid at home alone, when we went to meetings, and how the Lord preserved you, and kept you, so that no hurt came upon you. And I leave this charge upon you, Live in the fear of the Lord, and see you set him always before your eyes, lest you sin against him: for if I had not feared the Lord, and felt the comforts of his Holy Spirit, I never could have stood so great a trial, when so many judged, and said I was deluded, and that all the blood of my husband and children would be required at my hands; but the Lord was near to me, and gave me strength and courage, and faith to trust in him, for I knew his name to be a strong tower, yea, and stronger than any in the world; for I have oftentimes fled there for safety. O blessing and honour, and everlasting high praises, be given to the Lord, and to his dear Son, our Saviour and Mediator, Christ Jesus. Amen.

"MARY DOE."

A neighbour of the aforesaid people told me, that as he was at work in his field, the Indians saw and called him, and he went to them. They told him, that they had no quarrel with the Quakers, for they were a quiet, peaceable people, and hurt nobody, and that therefore none should hurt them. But they said, that the Presbyterians in these parts had taken away their lands, and some of their lives, and would now, if they could, destroy all the Indians.

Those Indians began about this time to shoot people down as they rode along the road, and to knock them on the head in their beds, and very barbarously murdered many: but we travelled the country, and had large meetings, and the good presence of God was with us abundantly, and we had great inward joy in the Holy Ghost in our outward jeopardy and travels. The people generally rode and went to their worship armed, but Friends went to their meetings without either sword or gun, having their trust and confidence in God.

After having had divers good meetings in those eastern parts of New England, I returned to Salem, Lynn, Boston, and so on towards Rhode Island, and at divers adjacent places; as in the Narraganset country we had divers meetings; also at Dartmouth, Sandwich, and Scituate. As I was entering into the town of Boston, in company with many others, a man rode up to me, and asked in a scoffing manner, Whether I saw or met with any Quakers on the road? I pleasantly told him, We should not tell the Presbyterians, lest they should hang them. He not thinking of such an answer went sneakingly away.

Now having thoroughly visited Friends in those parts, in company with my friend Thomas Story, I travelled through Connecticut government, and had several meetings in that colony; and came to Long Island, where we had divers meetings to the satisfaction of ourselves and friends. From Long Island, after we were clear of the service and exercise of the work of the ministry, and had visited Friends' meetings as we travelled, and in divers places found openness among the people who were not of our profession, (which sometimes came in great numbers to our meetings, and several were convinced in some good degree, and many comforted, strengthened, and edified in Christ our Lord,) we came to Philadelphia, the place of our habitation. Let, saith my soul, his name have the praise of all his works for ever.

After being at home some time, I visited Friends' meetings in our own country, and several parts of New Jersey, Maryland, and the lower counties on the Delaware. At Jones's I appointed a meeting at a public house near the court-house (general notice being given thereof) there came one —— Crawford, a priest, with many of his hearers, and in the beginning of the meeting he read a sermon, as they called it, which was a transcript of the work of some of our adversaries, which we desired to have from them to answer. They said, If I would answer it myself I should have it. The which I told them I should, if they would let me; but though they promised it, they did not perform, but were worse than their word. We heard them read it over patiently; and after they had done we had our meeting. The auditory was large, and most of the magistrates were at it. The priest's reading, and my testimony occasioned this meeting to hold long: after which as we were getting on horseback, the priest cried out among the people, That he did not think we should go away so sneakingly. We having twenty miles to ride that night, and he near his home, he having the advantage in that respect, some thought it made him the bolder, for he let me go on horseback before he uttered that sneaking expression. I told him, to challenge was enough to set a coward to work, and we were no cowards; for he knew we could venture our lives for our religion, which I questioned whether he would do for his; so I dismounted, and he having the bible open in his hand, I being near him, chanced, against my will and knowledge, to touch it with my foot. "Look you, gentlemen," says he, "he tramples the word of God under his feet." For which gross abuse his own hearers openly rebuked him, and put him to shame. Then he said, he would prove us no ministers of Christ. I bid him prove himself one, and he would do the business. "Well," says he, "how shall we know who are Christ's ministers?" "Why," said I in answer to him, "art thou willing to be tried by Christ's rule, for he hath given us a plain rule to know them by." "What is that rule? let us hear it," says he. "It is short, but full, namely, By their fruits you shall know them: for men do not gather grapes of thorns, nor figs of thistles; wherefore by their fruits they are known." "I deny it," says priest Crawford, (for that was the name he went by here, he going under another elsewhere), "that they are known by their fruits." I answered, "Then thou deniest the plain and naked truth of Christ." So I called aloud to the people to take notice what a blind guide they had; and indeed he was wicked as well as blind, and his fruits not good; which may make one suppose, that he was not willing to be tried by his fruits: for soon after, news came that he had a wife in England, and as he had another here, his fruits were wicked with a witness; and according to Christ's doctrine, no good could spring from his ministry, therefore he proved himself by his evil deeds to be no minister of Jesus Christ. Near the aforesaid place we got a meeting settled, which is called Little Creek meeting; and about the same time a meeting was .established, and meeting-house built at Duck Creek. The people in those parts about this time began mightily to see through the formal preaching of such as preach for money or hire, who love the hire, though they do not love to be called hirelings.

In the year 1706, having some concerns in the province of Maryland, I had divers meetings as I travelled on the road, as at Nottingham, Elk River, North-east, Susquehannah, Bush, and Gunpowder Rivers, at some of which places I do not know that there had been any meetings before. At one of these meetings were one Edwards a priest, and a lawyer, the attorney-general, and several of the justices of the peace. The priest was angry, and said, It was an unlawful assembly, the house not being licensed by law. The justices told him, that he and his people being there to hear, if any unwarrantable or false doctrine was preached, he had a fair opportunity to lay it open before all the people. So they desired him to hear patiently and quietly. He seemed to like the proposition, and sat down by me. We had not sat down long before I stood up, and spoke to the people some considerable time; and the lawyer sat opposite to me, and took what I said in short-hand, for about half-an-hour; but growing weary, he laid down his pen, and took out of his pocket a bottle of liquor, or spirits, and said, "Come, friend, here is to thee, or you, you have spoke a great while, you need something to refresh you." So I made a stop, and said to the people, "Here is your minister, and here are some of the fruits of his ministry, of which he and all sober people may be ashamed." And then I went on again without any opposition till I had done; but afterwards they were in a rage, and threatened what they would do to me, if ever I came to have a meeting any more there. But I told them, if they had power to take our lives from us, they were not dear to us for the sake of Christ and his gospel; and that we did not matter their threatenings. I desired the lawyer to give me a copy of what he had written: he went about it, but did not do it; neither was he candid in penning my words; for several of the people then present did bear witness he had not writ it verbatim, nor truly taken the sense of what I spoke, wherefore I charged him to be just, otherwise he had many witnesses against him; at which the priest bent his fist, and held it up to me, but did not strike me, and away he went in a fret. Soon after we had another meeting at the same place, which was large and quiet. The man of the house being an attorney-at-law, had got his house licensed; though the priest and lawyer threatened hard, they came not.

Aquila Pica, high sheriff for the county, living at the head of Bush river, near the main road, built a meeting-house at his own charge, and had it licensed, at which we had many good meetings. About this time also was built a meeting-house at a place called Nottingham, which is a large meeting, and greatly increases.

When I was travelling in those parts, I had a concern on my mind to visit the Indians living near Susquehannah, at Conestogoe; I laid it before the elders of Nottingham meeting, with which they expressed their unity, and promoted my visiting them. We got an interpreter, and thirteen or fourteen of us travelled through the woods about fifty miles, carrying our provisions with us, and on the journey sat down by a river, and spread our food on the grass, and refreshed ourselves and horses, and then went on cheerfully, and with good will, and much love to the poor Indians; and when we came, they received us kindly, treating us civilly in their way. We treated about having a meeting with them in a religious way, upon which they called a council, in which they were very grave, and spoke one after another without any heat or jarring; and some of the most esteemed of their women do sometimes speak in their councils. I asked our interpreter, Why they suffered or permitted the women to speak in their councils? His answer was, that some women were wiser than some men.

Our interpreter told me, That they had not done any thing for many years without the counsel of an ancient grave woman; who, I observed, spoke much in their council; for I was permitted to be present at it; and I asked, What it was the woman said? He told me she was an empress; and they gave much heed to what she said amongst them, and that she then said to them, She looked upon our coming to be more than natural, because we did not come to buy, or sell, or get gain, but came in love and respect to them, and desired their well-doing both here and hereafter; and further continued, That our meeting among them might be very beneficial to their young people, and related a dream which she had three days before, and interpreted it, viz. That she was in London, and that London was the finest place she ever saw, it was like Philadelphia, but much bigger; and she went across six streets, and in the seventh she saw William Penn preaching to the people, which was a great multitude, and both she and William Penn rejoiced to see one another; and after meeting she went to him, and he told her, That in a little time he would come over and preach to them also, of which she was very glad. And now she said her dream was fulfilled, for one of his friends was come to preach to them. And she advised them to hear us, and entertain us kindly; and accordingly they did. Here were two nations of them, the Senecas and Shawanese. We had first a meeting with the Senecas, with which they were much affected; and they called the other nation, viz. the Shawanese, and interpreted to them that we had spoke in their meeting, and the poor Indians, particularly some of the young men and women, were under a solid exercise and concern. We had also a meeting with the other nation, and they were all very kind to us, and desired more such opportunities; the which, I hope Divine Providence will order them, if they are worthy thereof. The gospel of Jesus Christ was preached freely to them, and faith in Christ, who was put to death in Jerusalem, by the unbelieving Jews; and that this same Jesus came to save people from their sins, and by his grace and light in the soul, shews to man his sins, and convinceth him thereof, delivering him out of them, and gives inward peace and comfort to the soul for well-doing, and sorrow and trouble for evil-doing; to all which, as their manner is, they gave public assents; and to that of the light in the soul, they gave a double assent, and seemed much affected with the doctrine of truth; also the benefit of the holy Scriptures was largely opened to them.*

After this we returned to our respective habitations, thankful in our hearts to the God and Father of our Lord Jesus Christ. Several of the Friends that went with me expressed their satisfaction in this visit, and offered themselves freely to go again on the like service.

I also was concerned soon after to visit the people about Egg-Harbour and Cape-May, and had divers meetings amongst them, and several meetings were settled in those parts, and the people somewhat reformed from what they had been before they were

* It is worthy of notice, that at the first settling of Pennsylvania, William Penn took great care to do justice to the Indians, and bought his land of them to their satisfaction, and settled a trade with them; so that whereas the Indians were destructive to other colonies, they were helpful to Pennsylvania; and to this day they love to hear the name of WILLIAM PENN.

visited by Friends, as themselves told me, after a meeting we had with them, that they used to spend the Sabbath-days in sporting and vanity, until Friends came among them, and now they met together to worship God, and his Son Jesus Christ. At our coming amongst them, some backsliders and apostates were displeased. One in a very bitter spirit, called us cursed and cruel devils. Another wrote against us. To him I sent an answer, for which he scandalized me in one of his almanacs, and publicly belied me in print; which lies I swept away with a "Small Broom," printed in this year 1706, to which I never understood that he returned any answer, nor that he wrote against Friends afterwards, though he had made it his practice before for several years.

At Little Egg-Harbour lived a Friend whose name was Edward Andrews, who as he himself told me, had been a leader of the people into vanity and folly, as music, dancing, &c. But the good hand of the Lord being upon him, wrought a wonderful reformation in him, and made him an instrument to lead people into truth and righteousness, and gave him an excellent gift in the ministry of the gospel of Christ; so that he was made instrumental in the gathering of a large and growing meeting, most of the people thereabouts being convinced, and a great reformation and change wrought in their conversations. This Friend told me, that when he was very rude and wild, he was mightily reached unto at the meeting we had under the trees at Croswicks,* so that he could not go on with his vanity as before, after which he had strong convictions on him, which

* See page 19.

wrought conversion in the Lord's time, after he had gone through many deep and inward exercises.

After these several journies were over, and I had cleared myself, I was some time at home, and followed my business with diligence and industry, and throve in things of the world, the Lord adding a blessing to my labours. Some people would tell me that I got money for preaching, and grew rich by it; which, being a common calumny cast upon our public Friends that are travellers, I shall take a little notice of it, and leave it to posterity. That it is against our principle, and contrary to our known practice and rule, to take money for our preaching the gospel of Christ, and the publishing of salvation through his name unto the people; for according to Christ's command, we, receiving it freely, are to give it forth freely: and I can say without vanity or boasting, I have spent many pounds in that service, besides my time, which was, and is, as precious to me as other people: and rising early, and lying down late; many days riding forty, fifty and sixty miles a-day, which was very laborious and hard for my flesh to endure, being corpulent and heavy from the 27th year of my age; and I can truly say, that I never received any money or consideration on account of these services, either directly or indirectly; and yet if any of our ministers are necessitous or poor, we relieve them freely, not because they are preachers, but because they are needy. And when we have done those things, we have done but our duty: and well will it be for those that have discharged themselves faithfully therein: such will, besides the earnest of peace in their own souls in this world, have a blessed reward in the glorious kingdom of the Lord and his

Christ in that world which is to come. It is well known that I have spent much of my time, since I have been free from my apprenticeship, in travelling and preaching the gospel, being out often many months, and sometimes a whole year and more; and at intervals I have been apt to think the time long, till I got to my business and family; and so have divers times made more haste than I should have done, which has brought trouble on my mind, and is a trouble to me unto this day; which may be a caution to those who travel in the work of the ministry hereafter, not to make too much haste from the work of Christ; and yet there ought to be discretion used; for a minister may stay too long, as well as return too soon, which may be perceived as we keep the eye of our mind to our Divine Guide.

CHAPTER III.

1707–1711.

AFTER VISITING FRIENDS IN THE WEST INDIA ISLANDS, HE EMBARKS FOR EUROPE ON THE SAME SERVICE—LANDS IN IRELAND—PROCEEDS THROUGH THAT NATION INTO SCOTLAND, AND THENCE TO ENGLAND—PASSES OVER INTO THE LOW COUNTIES—HIS TRAVELS THERE AND IN SOME PARTS OF GERMANY—RETURN TO ENGLAND, AND, IN THE FOLLOWING YEAR, TO PHILADELPHIA—DECEASE OF HIS FIRST WIFE.

AFTER I had staid at and about home for some considerable time, a weighty concern came upon me to visit Friends in the West Indies, and some parts of Europe, as it might please the Almighty to open my way; and as it was to be a long travel, both by sea and land, and hazardous, by reason it was war time, and many privateers out at sea, I settled my affairs by will, and otherwise, that if I should not live to come home again, things relating to my outward affairs might be done honourably and well; for at this time, as at many others, I can truly say, I gave up my life freely for my holy Master's sake, and in his cause, who said, "Go, teach all nations," &c.

On the 29th of the Sixth Month, 1707, I had a certificate from the Monthly Meeting of Friends at Philadelphia, signifying their unity with my undertaking, and desires for my welfare; and a tender concern was on my mind that I might live according to what my brethren had certified concerning me. I likewise laid my exercise before the General Meeting of ministers and elders held for the provinces of Pennsylvania and New Jersey, on the 22nd of the Seventh Month, who also signified their fellowship with my intended travels and journey, and recommended me to the grace of God; and in much love and tenderness I parted with my dear and loving wife, and my near and affectionate friends and brethren.

I had for my companion and fellow-labourer in the work of the gospel, my dear friend Richard Gove, who also had the approbation and unity of Friends in this journey and undertaking.

We went on board a sloop at Philadelphia, bound for Barbadoes, John Knight master, about the 27th of the Eighth Month, in the aforesaid year.

After a few days sailing down the river Delaware, we put to sea, and in about a month's time we came within sight of Barbadoes, where we met with a privateer, which chased, and had like to have taken us; but the good Providence of God preserved us out of the hands of those enemies, for ever blessed be his great name! In this chase the seamen were uneasy, and belched out wicked oaths, and cursed the Quakers, wishing all their vessels might be taken by the enemy, because they did not carry guns in them: at which evil I was grieved, and began thus to expostulate with them: "Do you know the worth of a man's life?" (guns being made on purpose to destroy men's lives;) "were this ship and cargo mine, so far as I know mine heart, I do ingenuously declare, I had rather lose it all, than that one of you should lose his life;"

for I certainly knew they were unfit to die. "Lives!" said they, "we had rather lose our lives than go to France." "But," said I, "that is not the matter; had you rather go to hell, than go to France?" They being guilty of great sins and wickedness, and convicted in their own consciences, held their peace, and said no more about the poor Quakers; and when we got within gun-shot of a fort on Barbadoes, the enemy left chasing us.

Next morning early we safely arrived at Bridge-Town, in Barbadoes, where our Friends gladly received us; amongst whom we laboured in the work of the gospel for about two months; and from thence, after having had divers good and edifying meetings for the worship of God, we sailed for Antigua, and staid some days there, having meetings, and visiting our brethren. From Antigua we sailed for Nevis, but the wind being contrary, we put in at Montserrat, an isle that hath a great mountain in it, on the top of which is a hot spring of water, which boils up, and the mud of it is clear brimstone, some of which we carried on board our vessel; the which is admirable, and shows the wonderful works of God. They say that the spring is hot enough to boil an egg. From this island we sailed to Nevis, and had meetings with those few Friends that were there, with whom we parted at the sea-shore with great love and tenderness. After which we sailed to an island called Anguilla, and were civilly treated there by the generality of the people; as also by the governor, George Leonard, at whose house we had meetings. I remember, that after one meeting the governor went into his porch, and took the bible, and opened it, and said, "By this book, if people believe the holy Scriptures, I am able to convince the world, and prove, that the people called Quakers are the people of God, and that they follow the example and doctrine of Christ, and the practices of the apostles and primitive Christians, nearer than any people in the world;" *i. e.* generally speaking. At this island several people were heartily convinced, and did confess to the truth, among whom a meeting was settled. Here was never any Friend before, as the inhabitants said. I entreat the Lord Jehovah to preserve the sincere-hearted among them in his holy fear, whilst they remain in this world; and not them only, but all that love and fear him, in all kindreds and nations, and amongst people of all professions whatsoever. This, in the universal spirit of God's divine love, is the desire of my soul. Back from Anguilla we went to Nevis, and from Nevis to Antigua; and notwithstanding our sloop was a dull sailer, yet we were preserved from the enemy to the admiration of ourselves, friends, and others, our course being in the very road of the privateers. Just as we got into the harbour and were landed, a privateer came by with a prize along with her, as we supposed, which excited our thankfulness to the Lord for our preservation. Here we met with the packet boat for Jamaica, and thence for England. We staid a little at the island called St. Christopher's. In our way to Jamaica we saw a small privateer, that gave us chase, and it being calm, she rowed up towards us. The master prepared the vessel to fight, hoisting up his mainsail, and putting out our colours. In the interim some were bold, and some sorrowful. One came to me, and asked, "What I thought of it? and what I thought of the Quakers' principles now?" I told him I thought I was as willing to go to heaven as himself was; to which he said nothing, but turned away from me. Another asked me, "What I would do now?" I told him, I would pray that they might be made better, and that they might be made fit to die. Then in the midst of their noise and hurry, in secret I begged of the Almighty, in the name, and for the sake of his dear Son, that he would be pleased to cause a fresh gale of wind to spring up, that we might be delivered from the enemy without shedding blood; (well knowing that few of them were fit to die;) and even whilst I was thus concerned, the Lord answered my desire and prayer, for in a few minutes the wind sprung up, and we soon left them out of sight, our vessel sailing extraordinary well, and the next day we got to Jamaica, and had divers meetings, viz. at Port Royal, Kingston, and Spanish Town, &c. At a meeting at Spanish Town, there were divers Jews, to whom my heart was very open, and I felt great love to them, for the sake of their fathers Abraham, Isaac, and Jacob, and they were so affected with the meeting, that they sent us some unleavened cakes, made with fine flour and sweet oil, it being a festival time with them. We had a meeting at Port Royal, in a place where the earthquake had destroyed a large building, in which meeting I had occasion to remind them of the righteous judgments of God, which had been justly inflicted on them for their sins and wickedness. Some wept, and some were rude. The people here, as I was informed, were generally very wicked. After having had divers meetings, the packet in which we had taken our passage, being obliged to stay but ten days, we went off sooner than we otherwise should have done, and solemnly taking leave of those Friends that were there, we went on board our vessel, in order for England, by God's permission. We got readily through the Windward Passage, which is between the islands of Cuba and Hispaniola; and divers times after we left Jamaica, we were chased by several ships, but they could not come up with us. One ship of twenty-eight guns, gave us chase after a great storm, and was almost up with us before we could well make sail; they being eager of their prey, sent their hands aloft to let their reefs out of the topsails, in order to make more speed, and came running mightily towards us, and gained much upon us; we fearing to make sail, by reason of the storm, and the sea running very high, and our masts being therefore in danger, we were some time in doubt, whether we should escape or not: but while we were in this consternation, down came the French ship's three topmasts at once, so we escaped, and left her, and went rejoicing on our way, that we were thus delivered. This was one of the great and remarkable deliverances among the many I met with, by the good hand and providence of the Lord, my great and good Master, whom I hope to serve all my days.

After having been at sea about six weeks, we began to look out for land, and in two or three days we sounded, and found ground at about ninety fathoms; after which we saw two French privateers, that gave us chase about four o'clock in the morning, and pursued us vigorously; but sailing better than they, we ran them out of sight by eight o'clock the same morning, and in about two hours after we saw the land of Ireland; it being misty weather, with rain and wind, our master thought it best to lie by and forbear sailing, that coast being rocky and dangerous, by which means the two ships that gave ns chase, came up with us, and found us not in sailing order, and were in gun-shot of us before we were aware of it. What to do now we could not tell, until they began to fire at us; but in this emergency and strait, our master resolved he would rather run the vessel on shore than they should have her, she being richly laden with indigo, silver, and gold, reckoned to the value of fifty thousand pounds. In this strait, we must either fall into the hands of the French, who were our enemies, or run against the rocks; and we thought it best to fall into the hands of the Almighty, and trust to his providence; so towards the rocks we went, which looked with a terrible aspect. The native Irish seeing us, they came down in great numbers, and ran on the rocks and called to us, saying, that if we came any nearer we should be dashed to pieces. Then our master ordered the anchor to be let go, which brought her up before she struck; and, with much ado, he put his boat out into the sea, and put in all the passengers, in order to set them on shore, the waves running very high, so that it looked as if every wave would have swallowed us up; and it was a great favour of Providence that we got to land in safety. The privateers not daring to come so near the shore as we did, after firing at us, went away, and our master carried the ship into the harbour of Kinsale in Ireland. Thus through many perils and dangers we were preserved, and got safe on the Irish shore, for which, and all other, the mercies and favours of the Most High, my soul and spirit did give glory and praise! In this voyage we were about seven weeks at sea.

When I came from my home at Philadelphia, I

did intend, the Lord permitting, to visit Friends in Ireland, and being accidentally cast on shore there, I thought it my place first to go through that nation. I had been in Ireland about nine years before, and then being but young, and now being more grown in body, my old acquaintance and friends did not at first know me; but we were kindly and lovingly received by our Friends and brethren in that nation, where there is a great and numerous people, that serve and worship the Father in spirit and in truth, and who have divers good and wholesome orders established among them, in the unity and fellowship of the gospel. In this nation we had many and large meetings after our landing, visiting Friends' meetings along to the north, many not of our Society, coming to them, among whom we often had good service, to our and their satisfaction, as they often declared, Richard Gove being still with me. Friends from their national meeting certified to our brethren in America, of our service and labour of love among them, after we had travelled several hundred miles, and visited Friends' meetings generally, and some other places where it was not usual. While I was in Ireland, under a concern for the prosperity of truth and religion, I wrote an Exhortation to the youth, and others, which was afterwards printed there.

We took ship in the north of Ireland, at a town called Donaghadee, being accompained with divers brethren, who brought us on our way after a godly sort. We got to Port Patrick in Scotland, after about five hours' sail, in order to visit those few Friends that were scattered about in that part of the nation. People in those parts looked very shy on us, and did not care to discourse with us on matters civil or religious, which I thought unreasonable. The first town or city we came to, in which we had a meeting, was Glasgow, accounted the second city in North Britain, where, in our meeting for the worship of the Almighty, we were shamefully treated, by the people throwing dirt, stones, coals, &c. amongst us, and by divers other actions unbecoming men, though heathens or infidels, much more people professing Christianity; so that I was constrained to tell them, that though I had preached the gospel to many heathens, and to divers Jews, as also to Indians and Negroes, and had travelled in many countries and nations in the world, in several quarters thereof, and many thousands of miles, yet I must needs say, that I never met with the like incivilities, and such scurrilous treatment, no, not in all my travels. I also told them, that I had preached the gospel of Christ among their brethren in New England, and in Boston, where they formerly hanged the Quakers, and cruelly persecuted them for their religion, and yet they did not treat us so brutishly even there. And further I told them, that I lived in those parts of America, and what account I should have to carry home to their aforesaid brethren, of our treatment in Glasgow, the second city in Scotland. I desired them to consider of it, and be ashamed, if they had any shame. This a little abashed them for the present, but afterwards they were as bad as ever. There were at this meeting divers collegians, who were very rude. I asked if that was their way of treating strangers? and that I believed their teachers in the university did not allow of such ill manners, by which they scandalized themselves, their city, and country. From this city we went to Hamilton and Gershore, where they were more civil. At Gershore a man of letters, and sober conversation, begged that I would pray to the Almighty, that he would establish him in the doctrine which he had heard that day. This being rare in those parts, therefore I thus minute it here. We went on towards the north of Scotland, to Aberdeen, and thereabouts, where there is a tender-hearted people, among whom we had several large gatherings, and some that were not of us, expressed their satisfaction. In the north, I met with a gentleman, who coming from a nobleman's house, joined me, and asked me, if I knew Robert Barclay. I said, not personally, but by his writings I knew him well. He told me, that he, Barclay, had not left his fellow in Scotland. We afterwards travelled southward, where there were but few Friends, and small meetings; yet we may say, that the goodness, love, and presence of Him, who said, "Where two or three are gathered in my name, there am I in the midst of them," was oftentimes witnessed to be with us, blessed be his holy name. Oh! that the children of men would praise him in thought, word, and deed, for he is worthy. So in great reverence and holy fear, we travelled along towards South Britain; had several meetings at Edinburgh, and divers other places; also at Berwick-upon-Tweed, where there were many soldiers who were very rude. The devil hath had many battles with us, ever since we were a people, in order to hinder us in our worship, but we generally came off with victory, as we did here also, through faith in his name who hath loved us, and manifested himself to us. Those rude soldiers threw their hats into the congregation, in order to disturb us, and hinder us in our service, but were at last ashamed and disappointed. At this place my dear friend and fellow-traveller Richard Gove, and I parted; (I was for going by the east sea-coast up for London, and he inclined towards Cumberland;) after we had travelled about a year in the work of the ministry, in great love and true friendship, in which work we were true helpers one of another; and as we had laboured together in the work of Christ, so we parted in his love. Now from Berwick I travelled along to Newcastle; had one meeting by the way, and several good meetings at Newcastle, Sunderland, Shotton, and Durham, and several other places in the bishoprick of Durham. The winter coming on apace, it began to be bad travelling; and I being already much spent by it, designed to go speedily up to London; and taking some meetings in my way, as at Stockton, Whitby, Scarborough, Burlington, Hull, and Brigg, [passed] on through Lincolnshire, where I went to visit a Friend that was prisoner in the castle of Lincoln, because for conscience' sake he could not pay an ungodly priest the tithe of his labour. From Lincoln I proceeded to Huntingdon, about which place we had several large meetings; so on to Baldock, where I met with my father and John Gopsil, who came from London to meet me, which was a joyful meeting, for I had not seen my father for about nine years. The love and tenderness between us, and the gladness in seeing each other again, cannot well be expressed; (but I believe it was somewhat like Jacob and Joseph's meeting in Egypt;) it was affecting and melting: blessed be the Almighty that gave me once more to see my tender and aged parent! So from Baldock we went to Hitchin, and had a meeting there, as also at Hertford, from whence, with several Friends, I went to Enfield, where I met with my dear and only brother George, and there were with us several of my relations, and divers others of our friends: we were heartily glad to see one another. From Enfield we went forward for London, and by the way we met with several Friends, of the meeting of Horslydown, to which I did belong from my childhood, who came to meet me, and accompanied us to London.

I staid in and about the city most of the winter, visiting meetings when I was well and in health; for through often changing the climates, I got a severe cold, and was ill for several weeks, so that I was not at any meeting, which time was very tedious to me; not so much because of my illness, as that I was deprived of divers opportunities and meetings, which are in that city every day of the week, except the last. When I was a little got over this illness, I went into Hertfordshire, and some parts adjacent, and had meetings at Staines, Longford, Uxbridge, Watford, Hempsted, Bendish, Alban's, Market Street, Hitchin, Hertford, Hoddesdon, and then returned again to London.

After I had been at London a while, I visited several other country meetings, as Winchmore-Hill, Tottenham, Wandsworth, Plaistow, Deptford and Epping, and then staid about London some weeks waiting for a passage for Holland, which I intended to visit, before I left my own habitation.

And on the 14th of the First Month, 1708-9, I with my companion John Bell, after having acquainted our friends and relations, having their consent, and taking our solemn leave of them, went down to Gravesend, and staid there two or three days for a fair wind. We went on board the ship

Anne, John Duck, master, bound for Rotterdam, in company with a fleet of vessels waiting for wind, &c. When the wind was fair, we sailed for the coast of Holland, and when we arrived on that coast the wind was contrary, and blew very hard, so that some of the ships in company lost their anchors; but on the 27th of the same month we arrived safe at Rotterdam in Holland. On the First-day morning we went to meeting at Rotterdam, where Friends have a meeting-house; and we staid at this city seven or eight days, and had six or seven meetings, and were comforted with our brethren and sisters, and greatly refreshed in the Lord Almighty. At this city we spoke without an interpreter, because most in the meeting understood English. From Rotterdam we travelled by the trek-schuit, or boat, being drawn by horses, which is a pleasant easy way of travelling, to a large town called Harlem, where we had a meeting, and spoke by an interpreter; to which meeting came divers of those people called Mennonists: they were very sober and attentive, and staid all the time of the meeting, and spoke well of it. From Harlem we went to Amsterdam, the metropolis of Holland, where Friends have a meeting-house. Here we had several meetings, and staid about a week. On the First-day we had a large meeting, to which came many people of divers persuasions and religions, as Jews, Papists, and others; and we had a good opportunity among them, and several were tender. A Jew came next day to speak with us, and did acknowledge, that Christ was the minister of that sanctuary and tabernacle that God had pitched, and not man; and that he was sensible of the ministry of Christ in his soul: "and," said he, "my heart was broken while that subject was spoken of in the meeting." I was glad to see the man tender and reached; but too generally speaking, the poor Jews, the seed of good Jacob, are very dark and unbelieving. I have met with but very few of them in my travels that have been tender: but I do love them for Abraham, Isaac, and Jacob's sake. At this meeting William Sewel, the author of the History of the Rise and Progress of the people called Quakers, a tender-spirited, upright man, interpreted for me. From Amsterdam we went to North Holland, and John Claus and Peter Reyard went with us to interpret for us; so by boat, or schuit, we travelled to a town called Twisk, where we had two meetings, Friends having a meeting-house there; from Twisk we went back again to Amsterdam, and had two large meetings there on the First-day; and Second-day in the evening, we went on ship-board, in order to cross the south sea to Herlingen, at which place we had two meetings, and we and Friends were glad to see one another: and, indeed we being as one family all the world over, are generally glad to see each other. From this place we travelled eastward through East Friesland, and went through several great towns and cities, until we came to Embden, the chief city in East Friesland, where we had a comfortable meeting by the bed-side of one of our Friends that lay sick; and several of her neighbours came in and staid till the meeting ended; some of them were very tender and loving, and wished us well, and were well satisfied. After meeting we set forward for Hamburgh, it being four days' journey by waggon, and passed along through divers towns and cities. We also travelled through the city of Oldenburgh, and a place of great commerce called Bremen. A magistrate of this city took notice of us, joined himself to us, and went with us to the inn, and then very lovingly took leave of us, and desired God to bless us. The people at our inns were generally very loving and kind to us, and some would admire at my coming so far only to visit my Friends, without any views of advantage or profit outwardly. When we got to Hamburgh, we had a meeting at Jacob Hagen's, and those that were there, were well satisfied with the doctrine of truth, blessed be God, who, I may say, was with us at that time and place! At Hamburgh there was at meeting one who had preached before the king of Denmark; who, as I understood by our interpreter, was turned out of his place for preaching the same truth that we had preached there that day; at which meeting were Papists, Lutherans, Calvinists, Mennonists, Jews, &c. All of them were sober, and generally expressed their satisfaction. I had so much comfort in that meeting, that I thought it was worth my labour in coming from my habitation, the answer of peace was such to my soul, that I greatly rejoiced in my labour in the work of Christ. From hence I travelled to Frederickstadt, it being two days' journey, where Friends have a meeting-house. We staid about ten days, and had nine meetings in that city. Some of the meetings were very large, and the longer we staid, the larger they were. This Frederickstadt is a city in the dominions of the duke of Holstein, and was the furthest place we travelled to eastward; and from hence I wrote a small piece, called, "A loving Invitation unto Young and Old in Holland and elsewhere;" which was translated into the German and Low Dutch languages; and divers impressions of it were also printed in England.

We travelled in this journey through some parts of the emperor of Germany's dominions, as also of the kings of Denmark and Sweden, and of the duke of Oldenburgh's and prince of East-Friesland's territories, besides some parts of the Seven Provinces of the United States. We parted with our Friends of this city of Frederickstadt, in much love and tenderness, and with our hearts full of good will one towards another, and so went back to the city of Embden a nearer way, by two days' journey, than to go to Hamburgh. We crossed the rivers Eyder, Elbe, and Weser; over which last we were rowed by three women. The women in those parts of the world are strong and robust, and used to hard labour. I have seen them do not only the work of men, but of horses; it being common with them to do the most laborious, and the men the lightest and easiest work. I remember that I once saw near Hamburgh a fair, well-dressed woman, who, by her dress or appearance, was a woman of some note, and a man, which I took to be her husband, walking by her, and she was very great with child, and the way difficult, being up a very steep hill, and he did not so much as offer his hand, or assistance to her; which, however it might look to a man of that country, it seemed very strange to me, being a Briton. For my part, I thought it unmanly, as well as unmannerly: on which I observe, that I never in any part of the world, saw women so tenderly dealt by as our English or British women, which they ought to value and prize highly, and therefore, to be the more loving and obedient to their husbands, the indulgent Englishmen; which indulgence I blame not, but commend, so far as it is a motive to stir them up to love and faithfulness.

In this journey between Frederickstadt and Embden, we had four days' hard travelling, and were twice overturned out of our waggons, but we got no harm which was admirable to us; for once we fell, waggon and all, over a great bank, just by the side of a large ditch, and did but just save ourselves out of the ditch. The next time we overset upon stones. We wondered that none of us were hurt, particularly myself, I being much heavier than any of the rest; but through the mercy of God, we got well to Embden the second time, and had a meeting upon a First-day, and immediately after meeting we took ship for Delfzuyl, which was from Embden about nine or ten English miles by water, and, with a fair gale of wind, got there in less than two hours' time. We spoke by interpreters all along, and were divinely helped to preach the gospel to the satisfaction of others, and our own comfort; and the friend who interpreted for us, was sensible of the same divine assistance, to his admiration, for which we were all truly thankful. But notwithstanding we were so opened, to the satisfaction of ourselves, our Friends, and the people, yet we were sometimes emptied to exceeding great spiritual poverty, and in the sense of our want and need, we did many times pour out our souls and spirits in humble prayer and supplication to the Most High, for his help and strength, that it might be made manifest to us in our weakness; and we found him a God near at hand, and often a present help in the needful time, and had a sweet answer to our prayers. Oh! that my soul, with all the faithful, may dwell near to him, in whom alone is the help and strength of all his faithful servants and ministers. Amen.

. .

From Delfzuyl we went to Groeningen, the chief city in Groeningland, and so on to a river called the Wonder, and to a town named Goradick, where we had a meeting with a few Friends there, and some of their neighbours came to the meeting. It was to us a comfortable meeting, and they were glad of it, they being but seldom visited by Friends. From this place we travelled by waggon to Hervine, where we lodged that night, and next day went by waggon to Leuwarden. It happened that we had generally very fine weather while in those open waggons, in which we travelled several hundred miles, so that Jacob Claus, our companion and interpreter, though he had travelled much, said he never had observed the like before: which observation I thought good to make, with thanks to the Almighty.

From the city of Leuwarden, we came by water to Herlingen, where Friends were glad to see us, and we them. We had a meeting in Friends meeting-house, and a good comfortable one it was, blessed be the Lord for it! From hence we crossed the South-sea, and had a contrary wind, which made our passage long and tedious. We were two days and two nights on this water before we got to Amsterdam, in all which, and the next day, I tasted no food, being three days fasting. I was willing to keep my body under, and found it for my health; neither had I any desire of food in those three days, in which time we had two meetings. We arrived at Amsterdam about the sixth hour, on the First-day morning, and had two meetings at Amsterdam that day, which were quiet, and many people came to one of them: but we could not be clear without going again to North Holland; so from Amsterdam we went to Horn, where we had a meeting in the collegian's meeting-house, and it was to satisfaction: the people were very loving, and divers very tender, even more than we had usually seen. They desired another meeting, but our time would not admit of it, we having appointed a meeting at Twisk the next day, which we had in the meeting-place, as also another at a Friend's house. The next day we returned to Amsterdam, and had a meeting, which began about the fifth hour, which was the last meeting we had in this city, and I hope it will not easily be forgotten by some. After it we solemnly took our leave of Friends, and departed for Harlem, where we were well refreshed in the love and life of Christ Jesus, our dear Lord and good Master. From Harlem we went with several Friends to Rotterdam, where we had two meetings, and in the evening we went to visit a Friend that was not well, with whom we had a meeting, and affecting time, and the sick Friend was comforted and refreshed, and said, she was much better than before; and we were edified, and the Lord our God praised and magnified over all, who is blessed for ever.

In those parts, viz. Holland, Friesland, Germany, &c. we travelled nine hundred and seventy-two English miles, all in waggons and vessels. We came not on a horse's back all the time. It was about nine weeks that we staid in those countries, travelling therein, and getting meetings where we could, which were to the number of forty-five, thus accounted:—

At Rotterdam . . .	10	At Horn	1
Harlem	3	Hamburgh . . .	1
Amsterdam . . .	10	Embden	2
Twisk	4	Frederickstadt	10
Herlingen	3	Goradick	1

all these are large cities except Twisk and Goradick.

From Rotterdam we took ship for London, and on the 30th of the Third Month, 1709, we sailed down the river Meuse to the Briel, in the ship *Anne*, John Duck master; but he missing the convoy, we took our passage in the packet; and so from Helvoetsluys we sailed over to Harwich, and thus safely arrived in our native land, blessing Almighty God for his many preservations and deliverances by sea and land.

About this time, after a long continuance of war, there was a great talking of peace, but the old enemy to peace, truth, and righteousness, broke it off by his evil working in man: neither can there be any lasting peace, until the nations come to the witnessing of the peaceable government and spirit of our Lord Jesus Christ, to be set up and established in themselves. The Lord bring it to pass, if it be his blessed will, with speed, for his holy name's sake! Amen.

As I have had great peace and satisfaction in my travels in Holland and Germany, so, for exciting others under the like exercise, I may truly say, that there is encouragement for faithful ministers to labour in the work of the gospel: for I know not that I ever met with more tenderness and openness in people, than in those parts of the world. There is a great people which they call Mennonists, who are very near to truth, and the fields are white unto harvest among divers of that people, spiritually speaking. Oh! that faithful labourers, not a few, might be sent of God Almighty into the great vineyard of the world, is what my soul and spirit breathes to him for!

After lodging one night at Harwich, we came to Ipswich, and from thence to Colchester, and staid there the First-day, and had two meetings; and had a meeting at Birch and Coggeshall, and then back to

Colchester, where we took coach for London, to the Yearly Meeting of Friends, which was very large. I gave some short account of my travels to the said meeting, with which Friends were satisfied, and made a minute thereof. I had been about twenty months from my habitation, and from my dear and affectionate wife, and from any manner of trade and business, either directly, or indirectly, being all that time wholly given up in my mind to preach the glorious gospel of God our Saviour, without any outward consideration whatever, taking my great Master's counsel, as I had freely received from him, so I freely gave; and had that solid peace in my labours that is of more value than gold, yea, than all the world.

From the Yearly Meeting I travelled through some parts of most of the counties in England, and also in Wales: in which service I laboured fervently, and often travelled hard, in body and mind, until the next Yearly Meeting, 1710, having travelled that year about two thousand five hundred miles, and had near three hundred public meetings, in many of which there were much people, and oftentimes great openness. I being at so many Friends' houses, and at so many meetings, if I was to be particular in the same it would be too voluminous, for which, and some reasons besides, I only give a general account thereof here.

In this year, viz. 1710, my dear friend and fellow-traveller, Richard Gove, departed this life, at Uxbridge, about fifteen miles from London, at our friend Richard Richardson's house. He died of a consumption. We travelled together in great love and unity, and the Lord blessed his work in our hands. We were in company in the West India islands, Ireland,

and North Britain, till we came to Berwick-on-Tweed. We met together again at London, and he visited some other parts of Britain in the time I was in Holland and Germany. He was an inoffensive loving Friend, and had a sound testimony, which was serviceable and convincing, and was well-beloved in Philadelphia, where he lived. He left a good savour and report behind him, I think, wherever he travelled in the world.

Now at this general meeting in London, I had a good opportunity to take my leave of my dear friends and brethren in my native land, not expecting to see it, or them any more, in this world. Oh! I may truly say, it was a solemn parting! it was a solemn time to me indeed. After the Yearly Meeting was over, I took my passage in the *Mary Hope*, John Annis, master, bound for Philadelphia; and on the 29th of the Fourth Month, 1710, at Gravesend, after having taken my solemn leave of our relations, and several of my dear friends, we set sail, and overtook the Russian fleet at Harwich, and so joined them, and sailed with them as far as Shetland, which is to the northward of the isles of Orkney. We were with the fleet about two weeks, and then left them, and sailed to the westward for America. In this time we had rough seas, which made divers of us sea-sick. After we left Shetland, we were seven weeks and four days at sea before we saw the land of America, and glad we were when we got sight thereof. In this time we had divers sweet and solemn meetings, viz. on First-days and Fifth-days, wherein we worshipped and praised the great JEHOVAH, and many things were opened in the spirit of love and truth, to our comfort and edification. We had one meeting with the Germans or Palatines, on the ship's deck, and one that understood both languages interpreted it for me. The people were tender and wrought upon, behaved sober, and were well satisfied: and I can truly say, I was well satisfied also.

In this voyage we had our health to admiration; and I shall observe one thing worthy of my notice. Some of my loving and good friends in London, fearing a sickness in the ship, as she was but small, considering there were so many souls on board her, being ninety-four in number, they, for that and other reasons, advised me not to go in her; for they loved me well, and I took it kindly of them: but I could not be easy to take their advice, because I had been long from my habitation and business, and which was yet more, from my dear and loving wife: and notwithstanding the vessel was so full and crowded, and also several of the people taken into the ship sick in the river Thames, yet they mended on board the vessel apace, and were soon all brave and hearty, being perfectly recovered at sea, and the ship, through the providence of the Almighty, brought them all well to Philadelphia, in the Seventh Month, 1710: I think I never was in a more healthy vessel in all my time, and I thought this peculiar favour worthy to be recorded by me. We had a very pleasant passage up the river Delaware, to our great satisfaction, the Palatines being wonderfully pleased with the country, mightily admiring the pleasantness and the fertility of it. Divers of our people went on shore, and brought fruit on board, which was the largest and finest they had ever seen, as they said, viz. apples, peaches, &c.

I was from my family and habitation in this journey and travel for the space of three years, within a few weeks; in which time, and in my return, I had sweet peace to my soul, glory to God for evermore! I had meetings every day when on land, except Second and Seventh days, when in health, and nothing extraordinary hindered, and travelled by sea and land fourteen thousand three hundred miles, according to our English account. I was kindly and tenderly received by my friends, who longed to see me, as I did them, and our meeting was comfortable and pleasant.

After this long travel and voyage I staid at home, and looked after the little family which God had given me, and kept duly to meetings, except something extraordinary hindered. Divers people, when I came home, raised a false report of me, and said, I brought home a great deal of money and goods, that I had got by preaching; which was utterly false and base; for I brought neither money nor goods, so much as to the value of five pounds, except my wearing apparel; so much the reverse, that I borrowed money at London, to pay for my accommodations home, the which I faithfully remitted back again to my friend that lent it me, to whom I was much obliged for the same: and if I might have gained a hundred pounds per annum, it would not have tempted me to undertake that, or such another journey. Soon after my return home again, I visited a few neighbouring meetings, which were large and edifying, Friends being glad to see me again returned home from that long journey. And I did, as I had reason to do, bless the holy name of the Lord, for his many preservations and deliverances by sea and land.

After some stay at Philadelphia, I went down with my wife and family into Maryland, to a cornmill and saw-mill which I had there, in order to live some time, and settle my affairs: and after being there some time, my dear wife was taken ill of a sore disease, which some thought to be an ulcer in the bladder, and I had her up to Philadelphia, she being carried as far as Chester in a horse-litter, where she continued for some months in much misery, and extreme pain, at the house of our very kind friends, David and Grace Lloyd, whose kindness to us in that sore, trying, and exercising time, was great, and is not to be forgotten by me, while I live in this world. From Chester we removed her again in a litter, being accompanied by our friends to Philadelphia, where she continued very ill all that winter, often thinking that death tarried long, and crying mightily to the Lord, Oh! come away, come away! This was her cry day and night, until at last she could speak no more. As we lived together in great love and unity, being very affectionate one to another; so being now left alone I was very solitary, and sometimes sorrowful, and broken into many tears, in the sense of my loss and lonesomeness. This my dear wife, was a virtuous young woman, and one that truly feared God, and loved his dear Son; from whom she had received a good gift of the ministry, and was serviceable to many therein. I had five children by her, four sons and one daughter, all which I buried before her, under three years old. At the Yearly Meeting before she died, she was so wonderfully carried forth in her ministry, by the divine grace, that divers of her friends believed she was near her end, she signifying something to that effect in her testimony, and that she should not live to see another Yearly Meeting: and so it came to pass; for she died before another Yearly Meeting, being aged about thirty-five years, and a married woman about thirteen years. Her body was carried to Friends' meeting-house in Philadelphia, and buried in Friends' burying-ground, being accompanied by many hundreds of our friends, in a solemn manner: and my heart was greatly broken in consideration of my great loss; and being left alone as to wife and children, I many times deeply mourned, though I well knew my loss was her and their gain!

Here I shall end the first part* of the Journal of some part of my life and travels, omitting many meetings, and lesser journeys, which I performed: and the accounts here given, have been mostly general, not descending into many particulars; though the adding some things might have been instructive and agreeable: the whole being intended as a motive to stir up others to serve, love, and faithfully follow, and believe in Christ.

* [The original distribution into Parts (three in number) is superseded in the present Edition by a more minute division into Chapters. This new arrangement, with the epitome that is given of the contents will, it is hoped, be found convenient.]

CHAPTER IV.

1712–1720.

EXTENSIVE TRAVELS IN AMERICA—SECOND MARRIAGE—VOYAGES ON BUSINESS TO THE BERMUDAS—VOYAGE PARTLY ON THE SAME ACCOUNT TO BARBADOES AND ENGLAND—RETURN HOME—A SECOND VOYAGE BY WAY OF BARBADOES TO ENGLAND, AND RETURN—VISIT TO FRIENDS IN MARYLAND, &c.

I NOW gave up my time mostly to travelling, for about the space of two years, in which I visited the meetings of Friends in the provinces of Pennsylvania, East and West Jersey, Maryland, Virginia, and North Carolina, and back again to Philadelphia, and then to New Jersey again: also to Long Island, Rhode Island, Conanicut Island, Nantucket Island, and New England, and through those parts on my return to Philadelphia. In these provinces, &c., I travelled some thousands of miles, and had many large meetings, some in places where there had not been any before, and some were convinced, and many would acknowledge to the testimony of truth, which was declared by the help and grace of Christ; and many times my heart was, by the assistance of that grace, wonderfully opened to the people. If I should be particular in the account of these journeys, it would enlarge this part of my journal more than I am willing.

In Virginia I had a meeting at James river, where a priest of the church of England, with some of his hearers, made some opposition, after our meeting was over, and were for disputing about religion; and he openly declared, The Spirit was not his guide, nor rule; and he hoped, never should be; but he said, the Scriptures were his rule, and that there was no heed of any other; and that they were as plain as Gunter's-line, or as one, two, three. I told him, the Scriptures were a good secondary rule, and that it were well if men would square their lives according to their directions; which we, as a people, exhorted all to: but that the Holy Spirit, from which the holy Scriptures came, must needs be preferable to the letter that came from it; and without which Holy Spirit, the letter kills, as saith the apostle. I also asked him, How he, or any else, without the light, or influence of the Holy Spirit, could understand the Scriptures, which were parabolically and allegorically expressed, in many places? And further, to use his own expression, How could any understand Gunter's line, without Gunter's knowledge; or, without they were taught by Gunter, or some other? Neither can we be the sons of God, without the Spirit of God. Which he answered not, but went away.

In New England, one Joseph Metcalf, a Presbyterian teacher at Falmouth, wrote a book, entitled, "Legal forcing a Maintenance for a Minister of the Gospel, warrantable from Scripture," &c. Which book, a friend of Sandwich gave me, and desired I would answer it; which, after finding some exercise on my mind, for the cause of truth, I was willing to undertake; and accordingly wrote an answer thereto, which I called, "Forcing a Maintenance, not warrantable from the holy Scriptures, for a Minister of the Gospel." In which I endeavoured to set the texts of Scripture in a true light, which he had darkened and misrepresented by his chimerical doctrines.

In this year, 1713, I went from Philadelphia, in the *Hope* galley, John Richmond, master, for South Carolina. We were about a month at sea; and when it pleased God that we arrived at Charleston, in South Carolina, we had a meeting there, and divers others afterwards. There are but few Friends in this province; yet I had several meetings in the country: the people were generally loving, and received me kindly. What I had to declare to them, I always desired to speak to the witness of God in the soul, and according to the pure doctrine of truth in the holy Scriptures; and there was openness in the people in several places. I was several times to visit the governor, who was courteous and civil to me. He said, I deserved encouragement, and spoke to several to be generous, and contribute to my assistance. He meant an outward maintenance; for he would have me encouraged to stay among them. But I told him, that though it might be a practice with them to maintain their ministers, and pay them money for preaching, it was contrary to our principles to be paid for preaching, agreeably to the command of our great Master, Christ Jesus, who said to his ministers, "Freely ye have received, freely give:" so that we are limited by his words, whatever others are: and those who take a liberty, contrary to his doctrine and command, I think, must be Antichrists, according to holy Scripture. The longer I staid there, the larger our meetings were; and when I found myself free and clear of those parts, I took my passage for Virginia in a sloop, Henry Tucket, master. I had a comfortable and quick passage to James river, it being about two hundred leagues. The master of the vessel told me, that he believed he was blessed for my sake. I wished him to live so as that he might be blessed for Christ's sake. And some reformation was begun on him in our voyage; which was the goodness of God, through Christ, to him, and not to be attributed to me, any further than an instrument in the Divine hand: for of ourselves we cannot do any thing that is good, it being by grace, through faith, that we are saved; which is God's gift to the soul.

After I had been some time in Virginia, I got a passage up the bay of Chesapeak, and had several meetings in Maryland, Friends being glad to see me; and we were comforted in Christ our Lord. I made some little stay at a place I had in that province, called Longbridge, and then returned to Philadelphia, where I lodged at the house of my very kind friends Richard and Hannah Hill; and was oftentimes at divers neighbouring meetings; and sometimes had good service therein.

About this time I had an inclination to alter my condition of being a widower, to a married state; and the most suitable person that I, with some of my good friends, could think upon, was Martha, the widow of Joseph Brown: and on the fifteenth of the Second Month, 1714, we were joined together in marriage, with the unity of Friends in general. We had a large meeting at our marriage, the solemnization thereof being attended with the grace and goodness of

God; and, for example-sake, we made but little provision for our guests: for great entertainments at marriages and funerals, began to be a growing thing among us, which was attended with divers inconveniences.

My wife was a sober and religious young woman, and of a quiet natural temper and disposition; which is an excellent ornament to the fair sex: and indeed, it is so both to male and female; for according to the holy Scriptures, A meek and quiet spirit is with the Lord of great price.

The first child we had I called Abigail (or the father's joy, as the word signifies) and while she lived, I had joy and comfort in her, even more than I could expect, her age considered; for she lived but about eighteen months, yet in that time gave frequent proofs of an uncommon capacity, and dropped such extraordinary expressions, that I have said to her mother, "This child is too ripe for heaven to live long on earth, therefore let us not set our hearts upon it." And I have thought, that in this child, the saying of Christ was fulfilled, even in the letter of it, "Out of the mouth of babes and sucklings thou hast perfected praise." Matt. xxi. 16.

I was at divers Yearly Meetings in 1715, viz. at Choptank in Maryland; at Shrewsbury and Salem in New Jersey; all which meetings were very large and comfortable, many things being opened therein, tending to the convincing and establishing the people in the truth and doctrine of Christ. I was likewise at divers other meetings in those provinces; which were large and satisfactory.

At Salem Yearly Meeting I was sent for to the prison, where there was a young woman that was to be tried for her life. She desired that I would pray for her, and charged me to warn the young people to be careful not to keep bad company: "For," said she, "it has been my ruin, and brought me to this shame and reproach." She had been tenderly brought up and educated; I knew her when she wore a necklace of gold chains, though now she wore iron ones: upon which subject I had afterwards a large opportunity to speak to the people in a very moving manner; which seemed to very much affect the youth, and others in the meeting, which consisted of many hundreds of people. I saw this young woman afterwards, the jury acquitting her; and I told her, that her life was given her for a prey; and reminded her, how it was with her when she was in prison in chains; and I advised her to walk more circumspectly for the future; which she said, she hoped she should do.

In the year 1716, I had some concerns which drew me to the island of Bermudas, to which island I went twice that summer. My family increasing, I traded a little to sea for their support and maintenance: and I can truly say, I carried on my affairs and business in the fear of God, having an eye, or regard therein, more to his glory, than to my own interest. We had a rough passage to this island in the first voyage, and were forced, by distress of weather, to cast some of our goods into the sea; and the storm being very violent, some of the seamen thought we should be devoured by the waves; and as for me, they had shut me up in the cabin alone, all in darkness, and the water came in so, that they were forced to take it out in buckets. When the storm was a little over, the master came to me, and asked, How I did all alone in the dark? I told him, Pretty well; and said to him, I was very willing to die, if it so pleased God: and indeed I did expect no other at that time. After this great storm was over, we arrived at Bermudas in a few days; but going into the harbour, the bottom of the vessel struck the rocks, but we got well in; for which I was thankful to the Almighty. I staid on the island about a month, and had several meetings, to some of which many came who were not called Friends. They were all sober, and some well satisfied; and the people of the island generally received me lovingly, and were very kind to me. Our ancients, who bore the burden and heat of the day, met with very different treatment. I tenderly desire that we who come up after them, may be truly humble and thankful to the Almighty for all his mercies!

By reason of my outward affairs, I had opportunities with some persons of great note and business on this island; and sometimes opened the principles of Friends to their satisfaction; some of them told me, they never understood so much concerning our Friends before; and if what I said was true, they had been misinformed. Divers such opportunities I had with several on this island, there being but very few of our society.

These are called the Somers Islands, or Bermudas, there being many little islands in the midst of the main island, in form like a horse-shoe, and are but two hundred leagues distance from the capes of Delaware. It is rare to see hail, snow, or ice there.

After I had done my business, and had been for some time on the island, I had a ready and comfortable passage home, where I was joyfully received.

After some little stay at home, I went the second

time, that summer, to Bermudas, and then also I had some meetings, and did some business on the island. It was my constant care, that my worldly affairs should not hinder me in my religious concern for the good of souls. It happened at this time there was a mighty hurricane of wind, so that it blew many houses to the ground, and very many trees up by the roots, and rent divers rocks asunder, which I was an eye-witness of: though it is to be observed, that those rocks in the Somers Islands, are not so hard as in some other parts of the world, particularly to the northward; for here they saw them with saws, and cut them with axes like wood. I was told there were sixty sail of vessels then at these islands, and all drove on shore but three, and ours was one of the three that rode out the storm; for which I was truly thankful. In this great storm, or hurricane, several sloops, there being no ships, were driven upon dry land, so that after the storm was over, one might go round them at high water, and several blown off the dry land into the water. One that was ready to be launched, though fastened on the stocks with two cables and anchors, put deep in the ground, yet the violence of the wind blew her into the water, and dashed her all to pieces.

About this time the Bermudas people had got a vast treasure of silver and gold out of the Spanish wrecks; and at a meeting which I had with a pretty many people on the First-day of the week before the hurricane, or storm of wind, it came weightily on my mind to exhort them. Not to be lifted up therewith, nor exalted in pride: for I declared to them, that the same hand that took it from the Spaniards, could take it from those who now had got it out of the sea; and if he pleased, by the same way; which was a storm that cast away the ships going for Spain. And indeed so it happened the same week; for it was reckoned by men of experience and judgment, that they had lost more by the storm, than they had gained by the wrecks of the Spaniards. A sober old man, not of our profession, told me the next day after the hurricane was over, that what I spoke in the meeting was soon come to pass: and he added, I was a true prophet to them. Many houses that were not blown down were uncovered. My landlord's house being old, several thought it would be down; but, by the good providence of God, it was one of them which stood. I was in my store, which stood also; though I expected every minute when it would have been blown down. It was by the mercy of God we were preserved, and not for any merit of ours. I entreated the Lord in the midst of this great wind, that he would please to spare the lives of the people; for many of them being seafaring men, were very unfit to die; at which time I thought I was sensible of the answer of my prayer, and he was pleased to be entreated for them: for, notwithstanding the violence of the storm, and the great destruction it made, yet not one man, woman, or child, nor creature was lost, that I heard of in all the island, which was to me very admirable. The Friend of the house came to me after the storm was abated, and said, The Lord had heard my prayers for them. Although they could not, by any outward knowledge, know that I had prayed for them, yet they had a sense given them, that I was concerned for them before the Almighty; which indeed was true. Oh! that they may never forget the merciful visitations of that high and lofty One, who inhabits eternity!

While I was on the island, I was invited to, and kindly entertained at the houses of several of the gentry, and at the governor's, who invited me several times to his house: and once I was with him and some of his chief officers at dinner, with divers of the first rank, where I was treated very kindly; and after dinner the governor's practice was to drink the king's health, and he hoped I would drink it along with them. "Yes," said the rest at the table, "Mr. Chalkley," as they called me, "will surely drink the king's health with us." So they passed the glass, with the king's health, until it came to me; and when it came to me, they all looked stedfastly at me, to see what I would do, and I looked as stedfastly to the Almighty, and I said to them, "I love king George, and wish him as well as any subject he hath; and it is known to thousands that we pray for him in our meetings and assemblies for the worship of Almighty God: but as to drinking healths, either the king's or any man's else, it is against my professed principle, I looking on it to be a vain idle custom." They replied, that they wished the king had more such subjects as I was; for I had professed a hearty respect for him; and the governor and they were all very kind and friendly to me all the time I was on the island.

After I had finished my concerns, I embarked in the sloop *Dove*, for Philadelphia, she being consigned to me in the former and this voyage. It being often calm and small winds, our provisions grew very scanty. We were about twelve persons in the vessel, small and great, and but one piece of beef left in the barrel; and for several days, the winds being contrary, the people began to murmur, and told dismal stories about people eating one another for want of provisions; and the wind being still against us, and, for ought we could see, like to continue, they murmured more and more, and at last, against me in particular, because the vessel and cargo was consigned to me, and was under my care, so that my inward exercise was great about it; for neither myself, nor any in the vessel, did imagine that we should be half so long as we were on the voyage: but since it was so, I seriously considered the matter; and to stop their murmuring, I told them that they should not need to cast lots, which was usual in such cases, which of us should die first, for I would freely offer up my life to do them good. One said, "God bless you, I will not eat any of you." Another said, he would die before he would eat any of me; and so said several. I can truly say, on that occasion, at that time, my life was not dear to me, and that I was serious and ingenuous in my proposition: and as I was leaning over the side of the vessel, thoughtfully considering my proposal to the company, and looking in my mind to Him that made me, a very large dolphin came up towards the top or surface of the water, and looked me in the face; and I called to the people to put a hook into the sea and take him, for "Here is one come to redeem me," said I to them; and they put a hook into the sea, and the fish readily took it, and they caught him. He was longer than myself; I think he was about six feet long, and the largest that ever I saw. This plainly shewed us that we ought not to distrust the providence of the Almighty. The people were quieted by this act of Providence, and murmured no more. We caught enough to eat plentifully of until we got into the Capes of Delaware.

Thus I saw it was good to depend upon the Almighty, and to rely upon his eternal arm; which, in a particular manner, did preserve us safe to our desired port: blessed be his great and glorious name, through Christ for ever!

I now staid at and about home for some time; after which I was concerned to visit Friends in several places, and in the adjacent provinces, as Maryland, New Jersey, &c., and was at many marriages and funerals, at which, many times, we had good opportunities to open the way, and also the necessity to be married to Christ Jesus, the great Bridegroom of the soul; and also to exhort the people to consider and prepare for their latter end and final change: which many times was sanctified to divers souls, and the Lord's name was glorified, who is worthy thereof.

In the year 1717, I went to Maryland, to look after my affairs in that province, and as I travelled, I had divers meetings at Nottingham, and at Bush River, about which time, at Bush River, several were convinced. The meeting I found in a growing condition in that which is good, several persons meeting together in silence to worship God, according to Christ's institution, which was, and is, and ever will be, in spirit and in truth: and for the encouragement of all such, Christ hath said, that such the Father seeketh to worship him: and again, "Where two or three are gathered together in my name, there am I in the midst of them." And if Christ be in the midst, there is no absolute need of vocal teaching, except it be the will of the Lord to call any to it. Let the spiritual Christian read and judge.

After my return I had several meetings in the country near Philadelphia; and about the latter end of the Eighth Month, I was at divers marriages, one of which was on the third day of the week, about fifteen miles above Philadelphia, over Delaware river.

The next was over the river again, about twenty miles below the city: the third was about twenty miles further down the river, and on the opposite side at Salem, on the following days; so that I crossed Delaware river three times in three days, and rode about one hundred miles. The meetings were all large, and matter suitable to the occasion freely opened to the people. These remarks are not intended to set up man, or exalt flesh, but to stir up others to come up to the work of Christ in their generation: all the glory and godliness of man is but as the grass, which soon withers, without we dwell in the root of true religion, and holy life of Christ; and that God may have the glory of all his works, is the end of all the labours and travels of the servants and faithful ministers of Christ.

In the tenth month, 1717, divers considerations moving me thereto, I took a voyage to Barbadoes, in the snow *Hope*, J. Curtis, master, and from thence to Great Britain and London; partly on account of business, and hoping once more, if it pleased God, to see my aged father, my brother, relations, and friends; which voyage I undertook in the solid fear of God. I desired the concurrence of my wife, and my friends and brethren of the meeting to which I did belong, in this undertaking, the which I had in a general way, and the good wishes and prayers of many particulars; with a certificate from our monthly meeting, signifying their unity with my conversation and ministry, and present undertaking; and felt the love and goodness of God therein, but in many respects it was a great cross to me, as the leaving my beloved wife and children, and many of my dear friends, whom I loved well in Christ: and the crossing of the seas always was troublesome to me, being sickly at sea, especially in windy or stormy weather; and the confinement was worse to me for the time than a prison; for it would be much easier to me to be in prison on land, upon a good account, than in prison at sea, I always looking on a ship to be a perilous prison, though my lot was to be much therein: and as for my natural life, I always gave it up whenever I went to sea; and I thought that was the least part of the hardship, never putting much value thereon; and I think I had rather die at any time, than go to sea, it being so contrary to my nature and disposition, as well as inclination: but to sea I went, for the reasons mentioned, and got from Philadelphia to Newcastle the first night, in the said vessel, and to Elsinburgh next day, where we lay for a fair wind about two days; and when the wind was fair, we sailed to Bombay Hook, where we met with two other vessels bound out to sea, who waited also for the wind. We lay there two nights, and then on the First-day morning set sail, the weather being bitter cold, and the ice very thick on the sides of our vessel, and on our ropes. The same day that we left Bombay Hook, we got out to sea, took in our boat, and went on our way; and in four or five days we got into warmer weather.

In this voyage I wrote something on the Common Prayer, used by some of the church of England, whose conversations were very loose and corrupt, which I entitled, "One truly tender Scruple of Conscience, about that Form of Prayer called the Common

Prayer, as used by the Church of England, and her Members," &c.

In this our voyage we saw several ships, but spoke with none; and in twenty-seven days from our capes, we arrived at Barbadoes, and came to an anchor in Carlisle Bay.

I had been twice in Barbadoes before, but this was the quickest passage by one day. Here I was lovingly and tenderly received by my friends. I took my good friend Joseph Gamble's house for my quarters, most of the time while I staid on the island; and I visited Friends' meetings several times over, there being five of Friends' meeting-houses in the island, and our meetings were sometimes large and open.

Our stay was longer here than we at first expected, by reason of a great drought, they having no rain for more than a quarter of a year, which was a great hindrance to trade on the island. While I was this time in Barbadoes, our ancient Friend George Gray died. I was at his funeral, at which there were many people; and on this occasion we had a large meeting at our meeting-house at Speights-Town, where I had a seasonable opportunity with the people, opening to them the necessity of preparing for, and thinking of their latter end; and pressed them earnestly thereto. They were generally attentive and sober, and some were broken into tenderness. While we were burying the Friend, there appeared a dismal cloud hanging over the island, such an one as I never saw before: it was to my thinking, of the colour of the flame of brimstone, and I expected there would have been a great storm, or some mighty gust, and much rain, they having had very little for many weeks, or some months; but it went over, and there was no rain, nor wind, as I remember. Soon after some people came in from sea, and they said, that from that cloud it rained ashes; and they brought some of the same to the Island, some of which ashes I have now before me: the taste of them seems to me to be a little sulphurous, and [they] have some glittering particles in them. In colour and smell I think they differed little from common ashes. Herein the Almighty and Infinite Being signally shewed his mercy and favour to poor mortals; for had not his mercy prevented, he could as easily have rained down the fire as the ashes, who rained down fire and brimstone on the cities and inhabitants of Sodom and Gomorrah, for their pride and idleness, much of which abounds among the inhabitants of Barbadoes; the people being very luxurious. Oh! may the luxurious inhabitants of that isle, as also all others, consider their ways and doings, and not provoke the great Lord, the Sovereign of heaven and earth, as many of them do by their evil lives, and voluptuous conversations; and that they would kiss the Son, though not with a Judas's kiss of profession, or speaking well or fair of him only, but with Divine love manifested through obedience; while his wrath is but a little kindled against them, before it break out into a flame.

After this funeral I was sent for to Bridgetown, to the burial of a master of a ship, a young man, who was very fresh and well a few days before. There was a great appearance of people, and I was pretty largely opened in the meeting, on the words of the prophet, where he says, "All flesh is grass, and all the goodliness thereof is as the flower of the field. The grass withereth, the flower fadeth, because the spirit of the Lord bloweth upon it: surely the people is grass. The grass withereth, the flower fadeth; but the word of our God shall stand for ever." Isaiah xl. 6–8. And I treated of this Word, its wonderfulness, its duration, and its work in man: as also of the fading constitution of mortal man, though young and strong, as that young man was a few days before, whose corpse was then before us.

I was at divers other burials on this island, which indeed doth prove a grave to many new comers. It being a hot climate, makes those who are not accustomed to it, very thirsty, and by reason of the extreme heat, it is not easy to quench their thirst; so that what is called moderate drinking, throws many strangers into a violent fever, and oftentimes is the cause of their death. I note this as a caution to any who may transport themselves there, that may see this, that they may shun that danger, which might be avoided by drinking cool drinks, of which they have many sorts very pleasant, viz. cane, sugar-reed and white sorrel, pine, orange, and divers others: and I advise such, as they love their health, to refrain from drinking much hot drinks or spirits.

I saw several curiosities in nature in this island, which among the great numbers of the works of God, do shew forth his praise and glory. One to the leeward part of the island, which is called the spout, sends up a vast body of water into the air, occasioned by a great cavity in the rocks under the water, which may be seen in calm weather, when the sea is low; but when the wind blows, a great body of water being pent in a large hollow place, it forces it up into the air, sometimes ten, fifteen, and twenty yards high, according as the strength of the wind is more or less, and makes a report like a cannon or thunder a great way off. I believe I have seen it ten or twelve miles out at sea. I was also at a place called Oliver's cave, which we got to with some difficulty, in going down the steep and craggy rocks. There is on the outward part next the sea, a very large vaulted place, in the form of a half circle, about one hundred feet high, as near as I could guess. In this large vault, behind a rock, is the mouth of the cave, not the height of a man at the first entrance; after one is in a few yards, one may walk upright comfortably, the bottom being pretty plain and smooth for about a hundred yards, and then we came into a large cave which is formed archwise, and about ten or fifteen yards high, as we thought, being much higher in the middle than the sides, but almost as regular as if it had been done by art, which we beheld with admiration, by the help of wax candles, and other lights, that we made and carried for that purpose.

When I had done my business in Barbadoes, having been about thirteen weeks there, our vessel being loaded, we sailed from thence the 10th of the Second Month, 1718, for London. We had a good passage, being five weeks and two days from Barbadoes to Great Britain, in which we saw divers vessels at sea, but spoke with none; and after sight of the land, we got in two days to Beachy-Head, which is about fifteen leagues from the Downs or Deal. We sailed along the shore by Folkstone, where we took in a pilot, and had a comfortable passage through the Downs, and up the river Thames to London, where I met with my dear and aged father, and loving brother, sister, and cousin, and many other of my near and dear relations and friends.

In this voyage I wrote some things which opened in my mind at sea, upon that excellent sermon of Christ's upon the mount, as it is recorded in the holy Scriptures of the New Testament, in the fifth, sixth, and seventh chapters of the Evangelist Matthew, but have since heard that the same is much better done by an abler hand; and therefore it may suffice here to give the advice, which in the course of my travels I have often had occasion to do, that the professors of Christianity should frequently read this sermon, and be careful to practise the same; that they may not only be Christians in name, but in deed, and in truth.

After visiting my relations, and some meetings of our Friends in and about London, and having finished my business, being ready to return homeward, divers Friends accompanied us from London to Gravesend; and the wind not being fair, we went to Rochester, and had a meeting there; and then back to Gravesend, and there took a solemn farewell of our friends, recommending one another to the grace of Christ; having this time made but little stay in Britain.

In the Fifth Month, 1718, we sailed from the Downs in the aforesaid snow *Hope*, divers Friends, viz. John Danson, Isaac Hadwin, John Oxley, Lydia Lancaster, Elizabeth Rawlinson, and Rebecca Turner, being in company with us: after about nine weeks' passage from land to land, having had meetings on First-days and Fifth-days, on board all the voyage, we came all safe and well to Philadelphia, through the blessing of God, where I staid with my family a few months, and then took another voyage for Barbadoes and Britain. I was under some concern more than ordinary, as to the support and well-being, or accommodation of my family, the circumstances thereof being a little changed by the increase of children, remembering the words of the apostle, that those who had not that care and concern, were worse than infidels; my Lord Jesus, whose servant I profess myself to be, also saying, "It is more blessed to give than to receive;" wherefore, an opportunity offering of the consignment of a vessel and cargo (the snow *Hope*, Warner Holt, master,) to Barbadoes, and from thence to London, and so to make returns home again for Philadelphia, I embraced it, though with reluctance, to leave my very loving wife, children, and friends, all whom I tenderly loved and respected. I also had in my eye an hope, through the blessing of God, to obtain wherewith to accommodate my friends, who were strangers and pilgrims in this world for Jesus' sake, as I also had been myself; and that they might find a place or home, and refreshment under my roof; not to excess, but to comfort and edification; which in sincerity, is all the grandeur I covet or desire in this world: so after due consideration, on the 2nd day of the Eleventh Month, 1718, we set sail from Philadelphia, many friends taking their leave and farewell of us for that voyage. Thus with hearts full of love and good-will, we parted with our friends, and went down the river about five miles, where we ran aground, but got off next tide, and next day came to an anchor at Chester. On the 4th day of the month we set sail, and got to Newcastle about the eleventh hour; it being meeting-day, we went to meeting, where our great Lord was pleased in some good measure to own us with his living presence, and comfort us with his love; blessed be his holy name! In the morning we sailed to Reedy Island, where we staid for the tide, and in the night our cable parted, which we knew not of till the morning, and then we had gone from the place where we anchored, about a league: but though the vessel drove about the river, yet she did not go on ground. We dropped our other anchor, and sent the boat to seek for that which was parted from us, but could not find it until the next tide, and then could not get it up, and were unwilling to go to sea without it; which occasioned us to stay several tides before we could get it: at last with much difficulty we weighed it, our men's clothes being much frozen; for it was very cold, and froze extremely hard. After this we went down to Bombay Hook, where was also another vessel going out to sea. Next day the wind was against us, and it snowed much and froze hard; and that night the river and bay were filled with ice as far as we could see, and it drove very hard against our vessel, so that we wished for day; for we thought sometimes it would have torn our bows in pieces; but our anchor and cable held us, we thought, to a miracle; for which we were thankful to the great keeper of all those who put their trust in him. When the tide turned for us we got up the anchor, and so let her drive with the ice down the bay; the other vessel did the same. It was now dangerous moving, go which way we would. The vessel in company with us attempted to go back again, but seeing that we did not, as we supposed, came to an anchor again, and we both went down the bay together; and the wind springing up fair, we got clear of the ice in a few hours time; but by this hindrance we could not get to sea that day, but were obliged to come to anchor near the middle of the great bay of Delaware, and the night being fair and calm, we rode it out safely, which if it had been windy weather, would have been dangerous. Early in the morning, of the 9th day of the month, we got to sea, and soon lost sight of the land. Next day the wind was high, and the weather proved stormy for several days, insomuch that our main-deck was under water most of the time, so that we were forced to go before it for several days together. We also shut up our cabin windows, and were tossed exceedingly, and I was very sea-sick; and we began in this storm to fear falling on the rocks of Bermudas, which we were near, as we imagined, and the wind set right on the island. But when we had passed the latitude of Bermudas, we met with fair weather and winds, all the remaining part of our passage being pleasant and comfortable, by which I was led to consider the vicissitudes which mortals may expect while on this unstable terraqueous globe, which is full of changes; and I strongly desired to be rightly prepared for that world which is eternal, and its joy and felicity permanent; at which blessed port, I hope in God's time, through his grace, safely to arrive. Thus through storms, tempests, ice, and snow, we left those frozen climes, and crossed the tropic of Cancer, between which, and that of Capricorn, there is neither frost nor snow at sea, at any time of the year, and the wind always within a small matter one way, viz. easterly, except in hurricanes and violent storms, which sometimes they have in those parts of the world. We arrived at Bridgetown, in Barbadoes, in one and twenty days, which was the quickest passage that ever I had, this being the fourth time of my coming hither, where I was always kindly received by my friends.

About this time war was declared against Spain by

the king of Great Britain, by proclamation in Bridgetown, which put such a damp on trade, that there was little business, and the markets low and dull, which made my stay longer than I would have chose; but my friends, among whom I had many opportunities, seemed rather pleased than otherwise; telling me, that they did not care if I was to stay there always, if it were my place: and when I left Barbadoes, Friends gave me better credentials than I thought I deserved. A friend of mine giving me intelligence that the market was better at Antigua than at Barbadoes, I dispatched my affairs, and took part of our cargo there, and was kindly received by our friends. We were about three days in our passage, and had fine weather therein. At Antigua I had divers meetings, my business, at no time, hindered me in my more weighty service; for I always, through Divine help, made that give way to my religious duty, in which I ever found peace and inward satisfaction. In about five weeks I finished my business in this island, having no small satisfaction in coming to it; and our vessel being now loaden, we took our solemn leave, and with the good wishes of many, departed for England.

Our friends there signified to their brethren, that they were glad of my company, and that I was serviceable to them, though I came upon business. My hand, when need required, was to my business, but my heart was, and I hope is, and ever shall be, freely given up to serve the Lord, in that work whereunto I believe he has called me. We have liberty from God, and his dear Son, lawfully, and for accommodation's sake, to work or seek for food or raiment; though that ought to be a work of indifferency, compared to the great work of salvation. Our Saviour saith, "Labour not for the meat which perisheth," but for that "which endureth" for ever, or to eternal life: by which we do not understand, that Christians must neglect their necessary occasions, and their outward trades and callings; but that their chief labour, and greatest concern, ought to be for their future well-being in his glorious kingdom; else why did our Lord say to his disciples, "Children, have you any meat?" they answered "No;" and he bid them cast their nets into the sea, and they drew to land a net full of great fishes; and fishing being their trade, no doubt but they sold them, for it was not likely they could eat them all themselves. Also the apostle of Christ says, he that doth not take care of his family, "is worse than an infidel;" and the apostle Paul, the great apostle of the Gentiles, wrought with his hands, even while he was in his travels, and in the work of the gospel; and others tasted of the benefit of his labour naturally, as well as spiritually. It is also written, that he that will not work shall not eat. By this, and much more, which might be noted, it appears that we not only have liberty to labour in moderation, but we are given to understand, that it is our duty so to do. The farmer, the tradesman, and the merchant, do not understand by our Lord's doctrine, that they must neglect their calling, or grow idle in their business, but must certainly work, and be industrious in their callings. We all ought to understand, that our hearts and minds ought to be out of the world, or above the nature and spirit of it. It is good and profitable for both soul and body, rightly to distinguish between earthly and heavenly things, and to be careful how they mix the one with the other; for it is an eternal truth, that God and mammon cannot dwell together, or join together in the heart. If our love is more to God than the creature, or to heaven than earth, then will he dwell in us and with us: but if our love is more to the creature than to Christ, or to earth than heaven, then will he not dwell with us, but will leave us to ourselves; for the Lord Omnipotent will not admit of any rival.

On the 11th of the Fourth Month, 1719, we left Antigua, stood close to the wind till we again crossed the Tropic, and got into those latitudes where the winds are variable. Sailing in the great deeps we saw the wonders of the Lord, particularly in divers kinds of fish, they living upon one another in the sea, the great fishes on the small ones; and mankind too much resembles them in that respect. About the latitude of thirty-three north, our master, Warner Holt, seeing a shoal of porpoises about the ship, though he was not very well, and had not been for most of the voyage, he took his harping-iron and struck one of them, and we took him into the vessel, out of which we got eleven quart bottles of oil; and we most of us eat heartily of this fish, which agreed with our people very well. They fried his liver for our mess, of which I eat a large meal, which was well tasted, and eat more like fresh beef than fish. I make this memorandum of it, that if any should take them when their provisions are scarce, they may eat freely without danger, according to our experience. When we had been at sea about three weeks, being near the latitude of forty north, and about the longitude of forty-two, though it was in the midst of summer, we saw an island of ice, at which we all marvelled, and judged that there had been a severe cold winter in those latitudes on the land of America. When we saw this island of ice we judged ourselves not far from the Banks of Newfoundland. Hitherto we had easy gales of wind, and many calms, which made our passage seem long to us. We saw two sail of ships about those latitudes, but spoke with neither, being willing to shun them as it was war time.

We had in this voyage weekly meetings for worshipping the Almighty, in which the great Lord, both of sea and land, was pleased greatly to manifest his name and truth amongst us, for which my soul often secretly and openly blessed and praised his Divine and glorious name and truth; for he bore up my drooping spirits, so that I could truly say with the royal Psalmist, not because he spoke it only, but also being an experimental witness thereof, "The floods have lifted up, O Lord, the floods have lifted up their voice: the floods lift up their waves. The Lord on high is mightier than the noise of many waters, yea, than the mighty waves of the sea." Psalm xciii. 3, 4. This the king wrote of his own experience in a spiritual sense; but I may say without boasting, I have witnessed the rage and noise of mighty waves and waters, both natural and spiritual; the one, as though it would swallow up my reputation among men, and the other, as though it would swallow up my person, in this my watery peregrination: but blessed be the name of Him that is Holy and Eternal, who indeed is stronger than the noise of many waters, or than the mighty waves of the sea, either inwardly or outwardly, I will through his strength, magnify his name, because he is worthy: and may I do it for ever!

About the 11th day of the Fifth Month, we saw great flocks of birds, which we judged came from the Azores, or Western Islands, near which we reckoned ourselves to be. The 21st day we saw, and came up with a French ship, which had been fishing on the Banks of Newfoundland, and was bound for Havre de Grace in France, the master of which came on board us, and our captain went on board them. We exchanged some rums and sugars, of our sea-stores, for their French wine and cider, and some of our provisions for some of their fish. The captain was a Protestant, and very courteous to us: the Regent of France at this time being kind to the Protestants, so that they increased much in that kingdom. The Frenchman seeming desirous to know what religion I was of, I told him by an interpreter, that I was one called a Quaker, or Trembler, and that our principle was to do good to all men, and not to hurt any man, according to Christ's doctrine, Not to render evil for evil, but to overcome evil with good. When they went away and took leave of us, they desired me to pray for them, the which I remembered with tenderness of spirit, and having but little wind, we kept company for several days; but the wind springing fair, we wished them well, and went on our way, our vessel outsailing most we met with; and a few days after we met with a New England ship, who came out six days before us from Antigua. We were then in the latitude of about fifty north, and twenty-nine and a half degrees of longitude from the Land's End of Great Britain. The 30th day of the Fifth Month, we sounded, and found ground at twenty-eight fathom, and on the 1st of the Sixth Month, we saw the Land's End of England, all our company being in health, and well; for which my heart was truly thankful to that great and infinite Being, whose providence is over us poor mortals in all parts of the world, and who reigns over sea and land, and is worthy of adoration, worship, service, and living praise for ever!

In a few days we came into the English Channel, and going up the Channel there came one of the king's yachts, and they pressed most of our men; the best hands we had they took from us, and carried them on board a man-of-war, after which we came to anchor at Folkstone, where I left the vessel, and got a horse to Dover, and from Dover took coach to London. In the coach were divers persons who began to talk about the Quakers, and spoke against their plain way of living and clothing, and said, that they did not understand their unfashionable way of conversation; neither was it the way to gain proselytes. Upon which I asked them, whether they understood Paul, the great apostle of the Gentiles? who said, "Be not conformable to this world," (*i. e.* the fashions of it) for this great reason, the world, and the fashions thereof, passeth away; which is a great truth, and it is plainly seen how fickle and changeable the world is in its vain fashions and customs, which, to follow, in all its foolish cuts and turns, or changes, must, of consequence, make a man or woman very foppish and apish. I told them, that our religion was agreeable to the holy Scriptures, which, if they did not understand, neither could they understand us; for the doctrine of Christ and his apostles, was generally therein very plain; and the doctrine in Christ's excellent Sermon on the Mount, is clear and plain to very low or mean capacities: so they discoursed no more of religion till we came to London, where once more I met with my loving and aged father, a man fearing God, and having a gift of the ministry of the gospel of Christ, and well-beloved of his friends and neighbours, who, with others of my near and dear relations and friends, received me gladly.

After some months' stay among my relations and friends in London, we sold our vessel, the snow *Hope*, and bought another ship, which we called the *Trine-Hope*, Warner Holt, master, and when I had done my business, I sailed in the same ship for Pennsylvania. We had meetings on board the vessel twice a week, in which the Almighty was pleased to favour us with his good presence.—Sobriety, and the fear of God, and faith in his beloved Son Christ, was often recommended to the youth then on board the vessel with us, of whom there were divers, who transported themselves to America, in order to settle there. At one meeting on board I was tenderly concerned to remind them of Jacob, who, in his youth, left his country and relations to sojourn in a strange land, and how in that undertaking, he sought the Lord, and his blessing, more than any outward thing; and that he was greatly blessed with many favours from heaven above, and also from the earth beneath, and they were advised to take him for their example: and many other things were tenderly opened to them in the love of God, and in his fear and counsel they were exhorted from time to time.

It being winter time, we sailed to the southward, and got into warm weather, and were on our passage seven weeks and some odd days from land to land, in which time we saw several vessels, and spoke with one, whose people said they were chased by a Turk, but got from him, at which they greatly rejoiced. We apprehended it was our ship that they saw over night, for we saw a sail that crowded from us as fast as she could, and it being near night, we shortened sail, and so she left us; but in the morning came up with her, and being pretty near, both they and we put out our colours, and being both Englishmen, we spoke to each other, and were glad to meet with some of our own nation upon the great ocean; but our vessel sailing best, we took our leave of them, wishing them a good voyage. We met with rough seas and high winds in the latter part of our passage, till we came to the capes of Delaware, which we were all rejoiced to see, and we had a pleasant passage up the bay and river to Philadelphia, where I had once more a comfortable meeting with my dear wife and family, which I gratefully acknowledged as a high favour from the hand of the Almighty.

We arrived at Philadelphia the 1st of the Second month, 1720; after which I staid at, and about home for some time, and I was not idle, but kept to my business, and to meetings, and having a desire to see my friends in the province of Maryland, at their general meeting at West River, I was accompanied by Isaac Norris and Thomas Masters, both sober young men. It had been a time of pretty much rain, and the waters thereby being out and high, going over a ford at Brandy Wine, my mare got among the rocks, it being a very rocky creek, she fell down, and the stream being very strong, she rolled upon me, and being entangled with the stirrup, I could not easily clear myself, but I gave a spring from her, and swam to clear myself from her; and when I was clear, I got to her again, and laid hold of her mane, and through the good Providence of God, got well out with the mare on dry land, which was a remarkable deliverance. In three days we got to West River, to the yearly meeting, which was large, and Friends were glad to see me, I having not been there for several years. I was out on this journey about two weeks, and rode about three hundred miles; and after my coming home, I travelled pretty much in and about the provinces of Pennsylvania and New Jersey.

CHAPTER V.

1721—1724.

SEVERAL JOURNEYS—REMARKABLE DEATH OF TWO ATHEISTICAL YOUNG MEN—REMOVAL FROM PHILADELPHIA TO THE NEIGHBOURING VILLAGE OF FRANKFORT — VISITS IN DIFFERENT PLACES — EPISTLE TO FRIENDS OF BARBADOES—VISIT IN LONG ISLAND—AFTER HIS RETURN, MEETS WITH AN ACCIDENT—A LETTER ON THE SUBJECT OF BAPTISM—GREAT LOSSES AND TRIALS—EXTRACT OF A LETTER FROM HIS AGED FATHER, WITH HIS ANSWER.

In the year 1721, Thomas Lightfoot and I, with William Browne, went to a meeting at Bush River, and going over Susquehannah-Ferry, the people were fiddling and dancing. When their dance was over, I asked them, believing them to be Protestants, If they thought Luther to be a good man? They replied, Yes, there was no doubt of it. "Well," said I, "and so do I; and I will tell you what he says concerning dancing, That as many paces as a man takes in his dance, so many steps he takes towards hell;" which spoiled their sport, and they went away, and we went on ours towards the meeting; and a good meeting it was! and we after it returned by way of Nottingham, and had a meeting there, and one at New-Garden, and so on to Philadelphia. I was from home about a week, and travelled in this journey about one hundred and fifty miles, and was well satisfied therein.

In the years 1721 and 1722, I went several journeys, and had many large meetings, travelling many hundreds of miles, of which I neglected to keep a particular account, hardly thinking what I did worth recording; but divers of my friends in many parts of the world, put me upon something of this nature, to which, at length, I gave up, and found some benefit and satisfaction therein, in looking back and considering the dealings of God with me in my youth, and upwards.

From Philadelphia I went to the general meeting at Shrewsbury, in East Jersey, where I heard of J. G.'s being wounded by a young man, with a sword, of which he died, lamenting that he did not take the counsel of his friends; as young men who slight the counsel of those that wish them well, commonly do, either sooner or later, if the day of their visitation be not over. Some few days after this meeting at Shrewsbury, I visited Friends on Long Island, and returned home again, having travelled about three hundred miles. In my stay at, and about home, I wrote something concerning perfection, in answer to a nameless author; as also something concerning predestination, or election and reprobation.

In the year 1722, I went back in the woods to Buckingham, the Great Swamp, Perkiomy, Manahatawny, and Oley, where I had meetings, travelling over great mountains, from which we could see many miles. I travelled in this journey about one hundred and fifty miles, and returned home in about two weeks; and after staying some time at home, and visiting neighbouring meetings, I went to the yearly meeting of Friends on Long Island, which meeting was very large, many people, not of our persuasion, being there, and were very sober. Many things were opened in the love of Christ, and his great love was declared to that great congregation. The parable concerning the Prodigal Son, came before me to speak of to the people in a very moving manner, and strongly to invite the youth to lay hold of the love of the Father in his Son, to poor souls: and indeed it is a wonderful parable, setting forth the infinite love of the great Lord of all to his poor creatures. Many were affected and reached to at this meeting, and the Almighty was praised and glorified, who alone is worthy.

From thence I went and had a meeting at New York, and then set forward to Woodbridge, where we had a comfortable meeting; Naaman, the Assyrian, being much the subject of that day's work: and that one thing loved and esteemed more than Christ, whatever it be, is to be avoided, and the people warned to be careful to keep close to the God of Israel, spiritual Israel, and to give up all which is contrary to his nature, and to take up Christ's cross, and follow him: for it is those who follow him in the regeneration, that are to be heirs of his kingdom.

In this year also, I was at the burial of our friend, Jonathan Dickinson, at which we had a very large meeting; he was a man generally well beloved by his friends and neighbours. In this meeting a passage, he had often told me in his health, was brought to my remembrance, I think worthy to be recorded to the end of time, which is as follows: "It happened at

Port Royal, in Jamaica, that two young men were at dinner with Jonathan, and divers other people of account in the world, and they were speaking about earthquakes, there having been one in that place formerly, which was very dreadful, having destroyed many houses and families. These two young men argued that earthquakes, and all other things came by nature, and denied a supernatural power, or Deity; insomuch that divers, surprised at such wicked discourse, and being ashamed of their company, left it; and at the same time the earth shook, and trembled exceedingly, as though astonished at such treason against its Sovereign and Creator, whose footstool it is: and when the earth thus moved, the company which remained were so astonished, that some ran one way, and some another, but these two atheistical young men staid in the room, and Jonathan with them, he believing that the providence of Almighty God could preserve him there if he pleased, and if not, that it was in vain to fly; but the hand of God smote these two young men, so that they fell down; and, as Jonathan told me, he laid one on a bed, and the other on a couch, and they never spoke more, but died soon after." This was the amazing end of these young men: a dreadful example to all Atheists, and dissolute and wicked livers. Oh! that young people might be warned, that the hand of God might be upon them for good, and that they would tenderly be concerned for their salvation.

On the 30th of the Fourth Month, 1723, my tenth child, named Thomas, died about midnight, having before buried nine. It was some exercise to me thus to bury my children one after another; but this did a little mitigate my sorrow, that I knew, that could I have all things relating to them according to my desire; could I see them grow up to be sober men and women, well married, have a competency in the world, &c., yet it was safer and better for them, and they more out of danger, being taken away in their infancy and innocency; and I fervently begged of the Almighty, that he would be pleased to take them away while innocent, rather than that they should live to be vicious or unrighteous men and women, and to bring scandal on the holy name of Christ, and upon our Christian profession; which consideration did mightily tend to settle and quiet my mind in my sorrowful exercise. The great Lord of all sanctify the sorrows and afflictions of his people and children, and grant them the fulfilling of that blessed portion of holy Scripture, that all things shall work together for the good of them that love and fear God: even so be it, saith my soul!

In the Sixth Month of this year, I removed from the city into the country, to a small plantation I had at Frankfort, in order to be more retired, and for health's sake, &c., finding some declining in my bodily strength, which I take to be very much owing to the severe colds and hardships I have sustained in my long and hard travels, more especially in the wilderness of America; for without vanity I may say, that I always loved temperance, and have been sometimes zealously concerned to preach against intemperance; and though I cannot now take so long journeys as I have formerly, my spirit earnestly travails for the welfare of Zion, and the peace and prosperity of all those who love, fear, and serve God, and believe in his Son.

On the sixth-day of the Eighth Month, it pleased

God to give me another son, whom I named George, after my father, brother, nephew, and king; and though this name is now a great name among men, I considered that no man can preserve life, so I gave him up to the will of him who gave him to me, and desire, if I have no name through children to posterity, I may have a name in the Lamb's book of life, which I have ever esteemed far above a name amongst men.

After my removal to this place I was not idle, but visited neighbouring meetings, and in the Eighth Month I went to Shrewsbury general meeting, where there were many hundreds of people, and the truth declared had good impressions upon the minds of many; some, after meeting, who were not of our society, acknowledged to the truth, and that they were glad they were there. In this meeting I was concerned for the welfare of mankind, and the exaltation of the holy name of the Almighty, to declare the universal love of God to man, from several texts of holy Scripture, as that passage concerning Jacob and Esau, and Peter and Cornelius, and something concerning the objection made against us the people called Quakers, that we do not acknowledge the holy Scriptures to be the word of God; for though we believe that the Scriptures came by divine inspiration, yet we are clearly convinced by their testimony, and by the Spirit of truth in our hearts, that Christ is the eternal Word of God, by whom all things were made and created, and do still exist.

From Shrewsbury, with divers other Friends, I rode to Croswicks, where on the Fifth-day, we had a very comfortable meeting, in which the ancient love and goodness of our heavenly Father was with us, to the tendering our hearts into tears of joy; some of us being likewise affected, in remembrance of the goodness of the Almighty to us, in the meeting we had in this place under the trees about twenty-five years since. The great subject of faith and works was spoken to; as that the Romans (Romanists) seemed to lay too much stress on works, and the Lutherans, Calvinists, and others, too little; but our principle led us to join both together; the Almighty having joined them together, none ought to separate them. This subject of faith and works having been much in debate amongst professed Christians, it is on my mind here to mention a few things deduced from the best authority:

The first is, Without faith it is impossible to please God. Heb. xi. 6.

Second, Faith is the gift of God.

Third, Faith works by love.

Fourth, Faith is the evidence of things not seen, and the substance of things hoped for.

Fifth, Faith without works is dead.

Sixth, The just live by faith.

Seventh, You believe (or have faith) in God, believe also in me. John xiv. 1.

And the author to the Hebrews speaks excellently concerning the power of faith, and the mighty wonders wrought by it. Note, this living, saving, true and divine faith, must be in the heart, through, and in Christ Jesus the Son of the living God, who is, and always will be, the author and finisher of it in every true believer.

After I came from Shrewsbury, I visited divers neighbouring meetings, and some in Chester county, where I had meetings for nine days successively, some of which were very large, particularly at Providence and Goshen, in which I was opened to exhort them to keep to that plain, honest way of life and conversation, which our fathers and elders were found in, and to remind them of the sufferings they endured for their testimony to the blessed truth, in the first breaking forth thereof in the last age; and I was concerned to shew them that the Almighty, who had blessed us with plenty of temporal blessings, would continue the same to us, if we were careful to live in his fear; but that otherwise, we might expect his judgments for disobedience.

And after my return I continued about home for some time, it being winter season and bad travelling, and I not so capable of travelling as formerly; but I had great peace and tranquillity of mind, in that I had freely given up my youthful days to serve my Creator; and the same love and zeal was yet fresh and warm in my heart, for the glory of his great name; and I still have a full resolution, through his strength and grace, to serve him, the great Lord of all, all my days, according to the light and strength given to me.

Our Yearly Meeting at Philadelphia this year was large, in which our friend Benjamin Kidd, from England, being with us, had good service. I cannot forget a concern which was upon me at this meeting, that the universal love of God, through Christ, might prevail amongst mankind, and to press Friends to manifest to all people the influence thereof, by their exemplary lives and conversation.

In the Second Month, 1724, I went into New Jersey, as far as Shrewsbury, where, on a First-day, we had a large meeting, to general satisfaction; and the next day we had another, wherein the love and good-will of God, through Christ, was opened freely to the people, and our duty to forgive one another was largely treated of; and it was plainly shewn, that without forgiving others, we could not be forgiven of God, as Christ saith, "If ye forgive men their trespasses, your heavenly Father will also forgive you; but if ye forgive not men their trespasses, neither will your Father forgive your trespasses," Matt. vi. 14, 15, &c., and much more to the same effect on that subject; as also Christ's answer to Peter, who asked, how oft a man should forgive his brother if he trespassed against him. Peter says, "till seven times?" Our Lord Jesus answers, "I say not unto thee, until seven times, but until seventy times seven," Matt. xviii. 22. And again Christ says, If thy brother "trespass against thee seven times in a day, and seven times in a day turn again unto thee, saying, I repent, thou shalt forgive him," Luke xvii. 4. Which hard-hearted people think a great hardship, but Christ's cross must be taken up, and borne daily, if we will be his disciples and followers in deed and in truth, as well as in profession.

After we had reconciled some differences at Shrewsbury, we went to a place called Menesquan, and had a good open meeting, and most of the people of that place were there. It was a good time, and I hope the opportunity will not soon be forgotten by divers that were there. From this place we travelled to Croswicks, and had a good meeting. After meeting, a Friend told me that some would say, I spoke by information, because I had opened some matters which were exactly to the state and condition of some there: but I knew nothing of their state and condition, otherwise than as it was then immediately opened in my mind; neither had I been told any thing concerning them, directly or indirectly: and from thence we travelled to Burlington, where the monthly meeting of our Friends had desired that I would be assistant to help to end a difference which had happened through mistake, and continued for seven years, since the first occasion was given, and through Divine assistance, our hearts being filled with the love of Christ, we so prevailed upon the differing persons, that they gave each other satisfaction, with hopes that they should live in love for the future; and Friends of the place greatly rejoiced at the end of that difference. As I went along this town, some Friends told me of a religious people some few miles distant, whom they desired I would have a meeting with. I desired them to see if it would be granted, and let me know; which was done, and we had a meeting, and were kindly received, and the Divine nature of the gospel of Christ was freely opened to them, and in great love we parted from one another. I travelled in this journey about two hundred miles; and when I came home, my dear wife and family gladly received me with hearts full of love: and this testimony I think proper, for several solid reasons, to leave behind me of my virtuous and loving wife, that since we were married, she never hindered me in the service my great Master called me unto, in all the time of our living together: we always parted, for the sake of the gospel of Christ, in pure love, and in the same love we always met again.

Soon after this time I met with several great losses by sea and land, and myself and my little daughter were dangerously sick, so that our recovery seemed doubtful; yet through the mercy of God we both recovered, for which I praise his name.

After some stay at home, I was again moved in the love of Christ, to visit the General Meetings of Duck Creek and Salem. At Duck Creek we had a large and satisfactory meeting. From Duck Creek I appointed a meeting at George's Creek, which was a good meeting. The next morning we went over to Elsinburgh, and so on to Cohansy, where I met with two of my fellow-labourers in the work of Christ, Thomas Lightfoot and Benjamin Kidd. We had a meeting together at Cohansy, in which the people were exhorted to sobriety and just dealing. The contrary of both is too obvious at such times as Fairs; there being divers of the Fair people there as well as others, the nature of Christ's work in the heart, was somewhat spoke to, but it was not so open a meeting as some others, the people thereaway being too slack and dull as to religion. Next day we had a meeting at Alloway's Creek, where we all three had some pretty close work; and from thence we went to the General Meeting at Salem, which was larger than common, on account of the said Friend, Benjamin Kidd's, being there; who, in the love of Christ came from England, to visit the churches in this part of the world. There were so many Friends and others here at this time, that some houses were so filled, that there was not room for all that came to lodge there. After this meeting I returned home, and in a few days went into Chester County, and travelled above one hundred miles; and when I came home I understood, that some, for want of a true sense of the work of Christ, had been censuring me for my travelling and hard labour in the work of the ministry of the gospel of Christ; though, by the same rule of judging, the apostles of Christ, and our ancient Friends, who travelled much, cannot escape their censure; for in all my travels, I have had an especial regard to the unity of the brethren, and never knowingly went abroad without it; but let this caution be recorded for the instruction of all such forward judges; let them be careful of judging Christ's servants, lest their words become their burden: "Judge not, that ye be not judged," saith our great Lord, "for with what judgment ye judge, ye shall be judged."

Soon after my return from Chester County, I was at a marriage at Abington, which was one of the most solemn I have been at; and on the 15th of the Third Month, at the youths meeting at German Town, to my great satisfaction; and on the 23rd of the same month, I went to the General Meeting of ministers and elders at Burlington; at which meeting, several things relating to the gospel ministry were declared: as its being a free, a clear, and a powerful ministry, reaching to the conscience, and convincing of the danger of continuing in sin: and Divine charity was much recommended, without which, all ministry is but as sounding brass, &c. From this meeting I went with Walter Herbert, into Bucks County, and at Neshaminy we had an open, tender meeting. From thence I went to Buckingham, and was at a marriage of a son and daughter-in-law of Thomas Canby's The meeting was large, and Friends well satisfied; and it was observable, though I was very hoarse, through a cold I had taken, and could hardly speak in common conversation, yet it was much taken away in my ministry, so that I was carried through the service to our admiration, for which I was truly thankful. After this meeting I returned home with true satisfaction, such as is much more valuable than silver and gold, two mighty idols in the world.

After a little stay at home, I went on a First-day to North Wales, or Gwynedd, where was a pretty large meeting, many young people being there, to whom I was concerned to shew, that Christ is the way by which we must come into the true church, through regeneration, and that all who invent other ways are thieves and robbers. I rode twenty-five miles that day, and the next day came to Frankfort, and was at the burial of an ancient Friend, Joan Orpwood, at which our friend John Salkeld was, with whom I was the next day at Philadelphia, at our Third-day meeting, which was a good meeting.

On the fourth day of the Fourth Month, intending soon to take a journey to Long Island, I thought it a proper time to alter my will, as I had kept one by me for divers years before, considering the uncertainty of life. On the 5th of the Fourth Month I went to Merion to visit an ancient Friend, John Roberts, who was sick near unto death, where I again met with John Salkeld. The Friend expressed his satisfaction in this visit, and we had a reward of peace in the exercise of that Christian duty of visiting the sick, which is recommended by the apostle to the primitive churches of Christ. After we had been some time with our said sick friend, we went to the meeting which had been appointed for us several days before, and was large and satisfactory; for which favourable visitation we blessed the great name of the Almighty, and parted tenderly in Christian love and good-will. The Friend we went to visit died the next day. He was a helper of the poor, and a maker of peace in the neighbourhood: of such, Christ said, "Blessed are the peace-makers, for they shall be called the children of God."

On the 10th of the Fourth Month, 1724, I had a concern to write the following epistle to Friends in the island of Barbadoes.

"Frankfort, *the* 10*th of Fourth Month,* 1724.

"DEAR FRIENDS,

"In the tender love of God, our heavenly Father, and of our Saviour Jesus Christ, do I, your brother, at this time greet you, and wish you health and salvation. Understanding by a concerned Friend, that of late several of our Friends are taken away from you by death, a concern came on my mind to put you in remembrance of your latter end, and of the cause of Christ; and also, of the prosperity of his blessed light and truth in your (in that respect poor, though in some others, rich and luxurious) island: the posterity of many that have been taken away there, as well as in divers other places, having gone astray; and that it may not be so with those who are left behind, let a weighty concern come upon you. O dear Friends! let your practices and expressions, manifest to the rising generation, that the welfare of their souls, more than of their bodies, is at heart with you; and do not indulge them in that which you in yourselves were convinced to be of an evil tendency, when your hearts were first reached by the power of truth. How many youths have been lost, through the looseness of the example of their elders, and through an undue indulgence of them in vanity, folly, pride, and idleness! Woful expericuce doth but too much declare that they are many —O they are many indeed, who have been lost by so doing! Wherefore, dear Friends, clear yourselves of your children; and, if they will obstinately go astray, faithfully bear your testimony against them, in life, doctrine, or expressions, and conversation, which will witness for you when you are dead and gone, and your heads laid in the silent grave. Thus will your youth, through the blessing of God, and your endeavours, come up in your places, or at least you will be clear, and their blood will be upon their own heads. A pure strict watch is required of you in conversation, in all those relations: First, That God may be glorified. Secondly, That your children may be exampled. Thirdly, That your neighbours may be edified, or built up in pure religion: and Fourthly, That you may die in peace with Him that created you, and died for you; remembering the blessed doctrine of Christ Jesus, Let your light so shine before men, that others seeing your good works, may glorify your Father which is in heaven. And again, You are as a city set on a hill, which cannot be hid. And as you thus train up your children in the way which they should go, when they are young, you may have reason to hope they will not depart from it when they are old; for many have been convinced of the truth, as it is in Jesus Christ, through the good conversation of his followers. And how can we expect to die well, if we do not live well? Or can we expect the answer of "Well done," if we are not in the practice of doing well?

"And I do desire and earnestly exhort Friends to read the holy Scriptures, and wait to feel the power from which they sprung, through the holy writers, and also to teach them to their children. And, dear Friends, let me prevail with you in the love of God and his dear Son, to keep close to your meetings for the worship of Almighty God, and for the well-ordering of your Society; and do it in the meek spirit, for that is of great price with the Lord; and, when in your meetings, get into a religious exercise, and lively concern for God's glory, and your souls' peace and prosperity. I pray the holy Lord of Sabaoth, to open your hearts to him in the reading of this epistle, as mine is open to you, my beloved Friends, that you and I may be edified, (though outwardly separated,) as we were when together; and if we should never meet more in this world, that we may meet in the kingdom of God, where we may never part more. Amen. Hallelujah, saith my soul.

"I desire this may be copied and read at the close of one of each of your particular meetings, and if it could be readily, in every family of Friends; to all whom is my very dear love in Jesus Christ, whose servant I am, and hope to be to the end, and I am an entire lover of souls, and a well-wisher of Sion's prosperity.

"T. CHALKLEY."

On the 11th of the Fourth Month I left home on a journey to Long Island, in order to visit Friends' meetings, and also to negotiate some business I had there; the first meeting I had was at Burlington, where I had occasion to advise them to keep in remembrance that ancient love which first united our society together, and in which, in times of cruel persecution, some freely offered to suffer the imprisonment of their bodies to obtain the liberty of their friends in confinement. From thence we travelled to Amboy, and so over to Staten Island. The day being very hot, and the evening cold, I got a severe cold, which I did not get clear of for about two weeks, notwithstanding which, I went to meetings, though ill in body. The first meeting I had on Long Island, was at Flushing, on a First-day: a comfortable meeting it was! in which was closely pressed, the taking up the cross of Christ, by all who desire to be his disciples, and that without it we could not be true Christians. From Flushing we went to Musketto Cove, and had a meeting there on Third-day, which was large, and to general satisfaction, and some were there that were newly convinced. I seeing the openness of the meeting, advised Friends to build a meeting-house there, which they approved of. On Fourth-day we had a meeting at Westbury, and on Fifth-day at Cowneck. From Cowneck I went to the south-side of the island, and had a meeting at Captain Hicks's. The neighbours who were not of our society, came generally to this meeting, and they were pressingly exhorted to come to Christ, and the way opened unto them. It was a good time, and I thought a time of love to us all; though before the meeting I was exceedingly shut up in myself, so that the meeting was very beneficial to me, among the rest, to see how the Lord could work by his power, and unlock the soul, as in a moment, as he did for my poor soul at times. O, may I, with Christ's followers and ministers, ever depend upon him, is my petition! From Rockway, for so is the place called, we went to Westbury, and had a very large meeting on a First-day; and, as I was informed, some were convinced there that day.

From hence I went to a place called Foster's Meadows, where we had a large meeting in one Duesbury's barn. After this I went over to the main land, and had a meeting at a place called Westchester. From thence we went to Flushing, and had a large meeting on a Fifth-day of the week, in which the right training up of children, and careful education of youth, was zealously recommended. From Flushing I went to Huntingdon, where some were lately convinced of the principle of truth as it is in Christ Jesus, some of whom were excommunicated by the Presbyterians, with whom they had formerly joined. We had a pretty large meeting in a Friend's barn, where one priest Prime opposed me, as he also had my friend Benjamin Kidd some time before, of which, by letter, I gave an account to my dear friends Thomas Lightfoot and Benjamin Kidd, desiring them, in their return from New England, to have an evening-meeting there. The grounds of this priest's cavilling, or dispute, was, that I had declared, That it is the light of Christ, or his Spirit, which convinceth the world of sin, and not a natural light, or the light of a natural conscience; from whence he took occasion to charge me with denying a natural conscience; the falsehood of which I charged upon him before the auditory, and desired him, if he had anything on his mind, to write it to me, to which I promised to return him an answer.

From Huntingdon I went to the general meeting of Friends held at New Town, which was so large that the meeting-house could not contain the people, and the weather being extremely hot, the people without doors were some of them uneasy, and went to and fro; but those that were in the house, and so near as they could hear, were very attentive, and as far as I could learn, generally satisfied. Our next meeting was at New York, which was the quietest meeting I ever had there; and those few Friends at New York, and some that were there from Long Island, parted with us in the love of Christ, and in the fellowship of his blessed gospel; and so I travelled homewards, having good satisfaction in visiting my friends; and when I came home, I found my dear wife and children in health, for which I bless God.

After this journey I kept to meetings at and about home as usual, and was at the Fifth-day meeting in Philadelphia, when Samuel Preston was married to Margaret Langdale, the widow of my dear friend and fellow-traveller, Josiah Langdale: the meeting was large, and the parable of the virgins, and the bridegroom's coming at midnight, was opened, with an exhortation to the people to be ready against that hour, and that they should take care to have the holy oil of divine grace in their hearts.

After this meeting I had some affairs which called me into Chester County, and on the road my horse gave a sudden and violent start out of the path, and threw me down, and before I could get up again, he struck my face and my right eye with his foot, being newly shod, which stunned me for the present; but as soon as I opened that eye which was unhurt, I perceived that I lay on my back, under my horse's belly, with my head between his fore feet. He stood still, and I got on my hands and knees, the blood streaming out of my nose and right eye, and while I was bleeding, a man and woman came by, and staid till I had done bleeding, and saw me mounted on my horse again. I went forward, being about two miles from the house I intended to go to, and after riding about a mile, I met with a friend that knew me, and was surprised to see me so bloody, and went with me to Randal Mayling's, a faithful honest Friend, who was upwards of eighty years of age, and had suffered much for his profession of the truth in his younger years, where several tender-hearted motherly women dressed my wounded eye. I was truly thankful to the Lord for his providence towards me in this deliverance, among many others, which he in his goodness hath vouchsafed to me. I staid at this Friend's house three nights, and mended apace, and the Friend accompanied me to my house at Frankfort, where my loving wife, with some surprise, received me very affectionately; and through her care and continual application, I recovered, that I could see pretty well with spectacles, which I was obliged to use for some months. Such accidents plainly shew us the necessity of preparing for sudden death, as we know not when, or how, we may go off the stage of this life.

On the 25th of the Fifth Month, I received a letter from a person in the county of Burlington, relating to water-baptism, to which I made answer as follows:

"Thy lines I received last night, in the perusing of which, there was a Christian love in my heart towards thee, though unknown by face, and I have much freedom of mind to answer thine, according to thy request, and my small ability. First, then, We are near in sentiments to each other in the grand Christian principle of saving religion, which is the work of the Holy Spirit of Christ upon the soul, for that is the baptism which is Christ's, and is truly saving, and absolutely necessary to salvation: Christ's baptism being but one, which is with the Holy Ghost, and with spiritual fire or water; John's being the element, or figure; and Christ's being the spirit, power, and divine substance, and is to be with the church of Christ, and with his true ministers to the end of the world. Secondly, In answer to thy query, was water baptism, that is, the element, not commanded by Christ himself, in Matt. xxviii. 19. I answer, I believe not. My reason is this, because the Holy Ghost, or Spirit, is mentioned in the text, or that command, in express words, and water is not; and therefore we omit going into outward water, and for other reasons, as followeth. Thirdly, That water-baptism, which was John's, was practised by the apostles, is true; but it was not practised by Christ, who, no doubt, would have done it if it had been absolutely necessary; for he disdained not to wash his disciples' feet, a much more despicable office than that of the baptismal ceremony: so because Christ did not himself practise it, nor, as we conceive, command us to go into material water, we therefore forbear it. Fourthly, That the apostles did baptize with water, we deny not; and that they were circumcised, and did circumcise, is also undeniable. Now, must we circumcise because the apostles did, and were themselves circumcised? Consider that carefully, and I hope that will give thee some sight, or light into, or concerning the dispensation of water-baptism, which was John's baptism, and was glorious in its day and dispensation, in pointing at Christ's baptism, until it came, which was the substance, and was with spiritual fire, and spiritual water, and will continue for ever. To Christ, and his baptism, I heartily direct thee for further instruction, in whom is light, and that light is the life of men, or life, and that life the light of men.

"And further, I would write a little of my own thoughts concerning water-baptism, and on some texts of Scripture, being Christ's own words, viz. 'He that believeth, and is baptized, shall be saved, but he that believeth not, shall be damned,' or condemned, Mark xvi. 16. Now this must needs be understood of the Spirit's baptism; for it would be absurd to say, or believe, that all who are baptized with the element of water, are saved, or all who are not baptized with water, are damned; therefore it is the Spirit's baptism, that all professing Christianity ought to come unto to witness salvation. Again, Christ says, 'Except a man be born of water, and of the Spirit, he cannot enter into the kingdom of God,' or of heaven, John iii. 5. This divers will have to be a mixture of the element water, and of the Spirit; but Christ says, 'It is the Spirit that quickeneth, the flesh profiteth nothing: the words that I speak unto you, they are spirit and they are life,' John vi. 63; and 'That which is born of the flesh is flesh, and that which is born of the Spirit is spirit,' John iii. 6. According to which doctrine, I have faith to believe, that outward, fleshly, or elementary water-baptism, profits little or nothing to the soul. Again, why should the water in that place be understood of the element, any more than the fire in the other, viz., To be baptized 'with the Holy Ghost and with fire,' since Christ said, 'My words they are spirit and life.' Remember the well of water that springs up to eternal life in the believers: remember the water that Christ gave, whosoever drank of it was never to thirst more. This is all spiritual, which the carnal mind cannot comprehend or enjoy, but is witnessed by the spiritual man. And further, if we consider what confusion there is in the world about this water-baptism, it may well put a tender seeking soul upon further search into the nature of holy, saving baptism. The Papists have one way; the Lutherans and Calvinists another; the Baptists, they have another; and all differ so widely, that, generally speaking, they will not worship together; neither are they ever like to be reconciled, except they come to the holy Spirit and divine power of Jesus, the good Saviour and precious guide of souls. That saying of his hath often been a comfort to me in deep exercises and distresses of mind, when he said to his disciples, It is expedient for you that I go away; for if I go not away, the Comforter will not come; but if I go away, I will pray to the Father, and he will send the Comforter, the Spirit of truth, in my name, and when he is come, he shall lead you, and guide you into all truth; he shall take of mine, and give it unto you, and shall bring all things to your remembrance, that I have spoken unto you. And that he was to convince the world of sin; and that he shall abide with you for ever. May the precious gift of the Spirit be given to thee, and to all true seekers of God, his Christ and kingdom, is my real desire, and humble prayer to the Most High. (See the four Evangelists for the promise, they not wording it alike.)

"Having answered the most of thy letter, I would add a few lines more, viz. I have known some who could not be satisfied with words about this point of baptism with water, until Christ had by his Spirit given them satisfaction in themselves; and as thou comest more and more into close communion with his grace and Spirit in thy own soul, I hope thou also wilt have better satisfaction than that of words only. I have known some of the people called Baptists, who have been convinced of the truth, according to our way and principle, to whom all the writing, and disputing, and reading, and preaching, about this point, could never give ample satisfaction, until they had it inwardly and immediately from Christ, manifested to them by his holy Spirit in their hearts, as aforesaid. Though I would not be understood to be against satisfying one another as much as lieth in our power, and as we find openness in the love of God and Christ. And further, I never understood that any of our Society were absolutely against such practising of it, who could see no further, or did really think in their consciences it was their duty so to do: but we believe, that we see beyond the figure or shadow, and are come to the substance, for the reasons mentioned, and many more which might be given. Several treatises have been written upon this subject, one of which is very full, before we were a people, by William Dell, a wise and learned man, and one who had a large sense of the power of God: and among us, *Barclay's Apology*, and a treatise by John Gratton, who was a Baptist preacher, and one by Joseph Pike: and also here is a little book of Thomas Upsher's, a Baptist preacher before he came to join with us, which I send thee, with whom I was well acquainted, as also with those men who subscribed it. If thou appliest thyself to Richard Smith, of Burlington, he is as likely as any I know to help thee to those books, all which are larger on the subject, and have given satisfaction to thousands about it; though some, as I have said, could never be satisfied with words. In reading the latter part of thy letter, I was tenderly affected, and my prayers to the Almighty were, that he would please to direct thee by his power and Spirit, and the grace of his dear Son, who hath said, Him that cometh untome, I will in no wise cast off. Now, tender Friend, Christ is the true light, that lighteth every man that cometh into the world, by which light thou must walk to the kingdom and city of God. He is the door into the true sheepfold: he is the truth, in whom thou must believe: he is the divine life and light of the soul: he is the true Christian's all in all: and as the kingdom is within, as said Christ, so the king is also within, and without also. He is God omnipotent, omniscient, omnipresent, the immortal Jehovah, and is God over all, blessed for ever. And as a servant of his, I recommend thee, with my own soul, unto him for preservation and divine direction; for it is the great work of Christ's true ministers and servants, to direct the seeking travelling souls to him; to whom, with the Father, and the eternal Spirit, be glory, now, and evermore. Amen.

"From thy assured friend in Christ,

"T. Chalkley."

The person to whom I wrote this letter, some time after informed me, it gave him great satisfaction.

After I had staid at home some time, and pretty well recovered of the hurt I had by my fall, I visited some meetings about home, as Philadelphia, Abington, and German Town. In several of those meetings I was concerned to exhort Friends, as our meetings and worship was, in this province of Pennsylvania, a kind of national worship, to beware that they did not indulge themselves in the sins of the nations, but to be careful to keep to the holy, self-denying life of Jesus.

On the 5th of the Sixth Month, between the hours of nine and ten in the night, there was an earthquake, which divers people were very sensible of; and about this time divers people were taken off with a violent fever; and I was concerned in several meetings to put the people in mind of their mortality, and shortness of time here: and also of the uncertainty of it, and the necessity of speedy preparation for their final change, and future well-being In the aforesaid month I was at our youths' meeting in Philadelphia, where I was concerned to advise parents to do justly to their children, in the divers relations of a child's state; to be just in correction, and to be sure to give them learning, and train them up in reading of the holy Scriptures, they being able, through faith in Christ, to make us wise to salvation. I also was earnest in exhortation to the youth, to obey and honour their parents, and to have a care not to be disobedient to their fathers and mothers. I had a concern also to remind that large congregation, that the Almighty had stretched out his arm of power, with his rod, and had given the people of this land three strokes therewith, as a gentle admonition towards heart-preparation, to meet him, and to prepare for their latter end, or final dissolution; which was first, A sickness, or pestilential fever, which carried off many of the people. Secondly, An earthquake, of which divers in town and country were very sensible. Thirdly, A terrible whirlwind, such as we never before heard of in this land, that I remember.

They were admonished to take particular and special notice of those gentle strokes of the divine hand, for if he pleased he could as soon take away many by sickness, as a few, and if he pleased he could have made us a desolation, as well as the country about Mount Ætna, or Port Royal, in Jamaica, not very far from us; and he could also blow us away with a whirlwind of his wrath, and could as easily have blown down all our city, as those few houses in the country.

Next day after this meeting I went with John Rodman to the quarterly general meeting for worship in the county of Chester, which was large and satisfactory.

The 25th of the Sixth Month, I was at the burial of the wife of Richard Waln, a virtuous and good woman. Some of her last words were, "Some men's sins go beforehand to judgment, and some follow after them; and that her sins were gone before, which was a great comfort to her, now she was going to leave the world." It was a large meeting, and a seasonable opportunity that we had at the funeral. The people were called upon to work, while it was called to-day, because, as our Saviour said, "the night cometh, wherein no man can work."

In this and the foregoing year I met with various trials and exercises: As First, Great inward poverty and want. Secondly, Great losses in outward affairs. And Thirdly, The evil spirits of divers stirred up against me, to report falsehoods concerning me, with many other sore exercises both inward and outward. As to the first, I had been often tried that way, and found by experience that I must wait upon God my Saviour, for fresh and renewed visitations from above;

in which exercise, I had always in the Lord's time, comfort from him, as by the same exercise I had now the same comfort also; but I thought it very long, and the enemy did greatly endeavour to break in upon my patience now more than usual: but my heart still depended in faith and hope upon the Lord my Redeemer and Saviour, and in his time he was pleased to help me, blessed be his holy arm and power for ever! Many blessed saints and servants of Jesus were brought to my mind, who were in the like condition, so that I had a secret joy in their company, who met with the like in their travels to the holy city. Secondly, As to my outward losses, I thought with myself, peradventure it might be best for me: and I remembered that many, through the increase of outward riches, were exceedingly hurt as to their inward state; and though I, or any good man, might be concerned for our children, to get and leave something for them; yet I plainly saw, that generally speaking, much riches doth much hurt to youth. This was a melancholy observation that I had made in my life and travels, and I see at this day, that it is an universal distemper, a very few excepted, wherefore I cried mightily to God, that he would give to me and mine the gift of his grace and holy Spirit, whatever our circumstances might be in the world. In this also I saw that patience was an excellent virtue, and that the meek had the best inheritance of the earth, if they had ever so little of it; and that true happiness did not consist in earthly things, which my experience had largely taught me. And Thirdly, As to the base and evil treatment I met with, which was more than I had ever met with in all my life before, great endeavours were used to lessen my reputation, as a man and a Christian; all which proved false and fruitless, and in due time my innocence was made manifest; and I considered that they could not use me worse than they had done my Lord and Master, and that the Devil was angry with any who endeavoured to dethrone him, and pull down his kingdom, at the foundation of which, through the help of my Master, I had many a stroke or blow, with such weapons as he was pleased to furnish me withal.

The last of the Sixth Month, and the first of the Seventh Month, was the quarterly and youths' meeting at Burlington, at both which I was. At the quarterly meeting I was concerned to open to that meeting, how all along the church of God was governed by his Spirit, in the time of the law, and Moses was an instrument therein; and that when it was too hard, and too much work for Moses, he was advised to get the help and assistance of the elders, and that the same power and Spirit of God that was with him and upon Moses, was upon the elders who assisted him in the affairs of the church, and congregation of the Lord's people; so that it was governed by God's Spirit, and is to be governed by the same still, and not by the will of man, nor according to the will of man in his corrupt nature. And when Israel went from God's power and Spirit, the Lord left them, but at last sent to them his only begotten Son, our dear Lord and Saviour Jesus Christ; and he was, and ever is, to be governor of his church, through his holy Spirit, [respecting] which, he told his disciples, he would pray the Father, and he should send unto them the Comforter, the Holy Ghost, or Spirit, the Spirit of truth, and he should abide with them for ever, and should lead and guide them into all truth; which sweet and precious promises that he made to them, the true believers do witness to be fulfilled at this day. Glory to his name for ever! he is the wonderful Counsellor, mighty Saviour, and Prince of Peace! of whose peace and government there shall never be an end, and upon whose shoulder the government is to be for ever, for whose power, and Holy Spirit, Friends were exhorted to pray and wait, and to be sensible of it in the discipline and government of the church now in this gospel day, in which is a brighter manifestation of God's love, through his Son, than in the time of the law. The youths meeting was also large, and divers testimonies were borne, by way of exhortation and counsel to the youth. They were with much tenderness advised to take counsel of their elders, and were shown how it fared with some young men, who slighted the advice and counsel of the elders; and that one, when on a dying-bed, cried out in the bitterness and agonies of his spirit, Oh! that I had taken the counsel and advice of my friends, for then I had not been here, nor in this condition. The youth were advised to beware of keeping bad company, and spending their precious time in taverns, which hath undone many fair and promising youths: and it was shewn, how a young man might cleanse his ways, by taking heed thereunto, according to the word of God, which liveth and abideth for ever, and which the holy Scriptures proceeded from; and they were earnestly exhorted to read and practise what was written therein: and a very tender time we had in prayer to God, through his dear Son, to preserve us all in his fear, both young and aged; and so our meeting broke up, and we parted in the sweet love of God, and his Christ, our holy Saviour.

My troubles in the world, and in the things of it, being many, and my outward losses being great; as also was my inward poverty of mind and spirit, I took my pen, and wrote one day as followeth: "Oh! if it be right in the sight of God, how do I long to be unclothed of this frail and mortal body, that my soul and spirit might mount up into the ethereal plains, and repose itself into the vast expanding arms of its Maker, and most sweet Saviour for ever!"

Being at and near home some time after I came from Burlington, I visited the meetings of Germantown and Philadelphia, which were large, and some good sense of truth was in the hearts of divers. I was concerned at that meeting at Philadelphia, to let the people know, that as God had blessed the people of that city, and the province, with spiritual and temporal blessings, and made the land naturally fruitful, to the enriching many of the inhabitants, he now expected fruits from them of piety and virtue; and that if there was not a stricter walking with God in Christ Jesus, they might expect his Divine hand, which had visited them with favours from heaven above, and from the earth beneath, would visit them with a rod in it, and that he had already given them some gentle strokes therewith.

Our yearly meeting was this year at Burlington, for the provinces of New Jersey and Pennsylvania, the service of which our quarterly meeting appointed me, with divers others, to attend. It was a large and comfortable meeting, and many went home thankful to the holy name of God and Christ, that they were there.

I shall end the second Part * of the journal of my

* See the note at page 87.

life and travels, when I have transcribed part of a letter which my dear father wrote me, when eighty odd years of age, he having been a minister of Christ above forty years, which followeth:

"Loving Son, Thomas Chalkley,

"Thine, dated the 11th of the Tenth Month, 1723, I received, and was very glad to hear of your welfare, and that the Lord hath given you children: and I pray the Almighty God, that he may preserve them with you, that they may be a comfort to you in your latter days; and that if the Lord may be pleased to continue them with you, that they may, as they grow in days, grow in grace, and in the knowledge of our Lord and Saviour Jesus Christ; and that the Lord may be pleased to preserve us all to the end of those few days we may have in this world, that then we may lay down our heads in peace and in full assurance of everlasting blessedness for ever and evermore. I bless the Lord that he has preserved me sensible of his blessed and holy Spirit, whereby my understanding is indifferent clear and well, considering my age; and the Lord in his great loving-kindness I do feel to help me to my great satisfaction, in my little service for him.

"Having this opportunity by a friend of your town, was willing to let you hear of our welfare and health. I am in as good health at present as I have been for many years, and can make a shift to go over London Bridge, and to the meeting at Aldersgate, and to the Peel Meeting, from my house in Shad-Thames. And the Lord hath been pleased to be with me now in my poor aged condition.

"So, dear Son, my dear love is to thee and thine,

and to friends that may inquire after us. Divers Friends give their love to thee, whose names I cannot remember.

"With repeated love to you all, I rest thy aged, and, thereby through pain, afflicted father,

"GEORGE CHALKLEY.

"Southwark, London, *5th of the Sixth Month*, 1724.

"P. S. Thy brother George, his love is to you all, and I desire thee to let us hear of you as opportunity may serve."

To see my dear father's hand-writing, now he was above four-score years of age, was very affecting to me; and the more, because I expected it might be his last, which it was. The answer I sent to my dear father's letter is as followeth:

"Frankfort, *22nd of the Eighth Month*, 1724.

"My dear Father,

"Thine, per James Wilkins, I received with joy, and was greatly comforted to hear that thou wast yet alive; and especially that thou art favoured now in thy old age, with a sense of the gift of God, through the Holy Spirit of his dear Son, our blessed Lord and Saviour Jesus Christ.

"The reading of thine did mightily refresh and tender my heart and spirit, not expecting many more such epistles from thee, by reason of thy great age. But my very dear and truly honoured father, if we should never hear from, nor see one another more in mutability, yet are we, while here on earth, as living epistles in one another's hearts, wrote by the finger, or hand of God. I have hope also, that we shall meet where we shall never part more, in the glorious kingdom of God and his Christ.

"We are all in good health, I humbly thank the Lord, and if it be his will, should rejoice to hear that these find thee, my tender and loving father, with my dear brother and sister, and all my loving cousins, and our friends in general, in like health. I desire to know exactly, thy age in thy next, if thou art able to write to me, and if thou livest where thou did formerly, or with brother or cousin, which will be very acceptable to me.

"Thus, with unspeakable love from self, and wife, to thee my dear and aged father, and all relations and friends, I remain thy loving and dutiful son,

"THOMAS CHALKLEY."

CHAPTER VI.

1724–1726.

FURTHER LOSSES AND AFFLICTIONS—SEVERAL OCCURRENCES AND LETTERS—GENERAL VISIT TO FRIENDS IN LONG ISLAND—RELIGIOUS SERVICE NEAR HOME AND IN NEW JERSEY, &C.—DEATH AND CHARACTER OF HIS FATHER.

In this year, 1724, I met with various trials, afflictions, and tribulations; and had not the secret hand of the Lord, which I felt underneath, borne up my spirit from sinking, I think I could never have waded through them.

I was now removed, as already related, into the country for retirement, which I greatly loved and delighted in; but as soon as I was a little settled there, the enemy of all good endeavoured to disquiet my repose, by stirring up some bad people against me, who lived near, and in time past had fawned upon me: and, to add to my afflictions, I lost a vessel, in which, I suppose, I had upwards of five hundred pounds; and another vessel came in almost a wreck, in which I suffered in my interest several hundreds more, and a third I heard of, in which I had the like loss; and about the same time I had also a good new barn burnt to the ground in a few minutes; so that I was exceedingly stripped that way. And to add yet more to my exercise, I was sorely afflicted with sickness, having a swelling in my jaws, mouth, and throat, to that degree, that I could neither speak nor swallow for some time, nor eat nor sleep for about seven days, as I remember, without great difficulty. What the distemper was, we could not be certain: some supposed it to be the quinsy, others an imposthume. Also, my little and only daughter at the same time was likely to die; and as for my own part, I was very willing to go, if it so pleased God; for I saw through the deceit of the world, and that the friendship of it was not permanent; and in my sore afflictions in body, mind, and interest, it fared with me as with Job; for divers of my pretended friends added to my afflictions by undue reflections; whom I pray the Lord to forgive for his Son's sake! At these times the remembrance of that saying of Christ, "The very hairs of your head are all numbered," Matt. x. 30, at times supported me in hopes, that all would work together for good.

When I got a little well, so that I could go to meetings, I went to German-town, Abington, Philadelphia, and Derby. My first going abroad was to Philadelphia, where, on a First-day, we had a large meeting, and divers things were opened in my mind. I told them they had Moses and the Prophets, and Jesus Christ, who was arisen from the dead; for neither death, hell, nor the grave, could detain the Lord of life and glory. And I was opened to declare to them, that they had a great advantage of the coming of Christ, not only in his appearance at Jerusalem, but as he came to, and spoke to the heart, by his inward and spiritual appearance; and that this gospel dispensation was by his coming, made more conspicuous, bright, and glorious, than that which went before. Friends were very glad to see me abroad again, they having expected daily to hear I was dead, and there was tenderness over the meeting, and God over all, through his dear Son our Lord Jesus Christ, was praised and glorified, who is worthy for ever.

In this year two sober young women, Elizabeth Levis and Jane Fenn, were concerned to visit Friends in the island of Barbadoes, and they meeting with some discouragement, in Christian love I wrote them the following letter, to encourage them in the work of Christ.

"Frankfort, 1st *of the Twelfth Month,* 1724.

"My dear Friends, Elizabeth Levis
and Jane Fenn,

"Understanding by our friend Grace Lloyd, that you have proposed your intention of visiting those few Friends in the island of Barbadoes, and that you meet with some discouragement inwardly and outwardly, therefore it is in my mind to comfort and strengthen you in so great and good an undertaking and honourable work, as is that of the cause of Christ, who, for our sakes crossed himself abundantly beyond expression, more than is possible for us to do for his sake, or the sake of his people, whom we may so entirely love, as to lay down our lives for his and their sakes. But what are our lives, to the life of the only begotten Son of God? and truly, we must give them up often, if we have the cause of souls at heart; and then he often gives them to us again, glory to his holy name for ever! As Christ said, He that will save his life, shall lose it, and he that will lay down his life for my sake and the gospel, shall find it; which reacheth your case in this undertaking. And, indeed, some of our lives, in our own sense, are hardly worth mentioning, considering the cause of Christ.

"And, dear children of our heavenly Father, I may through some good experience, truly inform you, that there is much openness in many people on that island, and good encouragement I have had, from above, in my visiting the people there; though, true it is, the inhabitants, too generally, are luxurious, and much given to vanity: yet I have this seal in my heart, that the Lord hath a seed in that place who desires to serve him, and that seed will surely join with you in your exercise, and you will be comforted one in another, and in the Lord. And that there are differences among them, is also true; but they have the more need of being visited by such who are, through their wise conduct and healing disposition, likely to heal those breaches which are, or may be among them. Some, indeed, have gone among them and have done hurt, by a rash and turbulent way of management, and by so doing, have rather made the breaches wider, than, by a meek and loving, as well as lowly disposition, lessened their differences, and healed them.

"And, tender Friends, though it may seem hard for you in several considerations, to give up to go to sea, and also to divers who love you, and are nearly related to you; know ye, and such so concerned, that the Lord is stronger than the noise of many waters, and than the mighty waves of the sea. And I really believe that you, as well as my soul, with the servants of Christ, have, and will experience it to be so, as David did, whose words they are.

"I remember the words of our great Lord and Master Jesus, when he sent forth his servants to preach his word and gospel; I send you forth as lambs among wolves. No question but you, like innocent lambs, before your return, if it please God to give you to us again, may meet with the wolves' spirit, or the spirit of the beast, in some or others among whom you may travel; then will the counsel of Christ, added to his commission, be good for you to keep close to: Be ye wise as serpents, but innocent or harmless as doves.

"And, dear maidens, I look upon it, your cross is great, you being two innocent, chaste young women, to give up your names to cross the sea, which I know is a great cross to a chaste woman, or man either, the seamen, too generally, being rude, dissolute people; so your crown will be great also. I have known that by keeping near to Christ, and his truth and power, there hath been a wonderful reformation divers times in several of those rude seamen; and some have been so far convinced, as to be exceedingly kind, and to speak well of Friends and their conversation, when it has been coupled with the fear and wisdom of God. When I have gone to sea, I always found a religious and Christian concern upon me, for the poor sailors, the good effects of which, have been much more than I may speak of; but give this little hint for your encouragement and information.

"Well, dear souls, if you go, I believe the Lord will go with you; and sure I am, that my spirit will go along with you, which will not hurt you, if it do you no good. And although my exercises and tribulations of late have been very great, both spiritual and natural, yet my very heart within me affects the cause of Christ, according to the best of my understanding; and I heartily wish well to all my fellow-labourers, who are faithful, painful servants of Christ, and disinterested, except as to the interest which they desire in Christ and his kingdom, for the sake of which they love not their lives unto death.

"I must now take leave, after putting you in mind of remembering me, your poor friend and brother, when before the throne you are supplicating the Father of mercies in secret, even as my heart is tenderly bowed and broken into tears on your behalf at this time. The Lord be with you, and sanctify the present exercise and concern that is upon you, and you to himself, with all the faithful lovers and followers of the Lamb, through his word, whose word is truth. I am your friend and brother, in the fellowship of the gospel of Christ Jesus our great Lord and good master; and blessed are all those, who by their fearing to offend him, manifest him to be their Master, and by their honouring him, manifest him to be their Lord.

"T. CHALKLEY."

In the Twelfth Month I went to the quarterly meeting of Friends, held at Providence, for Chester county, for discipline and worship; which meeting was large, and a concern came upon Friends at that meeting to suppress excess in eating and drinking, and great entertainments at marriages and funerals, and spending time idly in tippling houses; as also in several other things for the well-ordering our society, in which appeared great love and unanimity. The people were reminded of God's love to them in this land, and many favours were recounted to them, which he had favoured the inhabitants of the land with, which were very singular, and that he expected that they should bring forth fruits that might be answerable to the labours of love, which the Lord had bestowed upon them.

About this time I had it in my mind to write to one who was conscientiously concerned to preach the gospel of Christ, but was under great exercise on that occasion.

"Frankfort, *24th of the Twelfth Month*, 1724.

"My Friend,

"Since I last saw thee and conversed with thee, thou hast often been in my mind, and thy exercise has come before me; and not having an opportunity to converse with thee personally, I take this way of communicating my mind, hoping in Christ thou wilt reap some satisfaction and advantage thereby. I think I know thou art concerned for Christ's cause, as also was that eminent minister Apollos, yet was instructed more perfectly by good Aquila and Priscilla. The subject on which I have it in my mind to write to thee, is the ministry of the gospel of Christ Jesus, which I believe to be very different from that which it is generally taken for, in most parts of the world, by many professing Christianity. First, The greatest part of Christendom, so called, calls and elects their ministers themselves, and will not call them unless they have school-learning, although Christ called and chose unlearned men, as to that sort of learning, and the apostles were called, not according to the will of man, but by the revelation of Christ Jesus. And Christ thanked his Father, that he had revealed the mysteries of his kingdom to babes and sucklings. And the wise Jews (the Scribes and Pharisees) admired at the apostles, who so wonderfully preached Christ, and were so wonderfully carried forth in their ministry, and yet few of them were men of learning; so that the call, election, and wages of Christ's ministers, is spiritual, and not carnal, and therefore their ministry is with Divine life and power, by which they are qualified for this service without either study or premeditation; though it is not denied, that Christ may shew a minister beforehand, what he shall, or is to speak, at such a time or place, as he may see meet; but that studying or writing sermons, and afterwards preaching, or rather reading them to the people, was, or is, the practice of the true ministers of Jesus, our great Lord and Master, is denied: of which, I do believe, thou hast a real sense.

"I shall impart to thee something of my own experience for thy edification in this great work, viz.: As in the work of conversion, or regeneration, there is a growth and increase from the state of a child to that of a man in Christ, so in the work of the ministry, or preaching the gospel, there is also a growth from a babe to an able minister; in all which, the power and grace of the holy Spirit must be our guide, our help, and support, keeping close to which, we shall increase in Divine wisdom and sound judgment, and our hearts and understandings will be more and more opened and enlarged. The apostle Paul said, When I was a child, I spake as a child, understood as a child, and thought as a child; and yet he was an excellent child of God, and minister of Christ; and as he grew in his gift, and Christ's grace, he became a wonderful, serviceable instrument in the hand of God. Now a child's state in the ministry is too much overlooked by many, some thinking to be men as soon as they are brought forth into the ministry; and, according to my observation, divers have been at a loss, and some quite lost, for want of a patient continuing in well-doing; and not waiting to feel a growth and increase from above, have gone on in their own strength and will, perhaps against the advice and instruction of a sound and honest Aquila and Priscilla, and have been hurt; and some who had received a gift, have had that same gift taken from them, even by the Lord who gave it them.

"As I take it, a true minister of Christ, is to take no thought what to say, but it will be given him in the same hour that which he should speak to the people; (that is, in a general way;) and if it is not given from above, I believe he or she ought to be silent: for they receive freely, if they do receive any thing from Christ, and so they ought freely to administer; and where little is given, little is required, all which is plain from Christ's own words in the New Testament; and Christ's cross is to be taken up by his ministers in their preaching, as well as in their conversation.

"It is a practice which the holy Scriptures have not acquainted us with, that the ministers of Christ should take a verse, or line, out of the holy Scriptures, and write, or study beforehand, a discourse on it, and preach it, or rather read it, to the people. The holy men of old (as we read both in the Old and New Testament) spoke as they were moved by the Holy Ghost, and by it they were gifted for the convincing, converting, and reforming the world, and for comforting and edifying of the saints; quite contrary to the latter practice of modern reading divines, who dispute, write, and preach against the immediate and divine revelation of the Spirit of Christ, and therefore cannot be of his ministers, but must be the ministers of antichrist, and ministers of the letter, and not of the Spirit of Christ, or of his gospel. And where the apostle says, 'When I was a child, I spake as a child,' I take him to point at the being brought forth newly into the work of the ministry, as well as the work of conversion, and that he useth those expressions by way of comparison, and therefore I compare it thus: A child when it first begins or ventures to speak, he speaks but a few words, and those stammering sometimes, and its judgment is weak, and must be put upon speaking by his father over and over, if he be a backward child; otherwise, if he be forward, and speaks too much, he is curbed by a wise father. And thus, according to my observation, it hath pleased our heavenly Father, to instruct his children in the ministry, and as a child in Christ, I would speak a little of my experience unto the child, or children of God. When I first felt a necessity on me to preach the gospel, I had but a few sentences to deliver, in great fear and tenderness, with some trembling, with which my brethren were generally satisfied and edified; and after some time I felt a concern to preach the gospel in other countries, and to other nations than that in which I was born, which to me was a very great cross; but feeling the woe of the Lord to follow me in not giving up to it, I in some time took that cross up, for Christ's sake and the gospel's. And in taking it up, I experienced the truth of the apostle's doctrine, That the gospel of Christ is 'the power of God unto salvation, to every one that believeth,' Rom. i. 16. Thus through a continual labour and spiritual travail, I witnessed a growth in experience, and an enlargement in expressions and heavenly doctrine; and my heart was mightily enlarged to run the ways of God's commandments, and divers were convinced, and some, I hope, thoroughly converted, and many comforted, and God, through the ministry of his dear Son, glorified, who is thereof only worthy for ever.

"In all which I have nothing to boast of nor glory in, saving in the cross of Christ; for what is Paul, or Apollos, or Cephas, but instruments? (I would not be understood to compare with those apostles, but to endeavour to follow them as they followed Christ.) Christ is All in all: He is the great Teacher of teachers, and the highest Schoolmaster of all. And he says, He that will be my disciple, must first deny himself, and take up his cross and follow me.

"We do not find anywhere in the New Testament, that Christ's ministers or messengers were only to speak or preach to one meeting of people, or that they were called or hired by men; for then it would have been necessary man should pay them; but Christ says, 'Freely you have received, freely give;' and Go forth, &c. Matt. xxviii. 19, 20.

"And, my friend, I find to this day that it is safe for me when I am ministering to the people: when the spring of Divine life and power, (from which sound truths and edifying matter springs and flows into the heart or understanding,) abates or stops, to stop with it, and sit down, and not to arise, or speak publicly to the people, without some spiritual impulse or moving, and openings.

"I would have this taken no otherwise, but as one friend and brother opening their states and condition to another for edification, and the strengthening each other in Christ. And as I fear lest I should exceed the bounds of a letter, therefore shall conclude,

"Thy real friend in Jesus Christ,

"T. CHALKLEY."

The 25th of the Twelfth Month I was at the burial of the wife of Randal Spikeman. It being our Fifth-day meeting, divers sober people were there not of our persuasion, and I was drawn forth to speak to the people of the death of Christ and his merits, and to shew that there is no merit in the works of man, as he is man, or in a formal righteousness or holiness.

In our yearly meeting at Burlington, it was agreed that the families of Friends should be visited, and soon after our monthly meeting appointed me, with other Friends, to visit the families of Friends of our meeting; in which visitation many were comforted and edified, both youth and aged; and we could truly say, that the power and grace of God, and the sweet love of Christ accompanied us from house to house, to our mutual comfort; and we were so extraordinarily opened and guided to speak to the states of the people in their families, (that were unknown and strangers to us,) that sometimes some of them were ready to think that we spoke by information, when in truth we were clear of any such thing, and only spoke from what was immediately given to us, without any information from man or woman; which to us was sometimes very wonderful, and caused us to praise the name of the Lord.

In the First Month, the general meeting at Philadelphia was a solid, good meeting, and ended in a sense of grace and truth, which comes by Jesus Christ.

Next day, being our week-day meeting, our dear friends, Elizabeth Levis and Jane Fenn, took leave of us, they intending for the island of Barbadoes; and it was such a parting meeting, that will not soon be forgotten by some of us then present.

After this meeting I went to Burlington, to visit one that was sick, and under some trouble of mind for going astray, and greatly desired to come into the right way; with whom I had a good, seasonable meeting, to her comfort and my own satisfaction. Upon this visit I would remark, that it is a great pity, that youth, when in health and strength, should put off the work of their salvation, and forget the Most High, till either sickness or death overtake them. And then, Oh! the bitter piercing cries and groans, and terrible agonies the soul is in, which, by timely repentance, and amendment of life, might be avoided.

I was afterwards at meetings at Philadelphia, Merion, German Town, &c. and had some service and satisfaction therein. And on the 2nd of the Second Month, 1725, the Friend whom I visited, as above, was buried, and the relations of the deceased sent for me to the burial. The person being well beloved, there was a large appearance of people of divers persuasions, and we had an opportunity at this funeral to exhort the people to live so as that they might die well; and that the way to die in the favour of God, was to live in his fear: and charity to those who dissent from one another, was pressingly recommended from the apostle's words, that, If we had faith to remove mountains, and to give all our goods to the poor, and our bodies to be burned, yet if we wanted charity, we were but like sounding brass, and a tinkling cymbal, 1 Cor. xiii. 1–3. And also our belief of the doctrine of the resurrection of the dead was asserted, in contradiction to that gross calumny cast on our Society of denying it.

The latter end of the Second Month, I was at a marriage at Horsham, (at which was present William Keith, our Governor,) and I was concerned to speak to the end of that great ordinance, and of the happiness of those married persons who fulfil the covenants they make in marriage, and what strength and comfort the man is to the woman, and the woman to the man, when they keep their covenants, and that they are the contrary when they break them. And I also opened the methods prescribed by our discipline, to be observed in marriages, and our care to prevent any clandestine marriages amongst us. After this meeting I returned home, without going to the marriage-dinner, as I generally avoided such entertainments as much as I could, having no life in, or liking to them, being sensible that great companies and preparations at weddings were growing inconveniences among us, the which I was conscientiously concerned to discourage. And a few days after my return home, at our meeting at Frankfort, I was concerned particularly to exhort Friends to keep to plainness in language, dress, &c., according to the examples given us in the holy Scriptures, particularly that of Daniel and his companions; and to caution against vain and indecent fashions, which with concern I have observed to prevail too much among some who make profession with us.

In this Second Month I went to the yearly meeting of Friends at Salem, and by the way had two meetings at Woodberry Creek. At Salem we had a large meeting, and our gracious Lord was with us, to the bowing many hearts before him, and many testimonies were given of the goodness, love, mercy, and the grace of God, and his dear Son our Lord Jesus Christ. From Salem we travelled to Alloway's Creek and Cohansy, and from thence to Elsinburgh, and ferried over the river Delaware, with our horses, to George's Creek, and had meetings at all those places. At George's Creek, one, not a Friend, came to me after meeting, and said, he thanked me for my advice and counsel; and seemed heartily affected with the doctrine of Christ. From George's Creek we travelled to Nottingham, and had a large meeting on First-day, and another very large on the Second-day, where were many people of divers persuasions. The house could not contain us, so that we met in an orchard. A solid meeting it was! wherein the mighty power of the Creator was declared of, as also the Divinity of Christ, and his Manhood; and the people were exhorted to be careful of forming any personal ideas of the Almighty; for the holy Scriptures do plainly manifest, that God is a wonderful, infinite, eternal Spirit, and therefore is to be worshipped in spirit and in truth, and outward representations of the Lord Jehovah border too much on idolatry. Pretty much was delivered on that head; and I was told after meeting, that divers Papists were there, though I knew nothing of it. From Nottingham I went to Newcastle, and had a meeting there, and then visited a sick Friend, with which he expressed much satisfaction; and then went on to Centre, Kennet, and Marlborough, and so to the monthly meeting at New Garden, where we had a large, open meeting, wherein were shewn, that those who meddled with our discipline, in the will, nature, spirit, and wisdom of man only, could do but little service; and that our discipline, as also our worship and ministry, ought to be performed in the wisdom and power of God, through the grace and Spirit of Christ. From New Garden we went to Birmingham, had a large meeting, and I was much drawn forth to the youth, of whom many were there. From Birmingham we went to the quarterly-meeting for discipline and worship at Concord, in Chester County, which was larger than I had ever seen there before. In the quarterly meeting for discipline, Friends were exhorted to keep to the cross of Christ, and to speak to matters in the fear of God, and to avoid and shun, as much as in them lay, self-will, humour, pride, and passion; shewing that the rough, crooked, unhewn, unpolished nature of man, could never work the righteousness of God, and is contrary to the meek, self-denying life of Jesus. John Salkeld, and Jacob Howell, then signified that they were going to visit Friends in Long Island and Rhode Island; the sense of the call, labour, and work of the ministry of the gospel, and of the love of Christ (in the freeness of it) to mankind, took some good hold on divers in that meeting; and the great name of God, and his dear Son, through the holy Spirit, was glorified.

From this meeting I came home, having been out on this journey near three weeks, at twenty meetings, and travelled more than two hundred miles, and found my wife and children in health, and we rejoiced to see each other; but my rejoicing was in fear, even almost to trembling, lest I should be too much lifted up when things were agreeable to me.

After my return home, I went to several neighbouring meetings; and on a Fifth-day was at Philadelphia, at the marriage of Richard Smith and

Elizabeth Powell. The meeting was large, and the marriage solemnly celebrated; and the people were earnestly entreated to love Christ above all, and to manifest that love by keeping his commandments, and that not in shew or word only, but in the heart and affections.

About the latter end of the Third Month, I went to the quarterly meeting of ministers and elders for the county of Burlington; and from thence to Stony Brook; where, on a First-day, we had a large meeting, in Joseph Worth's barn, which was crowded with people, and was a solid, good meeting. From Stony Brook I went to Croswicks, and was at their youths meeting, which was the largest I had ever seen in that place. I told them that they might say as the sons of the prophets did, That the place was too strait for them, and advised them to enlarge it. I was glad to see such a large appearance of sober people, and so great an increase of youth, in this wilderness of America, and exhorted them to live in the fear of God, that his blessings might still be continued to them; and an exercise was on my mind for the welfare of the young people, to shew them the danger of sin and vanity, and of keeping ill company, and following bad counsel; and that the young king Rehoboam (Solomon's son) lost the greater part of his father's kingdom, by following the company and counsel of vain young men; and that many young men in this age had lost and spent the estates their fathers had left them by the like conduct, and brought themselves to ruin, and their families to poverty and want. Divers lively testimonies were delivered in this meeting, and it ended with adoration and praise of Almighty God; and though the meeting held more than four hours, the people did not seem willing to go away when it was over: for indeed it was a solid, good meeting. The business of the quarterly meeting was carried on in peace and love, (that being the mark the disciples of Jesus were to be known by,) and Friends were exhorted with a great deal of tenderness to keep that mark.

In this journey I travelled about ninety miles, and was at four meetings, being from home four days, and was much satisfied in my journey; but met with some exercise when I came home, hearing of some losses and damage to my estate; so that I found after I had, according to my best endeavours, done the will of God, I had need of patience, that I might receive the promise. I was sensible of the messenger of Satan, the thorn in the flesh, which the apostle speaks of.

About this time a loving friend of mine informed me, that one whom I very well knew in Barbadoes, a minister of our Society, had gone into an open separation, so as to keep meetings separate from his brethren, and contrary to their advice. I was concerned in love to write a few lines to him, to remind him of the unhappy state and end of such, who, notwithstanding the brotherly love and kind treatment of Friends, had separated from us; and losing the sense of truth, which had made them serviceable in the church, were actuated by a rending, dividing spirit, by which the enemy of our happiness had so far obtained his end, as to make some disturbance for a time; but few, if any, of these separatists, have had further power than to promote and maintain their separate meetings during their own lives; such meetings having, in every instance I have known except one, and that lasted not long, dropped on the death of the founders. And though we think it our duty to testify against, and disown, all such; yet this disowning is only until the persons offending, from a real sense of, and sorrow for, their faults, acknowledge and condemn the same; then the arms of Christ, and of his church, are open to receive and embrace them. I therefore earnestly besought him to consider the danger of offending any who love and believe in Christ, though never so little in their own or other men's esteem; for we cannot have true peace in departing from the pure love of God, his truth, and people; to which I added the following sentences out of the New Testament.

1. "By this shall all men know that ye are my disciples, if ye have love one to another." John xiii. 35.——(Do not lose this mark.)

2. "We know that we have passed from death unto life, because we love the brethren. He that loveth not his brother, abideth in death." 1 John iii. 14.

3. "He that loveth not, knoweth not God; for God is love." iv. 8.

4. "He that dwelleth in love, dwelleth in God, and God in him."—16.

About the latter end of the Fourth Month I was at a meeting in Abington, occasioned by a burial: and in the beginning of the Fifth Month, I was at a marriage in Philadelphia; and was soon after, on the First-day, at two meetings at German Town, where I went to visit a Friend, who had not for some months been at meeting, being in a disconsolate condition. I invited her to meeting, where the love and goodness of Christ to the poor in spirit was largely manifested; and the Friend after meeting said she was better, and afterwards recovered, and kept to meetings. I was frequently at the week-day meetings at Philadelphia; for I thought that week not well spent, in which I could not get to week-day meetings, if I was in health.

In this month I was at the burial of George Calvert, who was one of a sober life, and just conversation; and being well-beloved by his neighbours, he left a good report behind him. Soon after which I was at Merion meeting, which was large and solid: the people were tenderly exhorted, that neither outward favours, nor spiritual blessings, might make them grow forgetful of God; but that in the sense of the increase and enjoyment thereof, they might be the more humble; and forasmuch as the Christian church in former ages was corrupted by temporal riches and power, it was intimated, that as we had favour shown us from the government, and increase of outward things, we should be very careful not to abuse those privileges, by growing proud and wanton, or envious and quarrelsome; but to do justly, love mercy, and walk humbly with God.

In this month I was at Middletown, in Bucks county, at the burial of my dear and intimate friend, John Rutledge, who died very suddenly; at which burial there were above one thousand people. He was well-beloved among his neighbours, and was a serviceable man where he lived. I admired to see such a number of people upon so short notice, he dying one day in the afternoon, and being buried the day following: divers testimonies were borne concerning the wonderful works and ways of God. It was a solid bowing time, wherein many hearts were broken, and melted into tenderness. After meeting, a young man came to me trembling, and begged that I would pray for him, for he had spent too much of his time in vanity, and had strong convictions on him for it, and had been greatly affected and wrought upon that day. I exhorted him to deny himself, and to take up his cross and to follow Christ, who hath said, He would in no wise cast off those who came to him in true faith. He went from me very tender and loving, being broken in his spirit.

From thence I went to Gwynnedd, (or North Wales,) where on the First-day of the week we had a very large meeting. In the morning of the day, a voice awoke me, which cried aloud, saying, REWARDS AND PUNISHMENTS FOR WELL AND EVIL DOINGS ARE SEALED AS AN ETERNAL DECREE IN HEAVEN, which confirmed me that mankind were happy or unhappy in that world which is to come, according to their deeds in this life. If their deeds be good, as Christ said, their sentence will be, Come ye blessed; if their deeds be evil, Depart from me all ye that work iniquity; and, Go ye cursed, &c. And, If thou do well, shalt thou not be accepted? and if thou doest not well, sin lieth at the door. And again, "I have no pleasure in the death of the wicked, but that the wicked turn from his way and live." These, with many more texts of the same nature, contained in the holy Scriptures, are contrary to the doctrine of personal election and reprobation, as some hold it. We had a meeting also in the afternoon of the same day, which was satisfactory to many; our hearts being filled with the love of God, for which we thankfully praised him. The next day we had a meeting of ministers, in which they were exhorted to wait for the gift of the Holy Ghost, without which there can be no true minister or ministry. I was concerned to put them in mind to keep close to Christ, their holy, sure guide and bishop ; to be cautious of going before, lest they should miss their way ; and of staying too far behind, for fear we should lose our guide : and to be careful to keep a conscience void of offence towards God, and also towards man ; that we might say to the people truly, Follow us, as we follow Christ ; that our conversation might confirm and not contradict our doctrine ; for our Saviour says, By their fruits ye shall know them ; men do not gather grapes of thorns, &c. And of such as say, and do not, he charged his followers not to be like them. Matthew xxiii. 3. The next day we had another very large meeting there, in which many things were opened and declared, tending to establish and build us up in our faith in Christ. After this meeting, parting with my friend John Cadwallader, who had accompanied me, I came homeward, lodging that night at Morris Morris's, whose wife was very weakly, with whom we had a tender time.

The 9th of the Fifth Month I was at the general meeting at German Town, which was a large and good meeting. Going home, I went to see Richard Buzby, who was not well : he said the company of his friends revived him. Next day I went to visit Jane Breintnall, who was seized with the dead palsy on one side ; and the Lord was pleased to comfort us together, as she expressed, to our mutual satisfaction.

On the 30th of the said month was our quarterly meeting of ministers at Philadelphia, where humble walking before God was recommended and prayed for, and it was desired that ministers might be exemplary therein, having Christ for their pattern.

On the 1st of the Sixth Month, I was at our meeting at Frankfort, which was a dull meeting to me and divers others; a lively exercise of spirit being too much wanting among many, and close walking with God in conversation. If we would really enjoy the love and presence of Christ in our religious meetings, we ought to keep near to him in our daily conversation, which that we might do, was humbly desired in supplication and prayer to God.

The young man who came to me under great concern of mind after the funeral of John Rutledge, wrote to me that he was followed with the judgments of God for his manifold transgressions, desiring that I would pray for him. In answer to his letter, I wrote him to the following effect:

"Frankfort, *7th of Sixth Month,* 1725.

"Thine from Burlington of the 26th of the Fifth Month I received, by which I perceive the hand of the Almighty hath been upon thee for thy vanity and folly; and I desire that thou may be very careful to keep close to that hand, and do not go from under it, but mind the light of Christ that hath discovered God to be great and good, and his dear Son to be thy Saviour, and sin and Satan to be evil; which evil, if thou follow it, will certainly bring thee to destruction and eternal woe: but if thou follows Christ, and walks according to that light by which he hath manifested sin to be exceeding sinful, in his time, as thou waits in patience, he will bring thee through his righteous judgments unto victory.

"Wait, O wait in patience upon God, if it be all thy days! 'I will bear the indignation of the Lord, because I have sinned against him,' said the prophet

Micah. Again, 'All the days of my appointed time will I wait till my change come,' says Job.

"Thou art young in years, and young in expericuce in the work of grace, wherefore advise with solid good men, If thou meets with inward or outward straits and difficulties, for the enemy will not easily let go his hold which he hath had of thee; therefore walk circumspectly, and shun evil company. As to praying in a form of words, without the Spirit helps, in order to open them according to thy state and condition, that will not avail: a sigh or a groan through the help of the Spirit, is much more acceptable to God, than any forms without it.

"That in the Lord's time thou mayst enjoy the reward of peace, is the desire of thy friend,

"T. CHALKLEY."

The young man took this counsel well, and kept to meetings, and behaved soberly for a time, but afterwards ran out, kept bad company, took to drinking to excess, ran himself in debt, and at length into a gaol; which hath been the unhappy case of many unstable youths, who, "When they knew God, they glorified him not as God, neither were thankful, but became vain in their imaginations, and their foolish heart was darkened."

In this month I was at Bybury and Abington meetings, in which we were favoured with the immediate power and presence of Christ, to our great comfort and edification, the visitation of divine love to the youth having a good effect on some of them; and the latter meeting ended with praise to the Almighty, after supplications for all men, from our king on the throne to the meanest of his subjects.

In my travels I met with a person who queried of me, how he should know which society had most of the Holy Spirit, since most of the professors of Christ do believe in the Holy Ghost, or Spirit.

To whom I made the following answer, viz.

Let the rule of Christ determine this question; he says, "By their fruits ye shall know them: Do men gather grapes of thorns, or figs of thistles?" Matt. vii. 16. The fruits then of the Spirit of Christ are love, faith, hope, patience, humility, temperance, godliness, brotherly-kindness, and charity; with all manner of virtue. Therefore the society of Christians, who brings forth most of the fruits of the Holy Spirit, consequently have most of Christ's grace and Spirit. But some object and say, We will not believe that any society have the Holy Ghost now, or the immediate revelation or inspiration of the Spirit, unless they work miracles. To which it is answered, That right reformation from sin, and true faith in Christ, cannot be wrought without a miracle; neither can we bring forth the fruits of the Spirit without the miraculous power of Christ.—Men by nature bring forth the works of nature, and that which is contrary to nature is miraculous. Sin is natural, but divine holiness, or the righteousness of Christ, wrought in man, is spiritual, supernatural, and miraculous. And as to natural men, that are in a state of nature, seeing outward miracles, if they will not, nor do not believe what is written in the holy Scriptures of the Old and New Testament, neither will they believe, although one were to rise from the dead. Notwithstanding Christ wrought out miracles, and did the works which none other could do; though he cured all manner of diseases, and fed many thousands with a few loaves, and a few small fishes, and what remained, when all had eaten, was more than there was at first; though he raised the dead, and himself arose from the dead, yet few, but very few, believed in him, so as truly to follow him. His birth, his life, his doctrine, his death, his resurrection, are all miraculous; and since all this was done in the person of Christ, and at the first publication of his religion to men, there is now no absolute necessity of outward miracles, though his power is the same now as ever: but he said to his disciples, "He that believeth on me, the works that I do shall he do also, and greater works than these shall he do," John xiv. 12. Upon which W. Dell says, This must be understood in relation to sin; for Christ had no sin in himself to overcome, but we all have sinned, and to overcome sin is the greatest of miracles. This will try the notional or nominal Christian, who says, We can never overcome sin in this world. Where then is our faith in the Son of God, who for this purpose was manifested, that he might destroy the works of the Devil? 1 John iii. 8. Heb. ii. 14.

Therefore let not Christians be slow of heart to believe in the glorious gospel of Christ; and if we truly believe therein, and live in the practice of his doctrine, we shall see miracles enough to satisfy us for ever.

The 16th of the Sixth Month I was at the weekly meeting at Frankfort, which, though a small meeting, was sweet, reviving, and comfortable, to some of us; so that we had a sufficient reward for leaving our business, it being the time of our hay-harvest. Week-day meetings are much neglected by many, more is the pity. The apostle's advice is necessary for men in our age, even of professed Christians, viz. "Let us consider one another to provoke unto love and good works; not forsaking the assembling of ourselves together, as the manner of some is," Heb. x. 24, 25.

The 23rd of the Sixth Month, my cart-wheel, being iron-bound, ran over me, and my horse kicked me on my head; the wheel put my shoulder out, and the horse wounded my head, so that the skull was bare, and my leg was sorely bruised; the same day Dr. Owen and Dr. Graham, with the help of two of our neighbours, set my shoulder and dressed my wounds; and the Lord was so merciful to me, that the next day I was enabled to write this memorandum of this wonderful deliverance and speedy cure, for which, added to the many I have received from his gracious hand, I have occasion to be truly thankful: I was obliged to keep at home some time, and thought it long, because I could not go to meetings as usual; but many Friends came to see me, which was a comfort to me. One day upwards of thirty persons came from several parts of the country to see how I did, and were glad I was like to recover. The day before I was so hurt, being the first of the week, I was at meeting at Philadelphia, and was concerned to speak of the uncertainty of life, and the many accidents we are incident to in those frail bodies, and exhorted Friends to live so, that they might have a conscience serene, and clear of offence towards God and man, and then they might expect the comforts of the Holy Ghost, which in such seasons of difficulty, would be a great help and benefit to them, of which I had the sweet experience the next day, under great extremity of pain: and though the pain of my body was such, that I could not for several nights take my natural rest, yet I had comfort through the sweet influence of the Holy Spirit, which Christ promised his followers, John xiv. 26.

On the 18th of the Seventh Month, began our yearly meeting at Philadelphia, which was large, and our Friends John Wanton and William Anthony, from Rhode-Island, and Abigail Bowles, from Ireland, had good service therein. From this meeting an address was sent to king George, for his royal favour to us as a society of people, in giving his assent to a law made in this province for prescribing the forms of declaration, affirmation, &c., instead of the forms heretofore used.

The beginning of the Eighth Month, being a little recovered from my hurt, I had a desire once more to see my friends on the eastern shore of Maryland, at their general meeting at Choptank. The first day I set out, I travelled about thirty miles, and at night was very weary, being but weak in body, and I was almost ready to faint in my mind about proceeding any further; but next day, George Robinson, at whose house I lodged, offering to accompany me, we travelled about forty miles to Sassafras river, and both of us, though much tired, were comforted in each other's company and conversation. On the next day we travelled near twenty miles to the general meeting in Cœcil county, in Maryland, where we met with two Friends from Rhode Island, and two from Pennsylvania, who were there on the like occasion. The meeting was large and quiet, many people being there not of our own society, and were very sober: the meeting held several days, wherein the gospel-dispensation was set forth, and the love of God in Christ was exalted. From Cœcil we went to Chester river, and had a meeting there, at which the people were exhorted to come to Christ, the eternal rock, and true foundation, and to build their religion on him, against whom the gates of hell can never prevail; and they were so much affected, that they did not seem forward to leave the house after the meeting was over. From Chester river we went to Tred-Haven, to the general meeting of Friends for Maryland, which was very large; some Friends from Pennsylvania and Virginia being also there, and many people of other societies: many testimonies were borne to the operation of Christ by his Spirit in the soul, and Friends were earnestly desired to be diligent in reading the holy Scriptures, and to keep up the practice of our wholesome discipline; by the neglect of which, a door would be opened to loose living, and undue liberties. From Tred-Haven we travelled into the Great-Forest, between the bays of Chesapeak and Delaware, and had a satisfactory meeting; as yet there was no public meeting-house in this place, wherefore I told the people of the house, I was obliged to them for the use of it; but they tenderly answered, they were more obliged to me for my kind visiting of them; and truly we had a solid good meeting there: the people being generally poor, they had but little notice taken of them by the money-loving teachers, who preach for hire. From the Forest I went to Little Creek, in the territories of Pennsylvania, where was a general meeting for the counties of Newcastle, Kent, and Sussex. The meeting was large, and Friends parted in great love and tenderness. And I went forward to Duck Creek, where we had a meeting: divers persons of note being there, and all were quiet, and heard with attention. From

Duck Creek I went to George's Creek, and had a meeting, where a man of a sober conversation, said, that he never heard things so spoken to before; but that he could witness to the truth of all that was said. It was a good meeting before the conclusion; but I was very low and poor in my spirit in the beginning of it. From this place we set forward to Newcastle, where we had a meeting; it was the time of the sitting of the great assembly, and several members of the house were at meeting. The governor, who has from our first acquaintance been very respectful to me, hearing that I was in town, sent to desire me to tarry all night in Newcastle; but being engaged to a meeting over the rivers Christine and Brandy-Wine, and it being near night, I could not stay, but went away that evening, and sent my love to him, desiring to be excused. That night I lodged at John Richardson's, and next day went to George Robinson's, at Newark, where we had a meeting on a First-day, and on Second-day another at Providence; and went from thence to Derby, to visit our worthy aged Friend Thomas Lightfoot, who lay very weak in body, none expecting his recovery; I called as I went from home, and then he was very ill, and told me, he thought that illness would conclude his time in this world, but said, that all was well; and likewise, that he had a great concern upon his mind for the growth and prosperity of truth in the earth, and desired with tenderness of spirit, that I would give his dear love to all Friends; and he now said, "I never thought to see thee more, but am glad to see thee." I staid there all night, and in the morning we had a comfortable heart-melting time together, in which was revived the remembrance of the many favourable seasons of God's love we had enjoyed in our travels in the work of the ministry of the gospel of Christ, and we tenderly prayed, if we never met more in this world, we might meet in that which is to come, where we might never part more, but might for ever live to sing with all the saints and holy angels, Hallelujah to God and the Lamb. From Derby I went to Philadelphia Third-day meeting, and from thence to my house, where my dear wife and children with open hearts and arms received me, and I them with joy; at which time I had a gracious reward of peace for my labour of love, which far exceeded silver or gold. In this journey I travelled above three hundred miles, had nineteen meetings, and was from home above three weeks, in which time I recovered of my lameness to admiration; so that I had with satisfaction to remember the apostle's saying, that "All things work together for good to them that love God," Rom. viii. 28.

After my return home I was at the general meeting at Frankfort; and in the beginning of the Ninth Month, I was at meetings at Abington, German Town, and divers times at Philadelphia, particularly at the youths' meeting, wherein several testimonies were borne, and the youth exhorted to piety and humility.

On the 5th day of this month, in the morning, being under a consideration of the many sore exercises and trials I had met with from my childhood, I was much affected; but the following portions of Scripture being brought to my remembrance, afforded me some relief, viz. Whom the Lord loveth he chasteneth. And, If ye be without chastisement, ye are bastards, and not sons. And, In this world ye shall have trouble, but in me peace. So that I patiently bore my affliction, and praised God under it.

In this month I was at the funeral of our worthy ancient Friend, Thomas Lightfoot. He was buried at Derby; the meeting was the largest that I had ever seen at that place. Our dear Friend was greatly beloved for his piety and virtue, his sweet disposition, and lively ministry: the Lord was with him in his life and death, and with us at his burial.

After this burial I was at one at Abington; the meeting was large, and on that occasion, several things suitable to the states of the people were treated on.

I was also about this time at German Town, and at a general meeting at Plymouth, to my great satisfaction, being accompanied by my ancient friend Rowland Ellis; and at the Third-day meeting in Philadelphia, at the time of our Fall-fair; there were fervent desires and prayers, in several of us, that the youth might be preserved from the evils too prevalent at such times of liberty and profaneness.

About the 20th of the month I went for Long Island, being drawn in true love to make a general visit to Friends there; and likewise having some business to transact there. On the Fifth-day of the week, Thomas Masters and I set out from Frankfort, and in the evening we got to a Friend's house near the falls of Delaware, where we were kindly entertained, and our horses taken good care of: to take due care of travellers' horses, is a commendable thing, and more grateful to some travellers, than to take care of themselves. From the falls of Delaware we travelled next day to Piscattaway, and lodged at an inn; and on the next day we went to Woodbridge, to John Kinsey's, and on First-day we had a satisfactory meeting there, with Friends and others; and the next day John Kinsey went with us to Long Island, and that night got to John Rodman's, and next day we rested, being weary with travelling so far in the cold. Our dear friends in that island very lovingly and kindly received my visit to them; so that I had occasion to remember that saying of the holy Scripture, As iron sharpeneth iron, so doth the countenance of a man his friend!

The Fifth-day of the week we had a large meeting at Flushing, and another in the evening at Obadiah Lawrence's, which was an open, tender time. From Flushing we went to Cow Neck, to Joseph Latham's, who went with me to Westbury meeting, which, considering the cold, was much larger than I expected. From Westbury, Nathaniel Simmons, Samuel Underhill, and Phœbe Willet, went with us to Bethphage, where we had a comfortable evening-meeting at the house of Thomas Powell, who went with us next morning to a town called Setawket. It was as cold a day's travel as ever I went through in all my life; the wind was in our faces, and northerly; I do not remember, though I had been a traveller above thirty years, that ever I endured so much hardness by cold in one day; my chin and jaws were much affected with the frost for several days; but we had a good meeting that made up for all. After which we went ten miles to Amos Willet's house, where we had a serviceable meeting: he invited his neighbours, who came and received us with hearts full of good-will; and those not of our society, were well satisfied with the meeting; so that we went on our way rejoicing, that we were favoured with the good presence of God in our journey. Amos Willet and his wife went with us to Huntingdon, where we had a quiet, peaceable meeting, and the grace of our Lord Jesus Christ was with and amongst us, as many can witness that were there. From hence we went to Samuel Underhill's, and visited his weak brother ; in which visit the Lord mightily refreshed us together, and we blessed his holy name, for he is good to all them who put their trust in him. Next day we had a large meeting at Matinicock. After this meeting we went to Thomas Pearsall's, and had an evening-meeting at his house. The next day, being a snowy, stormy day, and one of the shortest in the year, we went, being eighteen in company, to Cow Neck, where we had a good meeting, and much larger than could be expected. After meeting we went to Joseph Latham's, and had a tender, open evening-meeting there, in which we were edified, and refreshed, in Christ Jesus. From Cow Neck I went to Flushing, had a large meeting there on the First-day of the week, and on Second-day we went over the Sound, which divides Long Island from the main continent, to Horse Neck, and had a meeting, where I understood there never had been one before; the people were sober and attentive, and some expressed their satisfaction. That evening we had a meeting at an inn near Byram river, where divers people came, and were attentive; the inn-keeper, his father, brother, wife, and several others, took our visit very kindly; though there was one restless man, who seemed to be out of order with drink before he came into the house, and when we were sitting in silence, waiting for the gift of Christ, and worshipping in spirit, as Christ instituted, he sitting by me, jogged me, and said, It was time to begin, for there is as many come as would come to night; though he was mistaken in that; but he not having patience to watch and pray, went away; after which we had a good meeting. These two meetings were in the government of Connecticut, where they formerly made a law imposing a fine of five pounds on those who should entertain any of our society, which law, I was informed, was repealed in Great Britain. From thence we travelled into New York government, and had a meeting at Rye, and another at Marrineck; from thence we travelled to West Chester, and had a meeting there on a Sixth-day of the week, intending to go over the ferry next day to Long Island; but the wind being high and boisterous, that we could not get over, we tarried three nights at the house of John Stephenson, where we were lovingly and generously entertained; and on First-day we were again at West Chester meeting, which ended comfortably, though I was in a low state, both of body and mind, in the beginning of it. On Second-day we all got well over the ferry to Long Island, parting with our friends at the ferry in much love and good-will. Joseph Latham having been my fellow-traveller on the main, I went to his house, from thence to Westbury, to a large meeting, and next to Bethphage, and had a meeting there, and in the evening, accompanied by Samuel Bowne and Joseph Latham, I went to Jerusalem, and had a large and satisfactory meeting: many of the people of the town, who were there, came the next day to our meeting at Hempstead, which was large; the great Lord of all was good to us that day, which, I hope, many that were there, will not forget; and some convincement was wrought on some that were of account in the world at these last-mentioned meetings, particularly one who lived at Jerusalem, with tenderness of spirit desired my remembrance, whom I pray to God to preserve, with all those who love and fear him, and believe in his Son, to the end.

From Hempstead I went to Matinicock, where, on a First-day of the week, we had a large meeting, and a solid, good opportunity it was; and from thence to Thomas Townsend's on the plains, at whose house we had an evening meeting; next morning a pretty many Friends from the plains, went with us to the south side of the island, to a place called Rockway, where we had a meeting at Hicks's, the neighbours coming to it pretty generally; there was great openness to receive the doctrine of truth in those not of our society, and they were very kind to us in those parts: this was the second meeting I had been at in this place, Benjamin Holme having the first there, since which they had not been visited by any Friend of the ministry except myself. From Rockway we went to Foster's Meadow, where was a large gathering of people, and Christ filled our hearts with divine love. From thence I went to Peter Titus's, and had a meeting at his house, to which came the neighbours, and were well affected; and next day we had a meeting in the meeting-house at Westbury, which was very large, and to our satisfaction. From Westbury, in the evening, we went to visit a young woman who had been in a despairing condition for several years. The family came together, and we put up our prayers to the Almighty, in the name of his dear Son; it was a good time to us all; and the young woman, and some others, expressed their satisfaction.

This evening we went to see another young woman, who was in a deep consumption, but in a very comfortable state of mind; having a great desire to see me before she died, she sent for me to come to her, and her desire was answered, her spirit being revived with a fresh visitation of the love of Jesus Christ, the holy Physician of value, and our supplications were, that the Lord would be pleased to be with her, and support her to the end, and grant her an easy passage from this life to his glorious kingdom, when it should please him to remove her; which prayer we have cause to hope was answered.

Though the days were short, we rode about fifteen miles, and made those two visits, after that great meeting at Westbury, and the season was exceeding cold; but our great and good Master supported us, and was with us in our exercises and service for his name and truth's sake. I lodged this night at Joseph Rodman's, and was next day at Flushing week-day meeting, which was very large and satisfactory, and had a meeting the same evening at Samuel Bowne's, and the next day went to New York, and had a quiet good meeting in the evening at Samuel Harrison's, and on the morrow had an evening-meeting at a place called the Kills, at the house of Richard Hallet, and the next day, being First-day, had a large meeting at New Town, to the edification of Friends and other sober people.

It being now generally known that I was on the island, the people flocked to meetings, though the weather was extremely cold, for the Lord manifested himself in the riches of his love unto us in our meetings for the worship of his holy name. The next meeting was at James Jackson's, at Rocky Hill, where was judge Hicks, the high sheriff, and a justice of peace, with several other persons of note, with whom and our Friends, we had a good time to set forth the work of grace and reformation, as I think, to general satisfaction, for which we blessed the holy name of God; and humble prayer was put up to him for all men, and particularly for our king George, as also for all in authority under him, and that they might be a terror to evil-doers, and the praise of them that do well. The next meeting we had was at Jamaica, which was also large, and several in authority were there, and were very loving and respectful after meeting. The next First-day we had a large meeting at the meeting-house at Cow Neck, which was somewhat crowded. I was right glad, though my exercises were very great, that there was such openness and room in people's hearts to receive the doctrine which I had to declare unto them, in the name and power of Christ; afterwards we had an evening-meeting with the widow Titus, to which divers Dutch people came, and were very attentive and sober. On the third of the week we had a meeting near the place called Hell-gate, a narrow passage in the great sound or bay, between Long Island and the main land, several justices and their wives were at this meeting, one of which had disowned his son, and turned him out of doors for coming among us; but beholding his son's sober conversation, grew more moderate, and after meeting he and his wife invited us to dine with them, but we were engaged to visit the widow Stevens that evening, at whose house we had a meeting. Going thither, it being very cold and stormy, my hands were touched with the frost, and perceiving it when I came to the fire, I called for a basin of cold water, which soon cured them; I note this that others may reap benefit thereby. Next day we went to the week-day meeting at New Town, and on the Fifth-day at Flushing meeting, which was large, and to edification, and in the evening had a meeting at our ancient Friend Hugh Copperthwait's, which was acceptable to him, as himself expressed when it was ended, and to us also Next day we had a very large evening-meeting at Thomas Pearsall's, and likewise a large, good meeting the day after, being First-day, at Matinicock, wherein the kingdom of Christ was exalted, and the deformed state of sin and iniquity represented, and the example and doctrine of Christ closely recommended, in order to the overcoming sin; this being not only possible, but the duty of Christians through the power of Christ, and true faith in his holy name; and the danger of believing, that it is impossible to overcome sin, was opened to them, and that such a belief is contrary to, and against Christ and his doctrine, and darkens and blinds the hearts of men; but the love of Christ enlightens the soul, and strengthens it to believe, that all things are possible with God: for this great work cannot be done in the will, wit, and power of man, but through the power and grace of Christ, which he promised to true believers in him. I was faint after this meeting, but resting a little I soon grew better, so that we had an evening-meeting at James Cock's, where one came and told us we must not eat any flesh, and produced Thomas Tryon's works for his proof; but I took the Bible, and shewed him a proof to the contrary, and told him, we were resolved to believe our book before his, and shewed him from the apostle, that the kingdom of God is not meat and drink, (nor divers washings,) but righteousness, peace, and joy in the Holy Ghost, Romans xiv. 17. Though at the same time, according to the doctrine of Christ and his apostles, I was for temperance in meats and drinks, as well as moderation in apparel. The next day we had a very large meeting at Oyster Bay, many being there, who were not of our society, who steadily gave attention to what was declared. Here being many young people, they were persuaded to give up their blooming years to do the will of God, and to remember him their Creator, in their youthful days. Friends said, there had not been such a meeting there a great while, for which opportunity I was humbly thankful to the Lord. After meeting we went to Samuel Underhill's, and had an evening-meeting with his brother, who, through sickness and lameness, could not get out for a long time. Next day, Samuel Bowne being with me, we went to visit a young woman that was weak in body, but lay in a comfortable frame of mind; she was thankful for our visit, and said the visits of her friends were comfortable to her. Next day, being the Fourth-day of the week, we had a meeting at the widow Taylor's, who desired it on account of her father, who was in the eighty-eighth year of his age, and so infirm, that he could not get to meetings; he was very clear in his understanding and memory, and was much refreshed with this meeting, as were divers of us also. Next day we had a meeting at Flushing, which was large and open, and the grace and power of Christ was with us in the ministration of the gospel. After this meeting, we had an evening-meeting with our ancient friend Joseph Thorne, who by reason of his age and infirmity, could not go abroad as far as to the meeting. The house was crowded with his neighbours and friends, and we had a solid, good time together.

While at Flushing I went to visit a young woman who was a most dismal spectacle to behold, an object of great pity: her face, hand and foot, being much eaten away by the king's evil: our prayers were, that now in her great misery, the Almighty would be pleased to support her soul by his grace and Spirit, and sanctify her affliction to her, that it might work for her a more exceeding weight of glory in that world which is to come. The next First-day we had a large meeting at Flushing, where many weighty truths were opened to the satisfaction and edification of the auditory, and in the evening we had a meeting with the wife of Matthew Farrington, who was too weakly to go abroad; the neighbours came in, and we had a seasonable opportunity. The next Third-day was the youths' meeting at Flushing, in which we were concerned to exhort them to obedience to God and their parents, and to follow their parents as they follow Christ; for where any leave Christ, there we are to leave their example, though they were our fathers and mothers; and the right honouring of our parents was set forth, and they exhorted not to despise the day of small things; and the happy state of the obedient, and the unhappy state of the disobedient, and many weighty truths were delivered to them in that meeting by several experienced Friends. From Flushing I went to the week-day meeting at New Town, and in the evening we had a meeting at the widow Way's; the neighbours coming in, we had a good time with them: the parable of the ten virgins was treated of, and the great disadvantage of wanting the Divine oil of grace in our vessels, was shewn to them.

The next day, being the fifth of the week, we had

a very large satisfactory meeting at the widow Alsup's at the Kills, and from thence with several Friends went to New York, where we had three meetings to our edification, the weather still remaining extremely cold, but we felt the love of Christ to warm our hearts, and though I think I never felt it colder, I never had my health better. Several Friends accompanied us to the boat at New York, the water being open on that side, we took our leave of each other, and put out for the other shore; but before we got there we were blocked up in the ice, and it was a considerable time before we could work our way through, but at last we got well on Long Island, where I waited some hours for company, who through some difficulty got on shore; after which we went to the Narrows, through a storm of wind and snow, but the wind being high, we could not get over that night, nor the next day, the ice having come down and filled the bay: when the tide had driven away the ice, we put out and got well over, and lodged at the ferry-house on Statengland. Next morning we went to the ferry at the Blazing-Star, over against Woodbridge, but it was all fastened with ice, and we not daring to venture over it, went to the ferry at Amboy, and got comfortably over; staid there that night, and next day went to Trenton, and lodged at Captain Gould's, who treated me very kindly, I being much tired with travelling. Next morning I went over the Delaware river on the ice, as we had also the day before at Rariton, and that day, being the 5th of the Twelfth Month, I got safe home to my loving spouse and tender children, where I found all well, and a hearty reception, having travelled six hundred miles, and attended above sixty meetings.

After having been at home, and at our own meeting at Frankfort, I went to the quarterly-meeting at Philadelphia, where Friends were glad to see me.

On the next Fifth-day I was at the marriage of Thomas Masters and Hannah Dickinson, where were many sober people, not of our society.

Having been lately among Friends at Long Island, and been comforted in the many opportunities we had together, it came into my mind to visit them with an epistle at their quarterly meeting at Flushing, which was as followeth:

"Frankfort, *Twelfth Month*, 1725.

"My dear and well-beloved Friends,

"Believing it might be acceptable to you to hear that I was got well to my habitation in such a difficult time of the year as I set out from you in; and also feeling the sweet influence of the Divine love of the heavenly Father, and his dear Son our Lord Jesus Christ, to arise and spring in my heart and flow towards you.

"It came into my mind to write a few lines to the quarterly meeting of Friends at Flushing, by way of epistle, well knowing also that many of us are as epistles writ in one another's hearts by the heavenly finger of the most High; and those characters of Divine love so written will not easily be erased. I could willingly have been at your quarterly meeting, but that I had been so long from my family, that I was much wanted therein, and my coming home was seasonable and acceptable, both to them and my friends; and I humbly thank the Lord, I found all well. Now that which is on my mind to your quarterly meeting, is after this manner, concerning the government of the church of Christ, of which church He is the holy head and lawgiver. Wherefore we are to seek and wait for counsel and wisdom from him, in all our monthly and quarterly meetings, for the well-ordering of our little Society, which is growing and increasing in the earth, and also in your island, notwithstanding the invidious attempts of some men of corrupt minds; and it will grow and increase more and more as we keep our places, our heavenly places in Christ Jesus.

"Dear Friends, The good order of truth and government of Christ in his church, is a great help to us and our children, when carried on in Christ's Spirit, (pray observe or mind that,) for if our order and church-government, be carried on in the spirit of man, as he is mere man, though he is never so crafty or cunning, it will do more hurt than good in the church of Christ. Christ's Spirit must govern Christ's church; and when, and where that is over all, then, and there, Christ's church and kingdom is exalted, of whose kingdom and peace there will be no end; and happy will all those be, whose end is in it. Moses, that man of God, governed in the Jewish church in the Spirit of God, and when he found the work too heavy for him, the Lord put his Spirit on seventy more, who were help-meets in the government; so that it was God's Spirit that governed; and while that ruled them, all was well; but when they went from that, they fell into error and disobedience; and at length the Messiah came, and he governed his own little flock himself; and when he ascended up on high, he promised his Spirit should be with, and in his church for ever, and be their holy Guide into all truth, in which he would also comfort them: and Christ fulfilled this his promise; for when his disciples waited at Jerusalem to be endued with power from on high, according to the advice of their Lord, they were filled with the gift and grace of the Holy Spirit: and when the brethren and elders met together about the affairs and government of the church, they gave forth rules and orders from that general-meeting to the particular ones; and the Holy Ghost presided amongst them, which they signified to the other meetings, saying, It seemed good to the Holy Ghost, and to us, to put you in mind of such and such things. And while this Holy Ghost, or Spirit, governed in the primitive Christian church, all was well: God and Christ was glorified, and his church and people edified; but by going from that, the apostacy came in.

"Wherefore, dear friends, keep close to the Spirit, power, light, and Divine life of Christ Jesus, in your monthly and quarterly meetings for the government of the church, as well as in your meetings for the worship of the Almighty; for if we go from that, he will go from us.

"And, dear friends, the testimony of Jesus, in the spirit of prophecy, opens in me after this manner, That if our Society keep and live up to the Spirit and truth of Christ, which hath been manifested to our forefathers, and to us also in this age, the great Lord of all will prosper his work in our hands, and bless both us and our children, as we and they keep therein.

"And as we have kept close to this our heavenly guide, how hath the Lord sweetly manifested his love and power to us in our meetings for the well-ordering of our Society? which many times hath filled our hearts with pure praises, and holy thanksgiving, to the high and lofty One, who inhabits eternity, and dwells in the highest heavens, and is light for ever: to whom, with the Lamb of God, who takes away the sins of the world, I recommend you, my dear and well-beloved friends, brethren, and sisters in Christ, with my own soul,

"T. CHALKLEY.

"P. S. Since my return, I have been thankful to God for the many favourable visitations and good opportunities he was pleased to grant me with you, and divers sober people on your island, in which there is an open door among many to receive the testimony of truth. I commend your nobility in building good houses, and making room for your sober neighbours to sit with you in your meetings; this is of good report concerning you, both far and near, and if I apprehend right, there is more work of that kind for you to do. I thought often, when among you, and now also, that there would be a large gathering, if there were a house built at the upper end of the Great Plains, not far from Foster's Meadow; but every one may not think or see alike; though I know some solid Friends among you, thought the same with me, about the prospect of a large gathering thereaway, if a house were built; to which friends, and well-inclined people, might come from Hempstead, Rocky Hill, Rockway, Foster's Meadow, &c.

"T. C."

After my service on Long Island, I had great sweetness upon my spirit for some time, which sometimes caused my heart to sing for joy; and yet I rejoiced in a trembling frame of spirit, and had the true sense of what is written in the holy Scriptures, where it is said, Serve the Lord with fear, (I take it, filial fear) and rejoice with trembling, for fear of losing that precious sense of the love of God, which is in Christ.

On the 20th of the Twelfth Month, the First-day of the week, I was at Abington meeting, in which the love of Christ was manifested to us, in the opening of his saying, "If I be lifted up, I will draw all men unto me," John xii. 32. The next day I was at German Town, at the burial of a son of Dennis Cunrad, at which also was our friend Abigail Bowles. On the Sixth-day following I went to the general meeting of ministers and elders at Burlington, where I again met with our said friend and divers others: the First-day meeting was large; and on Second-day was the quarterly meeting for the county; and on Third-day was their youths' meeting, which was large, and many weighty truths were delivered in that meeting. On Fourth-day we were at a meeting at Springfield; the house was pretty much thronged, and Friends were exhorted, thankfully to commemorate the mercies and favours of the Almighty to them, and desired to enlarge their meeting-houses as their number increased; for in those parts there was such an openness in the hearts of the people, and increase of their number, that Friends had already agreed on building two meeting-houses between Croswicks and Burlington; their zeal and unanimity therein, was worthy of commendation. Fifth-day being the week-day meeting at Burlington, Friends of the town desired I would stay at it; I thought we had just before had divers good opportunities, and my own inclinations seemed to lead to my family; but Friends being desirous of my staying, I did so, and we had a good, solid meeting. After meeting a solid good Friend said, he thought we had the best wine at last; and indeed the love of God, through Christ, is so sweet to his people, that the last often seems the best, when it is only a renewed visitation of the same love to his children. So I went home, rejoicing that I was in some good measure accounted worthy to serve so good and so gracious a master.

On the 6th day of the First Month, being the First of the week, I was at the morning and afternoon meetings in Philadelphia, wherein those who call themselves Free-Thinkers, were exhorted to be careful of drinking too freely, lest they might justly be called free-drinkers; for many times such, when they drink too freely of strong liquor, think and speak too freely their own corrupt notions, to the dishonour of God, and to the scandal of religion in general.

Soon after I was at the First-day meetings at Philadelphia; and in this month I went into the Jerseys, and was at three large meetings in company with Abigail Bowles, in which our said friend had good service, to the comfort of Friends, convincing of gainsayers, and confirming the weak; and the people were glad of our visit.

The 15th day of this month I was at Burlington, at the burial of my good friend and old acquaintance Abraham Bickley, at whose funeral were great numbers of people, he being well-beloved of his neighbours; Christ's raising Lazarus out of the grave, and his tenderness and weeping there, was spoken of, in order to stir people up to a tender, religious exercise of mind, which is too much wanting among many of the professors of his holy name, who have too little sense of that which should bring true tenderness over their minds, being more in earth than heaven; so that they are dry and barren, as to the things of God. The meeting ended, to satisfaction, with supplications to the Almighty.

A few days after, I was at our general spring meeting in Philadelphia, which was large; where our friends Robert Jordan and Abigail Bowles had good service.

This week I was at four very large meetings at Philadelphia, Frankfort, and Abington, much to my satisfaction, though I had no vocal service therein; yet my heart was broken into tenderness and tears, under the ministry of several weighty, solid testimonies that were borne by good and living ministers, qualified to preach the gospel in the demonstration of the Spirit, and with power.

The 26th of the First Month, 1726, I went to German Town meeting, which was large, and I was opened therein to speak of the vision of the prophet Ezekiel, of the holy waters which proceeded from under the threshold of the sanctuary, which the angel measuring, they grew deeper and deeper, until they became a river to swim in, Ezek. xlvii. 5. Which mystically sheweth the work of grace, conversion, and regeneration; and that these holy waters the soul must drink of, and be washed, and baptized in, are spiritual and supernatural, and therefore not to be measured by the spirit and will of man, in his natural state, according to the prophet Isaiah, chap. xxxiii. 21. Man before he can swim therein, must be stripped of all his self-righteousness, and artificial religion, though as splendid and beautiful as a gallant ship, or galley with oars, which in this respect is agreeable to the state of men swimming in elementary water, where the most skilful have sometimes lost their lives, for want of being naked or unclothed; and those who had not yet attained much experience, were advised not to go out of their depth, but to wait in patience and humility, to enjoy the medicinal virtue of the trees growing by the side of this river, whose fruit is for meat, and leaves for medicine. Ezekiel xlvii. 12. The people of this meeting were generally Germans, several of whom staid in the house after the meeting was over, and were broken into tenderness, in a sense of the presence and love of God unto us, for which I was also humbly thankful and bowed in spirit.

I was at the Third-day weekly meeting in Philadelphia, which was but small considering the large number of those professing to be of our society in this city; those present were closely and tenderly exhorted to be zealous for good works, and against bad works; not respecting the person of any man; the abominations committed by some under our profession, in this city and province, calling for humiliation; and as the promise of God's favour was to those who mourned with sighs and cries for the abominations among his people formerly, Ezek. ix. 4, 6, so now, as many as are under the same concern, may hope for preservation and salvation, if he should in like manner visit us, as at this time he doth some of our neighbours; there being a great sickness and mortality in some of the adjacent places.

In the Second Month I visited the meetings of Friends at Haverford, New Town, Radnor, and Merion, which meetings consist chiefly of ancient Britons, who are a religious, industrious, and increasing people; among whom my service was, as they expressed, to our mutual satisfaction. After my return home, I went to visit Friends at the Falls of Delaware, and was at a large meeting in their new meeting-house. After a satisfactory meeting at Frankfort, on the Fifth-day of the same week, I went with Ennion Williams to his son's marriage; and the next day he, and several other Friends, accompanied me to Woodberry Creek, and had a good, open meeting, and that night went to James Lord's, and next morning went towards Salem, and lodged at Isaac Sharp's; where I was informed of a great mortality at Cohansy. The 24th of the Second Month was the general meeting at Salem, which was a large gathering of people of different persuasions, from many parts of the country, where the doctrine of the gospel was preached in great love to the people, which they heard with solid attention. From Salem I went to Alloway's Creek and Cohansy, and had meetings there: I was informed that more than seventy persons had lately died here of a malignant distemper; though it seemed to abate, none dying while we were there. At Cohansy the meeting was large and solid, though but few of our society there; and they were earnestly admonished to a proper disposition of mind, to fit them either for life or death, and reminded of the regard of the Almighty to such as live in his fear, who will have peace in their death, and their exchange will be glorious, when they are taken out of this life; but with the wicked it is not so.

From Cohansy I went through the wilderness over Maurice's river, accompanied by James Daniel, through a miry, boggy way, in which we saw no house for about forty miles, except at a ferry, and that night we got to Richard Townsend's, of Cape

May, where we were kindly received; next day we had a meeting at Rebecca Garrison's, and the day after a pretty large one at Richard Townsend's, and then went down to the Cape, and had a meeting at John Page's, and next day another at Aaron Leaming's: several expressed their satisfaction with those meetings. I lodged two nights at Jacob Spicer's, my wife's brother.

From Cape May we travelled along the sea-coast to Great Egg Harbour, had another meeting, much larger than the first, at Rebecca Garrison's, and here I was much concerned to promote the settling a monthly meeting, for the well-ordering the affairs of our Society.

We swam our creatures over Egg Harbour river, and went over ourselves in canoes, and afterwards we had a meeting at Richard Summers's, which was as large as could be expected, considering the people's living at a distance from each other.

The next meeting we had at John Scull's; and on First-day we had a large one at Peter White's, and on Second-day at Japhet Leed's, and then we went five miles through a marsh to Little Egg Harbour river, and had a meeting in their meeting-house on the Fourth-day of the week, and 11th day of the month, which was the larger by the addition of the owners, masters, and mariners, of two Sloops from New York, who, hearing of the meeting, came to it. And the next day we had another meeting at the same place, and lodged at Jervis Faro's. After these two meetings I left Egg Harbour, accompanied by several Friends from thence, and travelled about forty miles, before we came to any house. In the evening we reached a Friend's house, where we were kindly entertained, and next morning we got to Burlington, and so home, where I found all well, and was therefore thankful to the Almighty. In this journey I travelled about three hundred miles, had twenty-one meetings, and was from home about three weeks.

In the Third Month I staid at and about home, visiting the meetings at Philadelphia, German Town, Abington, and Frankfort.

In the Fourth Month I left my family, and went back in the woods as far as Oley. I was from home nine days, travelled about one hundred and fifty miles, and had six meetings at Oley, Perkiomen, and divers other places, chiefly in barns and open places, there being large companies of people, and few meeting-houses yet built in those parts of the country. In this journey I suffered pretty much through the heat, The first meeting was at the iron-works, settled a little beyond a place called Mount Misery; I was concerned for those people, having heard of their rude doings before I left my habitation; and although some were rude, others behaved themselves soberly, and expressed their thankfulness for that visitation, as I do for the opportunity I had of clearing myself to them. On my return homewards I crossed Schuylkill, and went to Samuel Nutt's iron-works, where I had a large, quiet, solid meeting: and the next day I called to see my old friend David Meredith, who being about eighty-nine years of age, I thought it probable I might not have another opportunity of seeing him. He met me with gladness, and told me it was their meeting-day; so that I staid, and was much comforted and tendered by the power of Christ: after which I came home that night.

On the next First-day, after my return, I went to

Philadelphia, and, after the afternoon-meeting, to Derby, and from thence to a yearly meeting in Chester county, held at Goshen; though the season was wet, this was a large, good meeting; at which there were three young men, who were lately called to the work of the ministry, whom I was glad to hear declare the truth in the power and simplicity of the gospel of Christ, being of the mind of Moses, when he said, in answer to Joshua, "Would God that all the Lord's people were prophets, and that the Lord would put his Spirit upon them," Numb. xi. 29. After this meeting I went to Springfield, and the next day returned home.

On the 22nd of the Fourth Month I went to the marriage of John Leigh's daughter, at Springfield, in Chester county: the meeting was large, and I was concerned to speak mostly to the young people, advising them to seek the Lord in that great affair of marriage, that they be careful how, and on whom they set their affections, and not to draw out one another's minds if they did not intend an honourable marriage; and reminding them of the ill tendency of courting several at a time, or suffering several to court at once; and that they be chaste and true in their proceedings, duly regarding the advice of the apostle, "Be not unequally yoked;" for to be sure all such marriages are unequal, when those who marry are of different principles in religion. The meeting ended with tender supplication for preservation through whatever exercises, further troubles or trials, temptations or afflictions, we might meet with in the world, that we might end well at last, and live for ever to praise and glorify God and the Lamb, who through the holy, eternal Spirit, is worthy for ever.

On the receipt of the last letter from my dear father, which I sometime since mentioned, I was apprehensive it might be his last, which it proved to be, for the next letter from my dear brother gave me intelligence of his death, which I received the 25th of the Fourth Month this year. The news of my dear father's decease took such hold of my mind, though I daily expected it, that for some time I was hardly sociable. Oh! how have I been sometimes comforted in his loving and tender epistles! at the receipt of which I have cried to the Lord, that if it pleased him, I might have a double portion of the Spirit which he gave to my father: but oh! now I must never hear more from him in this world; yet in this I have some inward comfort, that I hope we shall meet where we shall never part more. Here follows a part of my affectionate brother's account of my father's death and burial.

"Edmonton, *25th of First Month,* 1726.

"Dear Brother,

"This comes with the sorrowful account of our dear father's decease, who departed this life the 7th instant, after having been indisposed about a fortnight. I have herewith sent a particular account of some remarkable passages, and his last expressions in his sickness; that part relating to his convincement, he desired should be committed to writing, which I have done, and sent it to thee.

"I was with him several times in his last illness, and most of the last two days of his life, as thou mayst perceive by the contents. Our worthy father was honourably buried on the 11th instant, being carried from his own house to the meeting-house at Horslydown, accompanied with his relations, where was a large meeting of many people, as many as the meeting-house could well contain, and many testimonies were there borne to the innocent, exemplary life, integrity and honest zeal of our dear father, so concurrent and unanimous, that I have hardly known any such occasion more remarkable. He was accompanied from thence to the grave very solemnly, and there in like manner, interred, where a further testimony was given to his honest life and conversation, and lively zeal for the holy truth, whereof he made profession.

"Dear brother, though it be a sorrowful occasion of writing, yet herein we may be comforted, in consideration that our father went to his grave in peace in a good old age: he had his understanding and memory to the last in a wonderful manner. I believe, as I have sometimes said, that he embraced death as joyfully as ever he did any happy accident of his life. I remember one passage of his cheerful resignation: finding him fine and cheery when I came to see him, a week before his decease, and he shewing me how well he could walk about the room, and would have went [gone] out of it, though he was very bad the day before, so that I said, 'Father, I hope thou wilt get over this illness;' but he answered me pretty quick and loud, 'No, but I do not though.' It is not long since he was at my house, and was cheerful and well, but spoke as if he thought it would be the last time. My wife said, 'Father, thou mayst live some years;' but he replied, 'Is it not better for me to die, and go to Christ?' So, dear brother, with dear love to thee, my sister, and thy dear children, and our relations, I conclude with earnest desires for thy health and welfare,

"Thy affectionate brother,
"GEORGE CHALKLEY."

My brother's account of my father's convincement, and of his last sickness and dying words.

"My father was born of religious parents at Kempton, near Hitchin, in Hertfordshire, the 1st of the Ninth Month, 1642; his father's name was Thomas Chalkley, by trade a dealer in meal, by profession, of the Church of England, and zealous in his way, as was also his wife.

"They had four sons and three daughters, Thomas, John, George, and Robert; Elizabeth, Sarah, and Mary. My father, being the third son, was convinced very young, at a meeting by Enfield Chace Side, near Winchmore Hill, through the powerful ministry of William Brend, who was an eminent minister in the Lord's hand in that day, and had been a great sufferer for his testimony in New England. He was preaching, as I heard my father several times say, upon the words of the preacher, Eccles. xi. 9, 'Rejoice, O young man, in thy youth, and let thy heart cheer thee in the days of thy youth, and walk in the ways of thy heart, and in the sight of thine eyes; but know thou, that for all these things God will bring thee into judgment.' Upon which subject he spoke so home to my father's state and condition, that he was convinced, and two others of his companions were reached and affected with the testimony of Christ's truth and gospel; my father and two young men had been walking in the fields, having religious conversation together, and were providentially directed to the meeting, by observing some Friends going to it, whom they followed thither. One of his companions was Samuel Hodges, who lived and died a faithful Friend, at whose house in succeeding times a meeting was settled, and is there continued, and a meeting-house built at this day at Mims in Hertfordshire.

"My father was the first of the family who received the testimony of truth as it is in Jesus, after which his father and mother were convinced, and all his brothers and sisters, who lived and died honest Friends, except one who died young, continuing in the Church of England persuasion. Soon after the convincement of my father and his two companions aforesaid, they met with a trial of their faith and patience; for being taken at a religious meeting of Friends, they were all three committed to the New Prison in Whitechapel, where having continued prisoners for some time, the magistrates observing their Christian courage, boldness, and innocency, and being touched with tenderness towards them, considering their youth, they discharged them.

"My father, about the twenty-fifth year of his age, married my mother, a virtuous young woman, who was the widow of Nathaniel Harding, a Friend, who died under the sentence of banishment for his profession of Christ; the above account I had from my father's own mouth; what follows fell within my own observation.

"My dear father met with great exercises and disappointments in his early days; he, dealing in his father's business, sold meal to some who broke in his debt, which brought him low in the world, in which low estate he was an eminent example of patience, resignation and industry, labouring with his hands for the support of his family, and conscientiously answered all his engagements; so that it may be justly said of him, he was careful that he might owe nothing to any man but love; and further, he was very constant in keeping to meetings, being a good example therein, though in very hot times of persecution; for when Friends were sorely and severely persecuted on account of keeping their religious meetings, and the prisons filled with them through the nation, and their goods taken away, and much spoil and havoc made about the years 1680 to 1684, my father constantly attended meetings, and never missed, as I remember, when well; and though he was sometimes concerned to speak by way of exhortation to Friends in their public meetings, when they were kept out of their meeting-houses, by the then powers, to stand faithful to the truth, and testifying of the solid comfort and satisfaction those had who truly waited on the Lord, which the faithful enjoyed, notwithstanding their deep and many sufferings for Christ's sake, and his gospel, it pleased the Lord to preserve him by his Divine Providence, that he did not suffer imprisonment, though the wicked informers were very busy in that time of severe persecution. I may further add, that when my father was about sixty years of age, he had a concern to visit Friends' meetings in the north of England, and some other parts of the nation; and in the seventy-fifth year of his age, he travelled to Chester, and from thence, in company with James Bates, a public Friend of Virginia, went over for Ireland; in all which services

P 2

he had good satisfaction, and was well received of Friends; divers other journeys and travels he performed not here noted; but this journey into another nation at seventy-five years of age, shews his age had not quenched his love and zeal for his Lord's work and service.

"In our father's old age he was attended with very great exercises. About the seventy-seventh year of his age, as he was assisting his men in the dusk of the evening, he missed his footing, and fell down and broke his leg; and soon after his leg was well, he met with another accident by a fall, which disabled him, and made him lame to his death, never recovering the hurt he had by that fall, which was after this manner: he was sitting in a chair by his door on a plank, which not being set fast, it fell, and he, to save himself from the stroke of the plank, fell with his hip on the stones, and got hurt exceedingly; notwithstanding he was remarkable for his activity: he would walk, though so aged, and also lame, as far as the Workhouse, Devonshire-house, and Bull and Mouth meetings, two or three miles from home. The last bad accident that befell him, was about three weeks before his death, when being walking in the timber-yard, a single plank, which stood against a pile, fell down, and striking him on the side, threw him down; he complained not much of the blow till about a week after, when he was taken with a violent pain in his side, on the very place where he received the stroke, and, when his cough took him, with which he was often troubled, the pain was very great; howbeit, through means of a sear-cloth he received some ease, and the pain of his side abated, and the cough went off; but a violent flux followed, and it brought him very low, and extremely weak, so that it was thought he could not continue long: upon which, notice was sent to me, and I went to see him, and found him very low; but he revived, and changed often in this last illness; I having been to see him five or six days before, having an account he was ill, I then found him cheerful, and thought he might recover. He continued all the time of his illness in a patient and resigned frame of mind; on a First-day in the afternoon he took his bed, being the 6th of the First Month, and in the evening, after the afternoon meeting, which was the day before his death, several Friends came to visit him, who, finding him very weak, after a little stay, went to take their leave of him, whom he desired to sit down, and after some time of silence, he broke forth in declaration in an intelligible and lively manner, to this effect, saying, 'We have no continuing city here, but seek one to come, which hath foundations, whose builder and maker is God: Friends, that we may all labour to be prepared for our last and great change, that when this earthly tabernacle shall be dissolved, we may have an habitation with the Lord, a building not made with hands, eternal in the heavens, and that it might be thus, the Lord hath shewed thee, O man, what is good, viz. To do justly, love mercy, and walk humbly with thy God. I do not expect but this will be the last night I shall have in this world, and I desire it may be remembered, as the words of a dying man, (which came to pass, for he died the next day) O that we may labour to be clothed upon with our house that is from heaven, so that when the finishing hour comes, we may have nothing to do, but to die.' About one or two o'clock the next morning, he began to change, and desired to see me, and I came to him, and found him very sensible, but expected his end quickly to approach; be saying, he was waiting for his change. My son-in-law, Samuel Thornton, being with me, and we sitting by the bed-side, with his nurse, his house-keeper and his man, about the fourth hour in the morning he prayed fervently after this manner: 'Lord, now lettest thou thy servant depart in peace, for mine eyes have seen thy salvation, which thou hast prepared before the face of all people; thou hast given thy Son, a light to enlighten the Gentiles, and to be the glory of thy people Israel; and now, Lord, be with thy people and servants, and preserve my near and dear relations, and keep them from the snares and temptations of the enemy, that in thy truth they may fear thy great name.'

"After a little time of silence, he desired me to remember his dear love, in the life of Christ Jesus, to my dear brother Thomas Chalkley, in Pennsylvania, and to all his old friends and acquaintance.

"About the eleventh hour in the morning he inquired how the tide was, which nobody present could exactly tell: some time after he asked again; his man then went out to see; returning, he told him it would be high-water about three o'clock in the afternoon; he then lay still awhile, and after some pause spoke cheerfully out aloud, so that all in the room might hear him, 'I shall go off about five;' his man said, 'Master, how dost know?' To which he answered, 'Know, I do not know, but I believe it.' After this the apothecary, one of his neighbours, among whom he was much beloved, about noon came to see him, and asked him how he was; father answered, that for three or four hours in the night he thought he should have gone. 'Why,' said he, 'sir, it will be no surprise to you, I hope.' 'No, no,' said my father very cheerfully.' He taking leave of father, said, 'The Lord be with you.' To whom father answered, 'And with thee also.' The doctor having ordered him a comfortable cordial to drink, he drank it willingly, and then said, 'I do not think to drink any more in this world; but I hope I shall drink plentifully of the river of life:' then drawing near his end, finding his strength fail, there being a cord by his order at the bed's feet, he raised himself up thereby, as long as he had any strength left in his hands, and when his hands and shoulders failed, and his head, when last lifted up, he spoke very low and faltering, yet so as I could understand, and said, 'Now I am a going;' and about an hour after, lying all the while without sigh or groan, departed this life as in a slumber, in sweet peace; according as he had foretold, just as the clock struck five; in a perfect enjoyment of that legacy our Saviour left his followers: My peace I leave with you, &c., leaving us of the succeeding generation, a good example to follow; who, as he lived, so he died, like a lamb, in the eighty-fourth year of his age, the seventh day of the First Month, 1725.

"GEO. CHALKLEY."

To which account I shall add the following short testimony concerning my dear and greatly beloved father, George Chalkley, viz.

"I have a great deal in my heart, more than I can write concerning my dear father's life, it having been a wonderful life to me from my youth up; his early care of me, and counsel to me, when I was too thoughtless and wild, melts me into tears now in the remembrance of it; and my tender mother was a partner with him in the same exercise, and she died in like peace: the last words I heard her speak, were, 'I long to be dissolved.' And as to my tender father, I would record a little briefly in memory of him, that he was,

"1st. A true and faithful servant of Christ.

"2nd. A tender and affectionate husband: I lived at home with my parents about twenty years, and I never heard, that I remember, an angry expression between them, only once something had troubled them, and they both wept, my father saying, 'I have been an indulgent husband unto thee,' and my mother answered, 'I have not been one of the worst of wives to thee;' which were the harshest words, and the greatest difference that I observed between them; for their life was a life of peace and love, and they were an excellent example to us their children. Oh! may we follow them therein to the end.

"3rd. He had a fatherly care for his children, in tender prayers for us, and in good advice to us, and in giving us learning, according to his ability, and teaching us, by his example, as well as precept, industry, humility, and the true religion of our blessed Saviour; endeavouring to plant it in us betimes, and to destroy the evil root of sin in us, while young.

"4th. I was his servant, as well as his son, and I can truly say, his service was delightful, and his company pleasing and profitable to me; and he was also beloved much by his other servants.

5th. He was universally beloved by his neighbours, and I do not remember any difference between him and them, in the many years I lived with him; but all was peace and love.

"6th. He was very loving to his relations, and true to his friends, and a hearty well-wisher and lover of his king and country.

"T. Chalkley."

CHAPTER VII.

1726–1728.

FURTHER RELIGIOUS SERVICE CHIEFLY NEAR HOME—VOYAGE TO BARBADOES ON BUSINESS—SEVERAL MEETINGS ON THE ISLAND—OCCURRENCES AFTER HIS RETURN—TWO OTHER VOYAGES TO BARBADOES, &c.

OUR general meeting at Frankfort, the 30th of the Fourth Month, was large, our friend William Piggot, from London, being there (in the course of his visit to Friends in America) and had close work and good service in this meeting.

In the Fifth Month, 1726, I visited the meetings of Friends at Philadelphia, German Town, and Bybury, in some of which meetings, as also at our own at Frankfort, I had very comfortable satisfaction: my testimony was pretty sharp sometimes to transgressors, and therefore some of them hate me, as the Jews did my great Master; because I was concerned to testify, that their deeds were evil, and to excite my friends to manifest a Christian zeal, by openly denying ungodly men, while they continue in their ungodly works; but when they become truly penitent, and reform their lives, the arms of Christ, and his church, will be open to receive them.

Being under some melancholy thoughts, because some persons, for whom I wished well, and to whom

I had been of service, were so envious and malicious as to tell false stories of me, tending to defame me; as I was riding to our meeting, it opened with satisfaction to my mind, The more my enemies hate me, the more I will love, if that can be; and I had hearty desires to come up in the practice of this resolution: and I then thought I should come up with them all, for if a man loves and prays for his enemies, if they are gained, he is instrumental to their good, and so hath cause of rejoicing; and if they are not gained, he heaps coals of fire on their heads; so that every true Christian, by keeping under the cross of Christ, and in the practice of his doctrine, gets the better of his enemies.

In the beginning of the Sixth Month, I was at the burial of Robert Fletcher, a worthy man, and one universally beloved by all sorts of people, as far as ever I heard. There was a large meeting at his funeral, wherein several testimonies, suitable to the occasion, were borne: some of his last words were mentioned, which were, that he had lived according to the measure of grace given him. And the doctrine of the resurrection was maintained according to the Scripture, and the people were exhorted to prepare for their final change. The death of this Friend was a loss to the country, to our Society, and to his neighbours, as well as to his family and friends.

After meeting I travelled towards Uwchland, had a meeting there on First-day, and on Second-day another meeting at Lewis Walker's, and on Third-day was at the general meeting at Haverford: Friends were exhorted to dwell in the love of God, one towards another; for if they lost their love, they would lose their religion, their peace, and their God; for God is love, and those that dwell in God, dwell in love.

My neighbour, Daniel Worthington, accompanied me in this rough travel, some part of the way being hilly, and very stony and bushy, and the weather wet. We had four meetings, and rode about fourscore miles; and though I had travelled much in this province, I had never been at some of those places before: but a few nights before I set out, I had a plain prospect of them in a dream, or night vision, as I saw them afterwards, which I thought somewhat remarkable.

The people inhabiting this province, are now become numerous, and make many settlements in the woods, more than I have observed in my travels in any of the British plantations; and there hath long been a desire in my mind that they might prosper in the work of true and thorough reformation; and a goodly fear and concern being upon me, I have sometimes put them in mind of the state of this land, when their fathers first came and settled in it; and to caution them of growing careless, and forgetting the Lord, lest he should forsake them, and turn their now fruitful fields into a barren wilderness, as this was so lately; which it is easy with him to do, if he pleases, for the sins of the people.

After my return home, I visited many meetings, as Abington (youths' meeting), Philadelphia, and Chester. At Chester I was concerned to direct the people to that power in themselves, which is the life of religion, and to be careful not to rest in the best forms without it; for if we had only the form of godliness, and had not the life and power of it, it might be as reasonable for people to turn away from us, as it was for our forefathers to turn away from other societies.

In the Seventh Month I was at our yearly meeting held at Burlington, for the provinces of New Jersey and Pennsylvania, which was a very large meeting, there being Friends from New England, Rhode Island, and Europe.

First-day morning I went to Evesham to the burial of our serviceable friend, Jervis Stockdale, he being in good esteem, there was much people. The meeting was in a good tender frame, and continued several hours so, in which divers testimonies were delivered, in order to stir up people to truth and righteousness, and godly living, that they might die well. I lodged the night before at Peter Fearon's, and in the morning I was awaked out of my sleep, as it were, by a voice expressing these words; HE THAT LIVETH AND BELIEVETH IN ME, SHALL NEVER DIE. This I took to be the voice of Christ; I do not know that it was vocal, but it was as plain as one. From these expressions I had to observe to the people, the happy state and privilege of those who live and believe in Christ, and that such must not live in sin.

During the time of our yearly meeting, some rude people came up the river in a small sloop, provided by them for that purpose, and spent their time in drinking, carousing, and firing of guns, to the grief and concern of Friends, who were religiously discharging their duty, in serving and worshipping the Almighty; and it is observable, that one of these disorderly persons had his hand shot off at that time, and that the chief promoters and actors in this riotous company were soon after cut off by death, in the prime of their days.

After the general meeting was over, which ended well, Friends in the love of God departed in peace for their several habitations, praising and glorifying God.

In the beginning of the Eighth Month, having some business at Cape May, I ferried over to Gloucester, and went the first night to James Lord's, lodged there, got up before day, it being First-day morning, and rode near thirty miles to Salem, where we had a good meeting, and so went to Alloway's Creek, Cohansy, and through a barren wilderness to Cape May, where we had one meeting, and returned by way of Egg Harbour home; in which journey I travelled upwards of two hundred miles. At Cape May I was concerned to write a few lines concerning swearing, as follows:—

"Christians ought not to swear in any case, for these reasons—1st. Because Christ, their Lord, forbad it; unto whom the angels in heaven must be subject, and, doubtless, so must mortal man, to whom he gave the precept. We must and ought to be subject to Christ, who is Lord of lords, and King of kings, and the judge of the quick and the dead. To him all mortals must be accountable for their disobedience. He says, in his sermon on the Mount, thus: 'I say, Swear not at all;' Matt. v. 34. Wherefore, how can Christians, or such who are his friends, swear, since he says also, 'Ye are my friends, if ye do whatsoever I command you,' John xv. 14. So consequently those who disobey his commands, must be his enemies. To this command it is objected, that Christ only spoke against common or profane swearing: but this must needs be a great mistake, because Christ says, 'It was said in old time, thou shalt perform unto the Lord thine oaths,' Matt. v. 33: alluding to the law of

Moses, which oaths were solemn and religions; therefore Christ did not only prohibit vain and profane swearing, but all swearing. If we understand the word ALL, and what all signifies, then all and any swearing whatsoever, is not lawful for a Christian, according to Christ's law and command, which is positive to his followers.

"2ndly. James, the holy apostle of Christ, our lawgiver and our king, says, 'Above all things, my brethren, swear not, neither by heaven, neither by the earth, neither by any other oath,' James v. 12. Christ says, Swear not at all; and James, his disciple and apostle, says, Swear not by any oath; wherefore, if swearing on the bible be any oath, or is swearing at all, it is contrary to the express doctrine of Christ, and his apostle James, as is plain from the above cited texts.

"3rdly. The primitive Christians did not swear at all in the first ages of Christianity. Query, Whether our modern swearing Christians are better than the primitive ones, who for Christ, and conscience' sake, could not swear at all, even before a magistrate, though legally called?

"4thly. Many Christians have suffered death, because they for conscience' sake could not swear, and so break the command of Christ their Lord; and do not our modern Christians trample upon their testimony and sufferings? Some of whom suffered death for not swearing before the heathen magistrates, and some were martyred by the Papists. Judge then whether the persecuted or persecutors were in the right.

"5thly. Many of our worthy friends and forefathers (since the former) have suffered to death in gaols for not swearing, when required by persecuting Protestants, because for Christ's sake and sayings, as above, they could not swear at all. And this hath been a testimony which our Society hath constantly borne ever since we have been a people; for the reasons above, and more also, if there were occasion, which might be given."

The 23rd of the Eighth Month, I was at the morning meeting at Philadelphia, on a First-day of the week, which was large; and I was concerned therein to exhort Friends to labour to purge and cleanse our Society of such under our profession who live in open profaneness, and are riotous in their conversations. I was at the Bank meeting in the afternoon, where we had a comfortable time. And the next Sixth-day of the week I was at our monthly meeting, where it was unanimously agreed, in consideration of some late indecent conduct of some persons pretending to be of our profession, that a testimony from that meeting should go forth against such disorderly doings, and unchristian practices; and that all such persons, who were irregular in their conversations, be disowned to be of our community, until they by repentance manifest their reformation: which was accordingly soon after published, and read in our First-day morning meeting, and in our youths' meeting. And about this time our Governor issued a seasonable proclamation against drinking to excess, gaming, swearing profanely, revelling, night-walking, and disturbing the peace, and other immoralities; which afforded some satisfaction to sober and well-inclined Friends and others: yet there remained a great exercise and concern upon my mind, that some young people, whose parents had been careful in training them up, were grown so wicked, that by their extravagant conduct, they not only disturbed our religious meetings, but likewise became obnoxious to the peaceable government we live under.

In the Ninth Month I was at divers meetings, at Merion, German Town, Fair Hill, Abington, and Philadelphia; in which were several marriages solemnized in a religious manner. And in the Tenth Month, I went into the county of Salem about my affairs. It happened to be at the time of the quarterly meeting for Salem and Gloucester counties; but I did not know of it, until I came to Salem, where Friends were glad to see me, as also I was to see them; there were some of us whose hearts were knit and united together as Jonathan's and David's, the Divine love of God being much shed abroad in our hearts at that meeting. When it was over, and I had finished my business, I could not be clear in my mind without having some meetings in the said counties of Salem and Gloucester; and though it was a sickly time, and people died pretty much in those parts where we were going, James Lord and I, in the love of Christ, visited the meetings at Alloway's Creek, Cohansy, Pile's Grove, Woodbury, Newton, and Haddonfield, having meetings every day in the week, except the last; and sometimes riding near twenty miles after meeting; the days being at the shortest, and the weather very cold; but the Lord was with us, which made sufficient amends for all the bodily hardships we met with.

I got home well, but weary; and was well and joyfully received by my loving spouse, children and servants; and I was truly thankful to the Most High for his presence and goodness continued to me: so that, though I perceived my bodily strength to decline apace, my sight, hearing, and voice, failing much, I have occasion to believe, at times I was helped even beyond nature in the work of Christ, my dear Lord and Master.

The 27th of the Tenth Month I heard the news of the death of my dear friend, John Lee, by one sent to desire my company at his burial. It affected me with sorrow, he being an old acquaintance and inward friend of mine, with whom I had travelled many miles. He was a living, serviceable minister of the gospel of Christ, and instrumental to convince divers of that principle of Divine light and truth, which we profess. I could not be at his burial, because of my indisposition, and the unseasonableness of the weather; yet I think it my duty to say this concerning him, that our love and friendship was constant and entire unto the end, having been acquainted about thirty-five years, as near as I can remember.

In the Eleventh Month, as I was meditating in my closet, on the duty and beauty of that great virtue of temperance, it appeared very bright to the view of my mind, and the great benefit of it to those who loved and lived in it: First, As to religion, it tends to keep the mind in an even temper, which is a help to devotion, and the practice of religious duties. Secondly, It is a great preservative to health and a good constitution. Thirdly, It is a blessing to posterity, in many considerations. Whereas intemperance destroys the health, stains the reputation, hurts posterity, (in respect to a healthy constitution of body and estate,) ruins many families, brings to poverty and disgrace, and what is yet worst of all, is a great let to religion and the true fear of God, and is a great scandal to any one who makes profession of the Christian religion.

In this month I accompanied William Piggot, (who lately arrived from London, on a religious visit to the meetings of Friends in America.) From Philadelphia we went to my house at Frankfort, and from thence to North Wales, and had two large satisfactory meetings on the First-day; next day we were at the monthly meeting at Abington, the Third-day at Frankfort, and Fourth-day at German Town; Fifth-day I went to Philadelphia week-day meeting, and the said Friend to Abington general meeting; and a few days after we met again at the quarterly meeting of ministers and elders at Philadelphia.

The 8th of the Twelfth Month was our youths' meeting at Frankfort; many dying about this time, I was concerned in the meeting to put Friends in mind of their mortality; and that I had told Friends lately at their meetings at Abington and Philadelphia, that as I was riding from my house to Philadelphia, about a mile from the city, I saw (in the vision of life) the hand of the Lord stretched over the city and province, with a rod in it, in order to correct the inhabitants for their sins and iniquities; which sight affected my mind greatly; and although I did not hear any vocal voice, nor see any visible hand, yet it was as plainly revealed to me as though I had: and that notwithstanding I understood some slighted that testimony, yet I observed to them, that since that time more people were taken away than common, as they now might see; and indeed that inward sight and sense I had of the displeasure of God for the sins of the times, made great impression on my mind; and that no flesh might glory, the

Lord took, from the evil to come, several sober, well-inclined young people, as well as divers whose lives and conversations were evil and vicious; so that all had need to be warned to be watchful, and turn to the Lord, lest he come at unawares, and call us suddenly out of the world unprepared. In the Twelfth and First Months many died, of all ages and professions; and now some, who would hardly give credit to what I had delivered in several meetings, began to see the fulfilling of it, and great talk there was about it. And many solid and large meetings we had with the people at divers funerals about this time, exhorting the people not to slight the present visitation of the Almighty, and to prepare for eternity, to meet the Judge of the quick and the dead, who stands at the door. And among many that were taken away by death, were some few of my particular friends; and first, dear Hannah Hill, who was a bright example of piety and charity; she was like a nursing mother to me in my afflictions, as was her husband more like a brother than one not related, whose generous entertainment I may never forget at times. Thomas Griffith, and Elizabeth his wife, died also about this time: Thomas was a serviceable man, and well esteemed in our Society; and his wife a noted woman for being helpful to, and visiting the sick. She chose the house of mourning, rather than the house of mirth. These were worthy ancients, who made peaceable and good ends, and to whom may be properly applied that remarkable text of Scripture, Mark the upright, and behold the just, for the end of that man is peace.

In the Second Month, 1727, I proceeded on a voyage to Barbadoes, on account of business, for the support of my family, and in order to discharge my just debts, which were occasioned by great losses by sea and land. Many of my friends were kind to me, and sent a cargo of goods in the sloop *John*, Anthony Peel, master, consigned to me for sales and returns. When the vessel was loaded, she proceeded down the river, and I went by land to Salem, and was at meeting there on First-day, and on Third-day went aboard the sloop at Elsenborough. On the 8th of the Second Month we took in our boat and anchors, and proceeded to sea. From Elsenborough and the Capes I wrote to my wife, giving her an account how it was with me, and encouraged her to bear my absence with patience: it was indeed very hard for us to part.

I may not omit taking notice of an exercise which I felt one night as I lay on my bed in Philadelphia, (on the 21st of the First Month, my sleep being taken from me,) which I recollected and wrote down on board the aforesaid vessel, and was in this manner, viz.

"That the Lord was angry with the people of Philadelphia and Pennsylvania, because of the great sins and wickedness which were committed by the inhabitants in public-houses, and elsewhere; and that the Lord was angry with the magistrates also, because they use not their power as they might do, in order to suppress wickedness; and do not, so much as they ought, put the laws already made, in execution, against profaneness and immorality. And the Lord is angry with the representatives of the people of the land, because they take not so much care to suppress vice and wickedness, and wicked houses, in which our youth are grossly corrupted, as they ought to do. And also the Lord is angry with many of the better sort of the people, because they seek after and love the things of this world, more than the things of his kingdom: and it was shewed me, that the anger of the Most High would still be against us, until there was a greater reformation in these things."*

For some days after we were at sea, the weather was pleasant, and we had our health, for which my heart was truly thankful. I exhorted the sailors against swearing; and though they had been much used to it, they left it off, so that it was rare to hear any of them swear; for which reformation, so far, I was glad. I lent and gave them several good books, which they read, and shewed much respect to me. But soon after the wind was contrary for some days, and some in the vessel were quarrelsome. I asked them what they thought of the saying of Christ, viz., If a man smite thee on the cheek, turn to him the other also. At which they were silent and better conditioned to one another afterwards, and we had some reformation both from fighting and swearing. This voyage I was not so sea-sick as I formerly had been, (though I had, before I left home, some uneasy thoughts about my usually being sea-sick,) which I took as a peculiar favour from heaven. About the latitude twenty degrees north, we met with calms and contrary winds, which was very hard for some

* It is worthy of commendation, that our governor, Thomas Lloyd, sometimes in the evening, before he went to rest, used to go in person to public-houses, and order the people he found there to their own houses, till at length he was instrumental to promote better order, and did, in a great measure, suppress vice and immorality in the city.

in the vessel to bear, they putting themselves much out of temper about it; as for my own part, I had been used to disappointment, and therefore did not so much mind it. I spent pretty much of my time in reading and writing, and God being gracious, it was in the main a comfortable time to me; and I enjoyed my health as well as ever I did at sea in my life, for which I often breathed forth inward thanks to the Almighty. On the 5th of the Third Month we arrived at Barbadoes, and I was lovingly received by our friends, but came to a very low market for my goods.

I visited Friends' meetings on the island, and had several open meetings at Bridge Town and Speight's Town, and likewise at Pumpkin-hill and the Spring. On the day of Pentecost, so called, we had a meeting at Bridge Town, in which was shewn the work and operation of God's Spirit on the old world, and under the law; and the everlasting duration and operation of the same Holy Spirit under the gospel dispensation, which, Christ said, should abide for ever. At the quarterly meeting at Speight's Town was judge Allen, and the Captain of the man-of-war stationed there, with several others, not of our Society. I was much drawn forth in this meeting to speak of the power of the Father, Son, and the Spirit, opening to the people how we had been misrepresented, in respect to our belief in the Trinity, or the holy Three which bear record in heaven, the Father, Word, and Spirit, which Three are One; for that it was clear and plain, that we are more orthodox in the belief in the Deity, than those who do not believe in the operation of the Holy Ghost; as also that none could be true Christians without it. It was queried, how could they be clear in their belief in the Holy

Trinity, or the Three that bear record in heaven, who believe the Holy Spirit is ceased in his operations, gifts, or immediate revelations, and if ceased, when, and where, to whom, and how? The people were very sober and attentive, and staid all the time; and after the meeting was done some time, divers expressed their satisfaction with what was said. My good friend, Peter Sharp, of Maryland, was with me at this meeting, on whose account some of the people came. He had good service in the meeting, and I was glad of his company in this island, where we joyfully met and parted in the love of Christ. At this meeting we had each of us a certificate from Friends, signifying their unity with our conversations and services. The last meeting I had at Barbadoes, was at Speight's Town, on a First-day; it was a solid, good meeting, in which I took my leave of friends there, and exhorted them to believe in and hear Christ, he being a Teacher that could not be removed from them, as men often were; and, though they were but few, they were desired to meet in Christ's name; and I had to shew them the difference between us and other Christian professors, who hold no public worship if there be no outward teacher. Whereas, if but two or three meet in the name of Christ, he has promised to be in the midst of them; and he is the best teacher we can have.

On the 14th of the Fourth Month we set sail from this island, and for the most part had fair weather and fair winds, and saw several ships, but spoke with none.

I was one evening leaning over the side of the vessel, as being very lonesome, having little conversation with any in the vessel for divers reasons, I turned from all outward things to the Lord, and was glad to feel his presence and goodness, which was a comfort to me in my lonesome state; and as my travels and concerns had called and caused me to be much on the seas, it also pleased my good and gracious God to support me thereon many times, in divers trials, temptations, and exercises; for all which, I bow in awful reverence before him, and return thanksgiving and praise to his great name.

The first of the Fifth Month about noon we came to the Capes of Delaware, and sailed up the bay; but in a little time we touched the ground with our vessel several times; there being little wind, we got no harm; but two hours after, or thereabouts, a gust, or storm of wind, took us, which if it had met with us on the shoals where we struck, in all likelihood we must have perished, which I took to be a remarkable deliverance. Next tide we got to Newcastle, and it being First-day, I had a meeting with Friends there, with which we were greatly refreshed in the Lord, and in one another. After meeting I went on board the sloop, and having a fair wind, we sailed for Philadelphia, where we arrived about the eleventh hour, lodged that night at Paul Preston's, and next day went home to my family at Frankfort, where my wife, children, and servants, received me with much rejoicing.

When I was in Barbadoes, P. M. who accompanied me from Bridge Town to windward to counsellor Weeks's, told me that when I was in the island before, he and I had some discourse concerning the use of the sword, he then (not being of our Society) wore a sword, but now had left it off, and his business also, which was worth some hundreds a-year. I had reminded him of Christ's words, that those who take the sword, should perish with the sword, Matt. xxvi. 52, and, Resist not evil; and, If a man smite thee on one cheek, turn the other also: Love enemies, do good to them that hate you, pray for them who despitefully use you, and persecute you. After I had used these arguments, he asked me, if one came to kill me, would I not kill rather than be killed? I told him, No; so far as I know my own heart, I had rather be killed than kill. He said that was strange, and desired to know what reason I could give for it. I told him, that I being innocent, if I were killed in my body, my soul might be happy; but if I killed him, he dying in his wickedness, would consequently be unhappy; and if I were killed, he might live to repent; but if I killed him, he would have no time to repent: so that if he killed me, I should have much the better, both in respect to myself and to him. This discourse had made so much impression, and so affected him, that he said, he could not but often remember it. And when we parted at Bridge Town, we embraced each other, in open arms of Christian love, far from that which would hurt or destroy.

After I had been at home some time, I visited the meetings at Philadelphia, Burlington, and German Town, in which places I had service of divers kinds, and was lovingly received by Friends and others.

In the Fifth Month, Joshua Fielding and John Oxley had a large and satisfactory meeting at Frankfort. Joshua came from London on a religious visit to America, and having been on divers islands, he landed on the main at South Carolina, and from thence travelled through the wilderness four hundred miles, or more, where no public Friend had ever travelled before. The journey was perilous, but the

Lord was with him; who may in his own time, make way for his servants in those desert places. John Oxley came on the same account from Barbadoes, and had good service among Friends in his public ministry.

In this month, we thinking it convenient to send our little children to school, and not having a schoolmaster of our Society near us, concluded to put our son and daughter under the care of Nathaniel Walton, to whom I thought it my duty to write a few lines about the salutation and language I would have them trained up in, which were on this wise, viz.:—

"Frankfort, 30*th of Fifth Month*, 1727.

"Loving friend, Nathaniel Walton.

"I hope thou wilt excuse this freedom which I take with thee, in writing this on account of my children, in these particulars, viz. respecting the compliment of the Hat, and Courtesying, the practice thereof being against my professed principle:—1st. Because I find nothing like it in the Bible; but, as I think, the contrary. Thou knows the passage of the Three Children of God, who stood covered before a mighty monarch; and Mordecai, who could not bow to great Haman. And, 2dly, I believe those practices derived from vain, proud man. And as to Language, I desire my children may not be permitted to use the plural language to a single person; but I pray thee to learn them to say *Thee*, and *Thou*, and *Thy*, and to speak it properly, divers using it improperly; and the rather I desire it, because it is all along used in the Divine inspired holy writings. I suppose thou art not a stranger of its rise being from the grandeur and apostacy of the Romish church; and, also, that

You to a single person, is not consonant to the Book of God, nor the true rules of grammar. I know it is generally objected, That the end of speech is to be understood: but it is understood better in and according to the language of God, Christ, and the Holy Ghost, in the Bible, and the language of kings, and all peöple, as we read it in the holy Scriptures; why then should we be ashamed of it, or shun it; and bring in and uphold a custom contrary to it? The same care I would have thee take about the names of Days and Months, which are derived from the names of the gods of the Heathens, and are not found in the Bible. I suppose I have the mind of all those of our Society in the above, it being consonant to our principle and profession, and I write in a motion of Divine love to all.

"As to the school-learning of my children, I leave to thy management, not questioning thy ability therein; and if they want correction, spare not the rod.

"I hope thou wilt observe this direction in teaching my children, in which thou wilt oblige thy assured friend,

"T. CHALKLEY."

The latter end of the Fifth and the beginning of the Sixth Months, the weather was exceeding hot so that divers people died suddenly of the heat, as it was supposed.

The beginning of the Sixth Month I was at the youths' meeting at Abington, which was large and open to many; and I not having been here since I came from sea, divers expressed their gladness to see me; and we were that day favoured with some showers, both celestial and elementary, to our comfort.

In the same month I was also at the youths' meeting in Philadelphia: it had been a sickly time, but many had recovered. That passage opened on my mind, to speak of in the meeting, concerning the lepers, which Christ cleansed and healed, being ten in number, and that but one came to return thanks to God, for being healed and restored to health, Luke xvii. 12, 19.—Friends were exhorted to prize their health, and to shew their thankfulness to God, the giver of it, by fearing and serving him, and taking heed to Christ, the Word in their hearts. The meeting was in a good, solid frame, and we praised the Lord together, and gave him thanks for his merciful visitation.

About this time I heard of the death of our king (George the First) a prince whom I loved and honoured; which news was very sorrowful to me on divers accounts: his love and kindness to our Society, was well worthy our grateful remembrance.

On a Third-day, being our week-day meeting at Frankfort, Elizabeth Whartnaby and Mary Smith, were there: it was a comfortable opportunity. They were two nights at my house. Elizabeth was preparing to leave this land for Barbadoes, and Europe, intending a religious visit to Friends.

The 20th of the Sixth Month, going into my closet, I there met with a paper of my son-in-law Isaac Brown's and finding the contents were religious, as I had done of several of his late writings, I found it on my mind to write to him after this manner:—

"Dear son Isaac,

"By several writings of thine, of late, I perceive that a good thing is at work in thy mind, the which

I pray the All-wise and Infinite Being to promote in thy heart, to thy eternal salvation, and his glory. I now begin to be in some hopes that my prayers and tears for thee, in the Lord's time, may be answered: and I do believe, if thou keeps low in thy mind, that God will more and more visit thee. The advice of David to his son Solomon, when he also gave him the kingdom, comes before my mind to give thee. 'My son, know thou the God of thy father, and serve him with a perfect heart, and with a willing mind; for the Lord searcheth all hearts, and understandeth all the imaginations of the thoughts; if thou seek him, he will be found of thee; but if thou forsake him, he will cast thee off for ever,' 1 Chron. xxviii. 9. Dear Isaac, this was counsel from one of the greatest and best of kings, to a wise young prince, who petitioned the Almighty for Divine wisdom, before riches, or honour, or long life; which petition so pleased God, that he answered his request, and over and above, blessed him in an extraordinary manner.

"I perceive thou art inclined to read pretty much; I pray thee, that thy chief study in books may be the holy Scriptures. Let all other books, though of use, and good, in their places, be subservient to them; for their authority, of all other writings, to the true believers in Christ, is most Divine; they having a supernatural spring and Divine evidence in them to the virtuous and pious readers. Thou, my son, wilt much comfort the heart of thy tender mother, and of me thy loving and careful father, if thou follow and persevere in the ways of virtue and truth; which, that thou mayst, is the prayer of thy affectionate father-in-law.

"T. CHALKLEY."

The latter end of the Sixth Month I went to the general meeting of ministers and elders for the East part of New Jersey, and to the quarterly and youths' meeting at Burlington, and to a general meeting at Stony Brook, and to the quarterly meeting of the county of Bucks. John Oxley, of Barbadoes, and Joshua Fielding, of London, were at divers of those meetings, wherein we had open, seasonable opportunities; and I had a large, affecting account from Joshua, of his long and difficult travels in the service of truth to the West India isles, and thence to South Carolina, from whence he came through the wilderness by land, through North Carolina, Virginia, &c. to this province.

The 16th of the Seventh Month began our yearly meeting at Philadelphia, which was attended with the gracious presence of God, to the comfort and great satisfaction of many souls. In this meeting divers young men and women appeared, who were lately come forth in the ministry, and, as I believe, had received a measure of the gift of Christ's gospel; which was cause of rejoicing to the faithful among us, and excited our thanksgiving and praises to the Almighty Lord of heaven and earth.

At this meeting we had the company of four ministers from Great Britain, and one from Barbadoes, and many from divers other parts, it being a very large gathering of some thousands of people, as was believed, in which many were strengthened in their faith in Christ, and comforted through the power of the Holy Ghost, that blessed Comforter, which Christ promised to his church, who should be with them for ever, and guide them into all truth.

Next First-day after the yearly meeting, I, with

several of my neighbours, went over Delaware, to a meeting up Pensawken Creek; in which the wonderful love of God was declared, in sending his Son upon earth, who, as he was man, died for man, and is now by his Spirit present with all those that truly believe in him; he being the messenger of the covenant of God to mankind. And on Second-day, being the 25th of the Seventh Month, I had the sorrowful tidings of the death of my beloved friend James Lord; who, on his death-bed, desired that I might be sent for to his burial. In the consideration of that Christian love that was between us, I think I may truly note, that we were always glad to meet each other; therefore the thoughts of this so sudden change, and final parting, brought, for the present, a sadness and heaviness over my mind; considering his station in that neighbourhood, and service in that congregation to which he did belong; for therein he was well-beloved, and very serviceable.

And oh! the loss that his dear wife and tender children will have of him, really affects me with sorrow in penning these notes; but the sorrow, in these things, is all on our side; for he, without doubt, is at rest with his great Master in heaven. We had a larger meeting at his funeral, than ever was known to be there before, (as an ancient Friend told me,) which was solemn and serviceable to many.

Some time after, having been at divers meetings about home, John Oxley and I, in company, visited Friends on Long Island. At Flushing, we were at the burial of Jonathan Dickenson: many people, of divers persuasions, were at the meeting on that occasion, and were very sober and attentive. I was at the yearly meeting for the south side of the island, at a place called Seccataug, which meeting was large, many Friends and others coming to it over the plains. I was afterwards at the yearly meeting at Shrewsbury, in East Jersey, which held three days, and was very large, and the last day the people were very still. Joshua Fielding was at this meeting, and was therein concerned to preach the gospel of Christ with good authority, and matter suitable to a true gospel minister; John Oxley was ill of a fever, so that he could not be there; but there were brethren from divers parts, and the power and presence of the Most High was with and among us: blessed be his name.

I was also at Rohaway river, where was a solid, good meeting. From thence I returned home having been abroad about a month, and at above twenty meetings, and travelled about three hundred and fifty miles.

In the Eighth Month, at Frankfort, we had three burials out of one house, at one time; the mother, daughter, and grandaughter, of which I had never known the like instance before; on this occasion we had the company of many neighbours, and a very solemn meeting at our meeting-house at Frankfort.

About this time I was at divers meetings at Philadelphia, Abington, and Burlington: we had an evening-meeting at Burlington with Richard Smith, junior; who had been so ill that he could not get out to meetings for some months: it was such a satisfactory meeting, that he, and I, and others that were there, will not easily forget, our hearts being broken together.

The world still continued to frown upon me; but, though my case was such in this world, yet, at times, I had great consolation in Christ; and, in the midst of my troubles, when I looked back, I could truly say, that I had not been extravagant, but frugal; not covetous, but charitable; not idle, but industrions; not willing to be such an infidel as not to take care of my family. It was some solid comfort to my mind; and I bless the Almighty, that I always preferred his work and service to my own, and therein had great peace. This I can also say, if it were the last I should say, That I never wilfully, or knowingly, wronged any man, woman, or child, since I came to years of discretion; and yet I have nothing to boast of; it is the Lord's grace and mercy which saveth us.

Having occasion to make another voyage to Barbadoes, I wrote to the teacher of my children as followeth:—

"Frankfort, 10*th of Tenth Month*, 1727.

"Loving Friend,

"I being going to Barbadoes, leave the charge of my little children to thy care, not doubting thy management of them, by their growing in their learning, please to instruct them to sobriety, and the fear of God, and faith in Christ; and, if I never should see them or thee any more, our lives being uncertain in this world, pray let them know, that it was their father's will and desire, that they should mind their learning, and, above all things, mind the fear of the Most High. When my little daughter hath read her Testament through, I would have her go to writing, and George the same, on the same terms. Please to learn them the use of chapter and verse, that if any ask them where they are learning, they may tell. And, kind friend, inasmuch as I perceive thou hast followed my former directions, I look on myself obliged to thee; therefore am so much the more free to impart my mind to thee, now on my departure; which, with real love, is from thy loving friend,

"T. Chalkley.

"P.S.—Although my care is great for my children's learning their books, yet it is much more so as to their learning true piety and virtue."

On the 25th of the Tenth Month we set sail from Philadelphia, in the sloop *Dove*, Oswald Peel, master, having taken a solemn farewell of my dear wife, children, and friends; in order for the support of my family, and answering my just debts, which I had contracted. On the 27th day of the month, in the evening, we took in our boat, and put to sea; had some rough weather in our passage, but lived comfortably; we being all loving and obliging one to another. On the 15th of the Eleventh Month we safely arrived at Speight's Town, in Barbadoes; and the 18th between the hours of five and six in the morning, we felt the greatest earthquake that I had ever felt; having been sensible of three, one at London, one at Jamaica, and one at Frankfort in Pennsylvania. I was thankful in my heart to the Lord for my safe arrival, and that we were all preserved safe in our stormy passage, and deep-loaded vessel; one vessel being lost that came out a little time before us, and another, which came from our port to this island a few days sooner than we, lost three men by the violence of the storm, and received much damage otherwise; one of them being a neighbour of mine, with whom I was well acquainted, it affected my mind very much. I visited Friends' meetings in Barbadoes, and some divers times over; and had occasion in some meetings to mention the earthquake, which I told them I did believe was a visitation from the Almighty, in order to put people in mind of mortality, and to reform them from the evil of their ways, and call them to repentance.

While I was in Barbadoes, Francis Gamble died, whom I went to visit several times in his sickness: at his funeral was a large gathering of his neighbours, and others; and divers not of our Society, expressed their satisfaction with the meeting. The people in and about Speight's Town, in Barbadoes, were very loving and kind to me, more than I ever had observed before; even some vile, profane men, whom I could not forbear to reprove for their swearing, and taking the sacred name in vain, yet they shewed respect, notwithstanding I reproved them sharply. Who can take the sacred name of God into their mouths in vain, and be guiltless? Or who can hear it and forbear reproving it, without being remiss in their duty? This great evil is too frequently practised in this rich (poor) island of Barbadoes, (rich in earthly, but poor in heavenly treasure,) which caused me many times to mourn in secret before the Almighty, praying him for the reformation of the people, for Christ's sake, and for the glory of his own eternal name.

The 27th of the First Month, 1728, having done my business in Barbadoes, and seen Friends generally, an opportunity offered for my return home, in the brigantine *Sarah and Mary*, Samuel Gallop, master, bound for Burlington, in company with William Dury and William Callender, both of Barbadoes. Our master was exceedingly kind to us in the voyage. The wind hanging northerly, we could not go to windward of Martinico, but drove to leeward, and sailed by the isles of Lucia, Martinico, Dominica, Guadaloupe, Antigua, Montserrat, Rodondo, Nevis, Christopher's, Eustatia, Saba, Martin's, Anguilla, Bartholomew's, Sombrero, and four other small islands which are called the Saints. It was very pleasant sailing by these islands, only some of them were so exceeding high, that in some places we were becalmed, and the clouds appeared below the tops of divers of the mountains. At Christopher's, which is accounted the highest of them, there being a small river of good fresh water, we sent our boat on shore for some, having none very good on board. We lay off and on about two hours, but did not come to. I was thankful for this water, it being my constant drink; it was also very serviceable to the people on board. After we left the isle of Sombrero, we saw a sail, which we thought stood after us, and hearing at Christopher's that several Spanish privateers were on that coast, our master, and some others on board, were a little surprised; but we soon left her out of sight, and we afterwards went pleasantly on our way, until we came to the latitude of Bermudas, where the winds blew fresh, and much against us; and this winter having been very hard, we felt the sharp blasts of the latter end of it. We had a passage of about thirty days, and came very pleasantly up the bay and river; and it pleased God that I got home once more to my beloved wife and children, and was joyfully received by all my family, whom I found in a good degree of health; for which I did, as I had occasion to do, bless and praise the great name of the Most High, who is worthy for ever.

After I came home, I was at many meetings in Pennsylvania and Jersey, viz. at Philadelphia, Burlington, Bristol, Biberry, Frankfort, German Town, New Hanover, Croswicks, &c., in all which meetings I had some service to Friends' satisfaction; and was comforted with the goodness of God in the midst of my afflictions. My business lying much at Burlington, I spent pretty much of my time there for several weeks; where my friends manifested a tender and hearty respect towards me, and sympathized with me in my troubles and travels; and there I prepared for another voyage; for I was fully resolved, through Divine assistance, to pay all my just debts, which I contracted, and lay on me, through my losses; or else to die in the pursuit of it: in which resolve I had inward peace and satisfaction; though such labour, travel, and separation from my family, was a great cross to nature.

On the 14th of the Fifth Month we went on board the brigantine *Sarah and Mary*, Samuel Gallop, master, for Barbadoes; and on the 16th we sailed down the bay, and put to sea, and I wrote a loving, tender letter to my wife and family, and another to my friends at Burlington. We had fair winds for about two weeks, after which they were contrary for several days, during which two of our men had a fever, and our vessel proved leaky, though tight in smooth water, which was some concern to us, and obliged us to pump every half hour; but the leak being much the same, while at sea, we were the more easy about it: I took care of those two people that were sick, who soon recovered. The 3rd and 4th days of the Sixth Month, it was very windy, with lightning, thunder, and rain; in which rough weather one of our best sailors put his shoulder out of joint, and they brought him to me to see if I could do him any service; I was not forward to meddle; but the man and the people believing, if I would undertake for him, I might help him; I told them that though I did not understand bone-setting, I would instruct them the best I could; then I ordered him to be set down upon the deck, and to be stripped to the waist, and got a round piece of wood as thick as his arm, and wrapped a piece of cloth about it, that it might not bruise his flesh, and put it under his arm, and ordered two men, one at each end of it, to lift up strongly, and a third man to stretch his arm out, and keep it down withal, which being done, the bone went into its place; for which I was thankful in my heart to the Almighty. About the 10th of the Sixth Month, we safely arrived at Speight's Town in Barbadoes, being the First-day of the week. From whence I had an opportunity, by Alexander Seaton, master of a vessel bound to Pennsylvania, to send an account of our safe arrival.

I had many meetings in the island, and made several visits to divers sick persons, one of which was particularly to the satisfaction of the person visited, and his relations: he died, and was buried at Heathcott's Bay, where we had a large meeting at our meeting-house, where was many people, and it was a good, seasonable opportunity, in which I had occasion to remind them of their mortality, and press them to a holy life, the way to a happy immortality. I had divers meetings at Bridge Town, Speight's Town, and the Spring; where the testimony of Christ's gospel was well received. And after a stay of three weeks, I left Barbadoes on the 1st of the Seventh Month, and took my passage in the *Amity*,

Charles Hargrave, master, who was very friendly to me in my passage, as were all on board. We arrived at our port without casting anchor at all in our voyage, and laid the vessel to the wharf at Philadelphia, and on my landing I immediately went into the meeting of the ministers and elders, it being just meeting time, where we were much comforted together in Christ; after which I went home, being lovingly received by my wife and family, having been from home about ten weeks.

After I came home from this voyage, I visited the meetings of Friends at Philadelphia, Frankfort, German Town, the Falls of Delaware, Burlington, New Hanover, Mount Holly, Fair Hill, &c.

The 2nd of the Ninth Month I was at the quarterly meeting of ministers and elders at Philadelphia, where I met with Joseph Taylor, a Friend who had visited our meetings pretty generally on the continent of America, in the ministry of the gospel, and was now on his return homewards; with whose visit Friends had good unity, and certified the same to our brethren of the meeting where he lived in Great Britain.

After this I was at divers meetings in Pennsylvania, and Jersey; and the latter end of the Ninth Month, Sarah, the wife of Jeremiah Elfreth, died very suddenly, having been the day before walking in her garden; she was a sober young woman, and her death much lamented; her burial occasioned my stay at Philadelphia, which I had at divers times shunned, because a concern had been on me for some time, to declare to the people of that city, That the Lord was angry with the legislators of Pennsylvania, because they were not so much concerned to promote religion and piety as they ought, and to make such laws as might prevent the excessive increase of public-houses, which often prove seminaries for Satan; but strove to promote parties more than religion: and that the Lord was angry with the magistrates, because they did not so much as they might, and ought to do, put those good and wholesome laws in execution, which were already made against vice and immorality; and that the Lord was angry with some of the better sort of people, because they seek and mind the things of this world, more than the things of God and his kingdom. But I was helped to clear myself in the morning-meeting, to the satisfaction of many of the honest-hearted, and unburden my mind of a great exercise that I had long lain under.

In the afternoon we had a large meeting at the Bank meeting-house, occasioned by the aforesaid burial; the resurrection of the dead was declared in that meeting, according to the doctrine of our Saviour Jesus Christ, the great author of the Christian religion, and also of that eminent apostle Paul; and that old and false calumny, that our Society denied the resurrection of the dead, was publicly denied and refuted. The people were exhorted to live well that they might die well; and then they need not doubt but that they would rise well at the resurrection in the last day. The meeting concluded with praise to the Almighty, for all his mercies, and prayer to him, that he would sanctify that day's service to the people.

In the Tenth Month I prepared for another voyage to the island of Barbadoes, and had the ship *Bristol Hope*, consigned to me, but the winter setting in sooner than common, caused our stay much longer than we expected, whereby I had the opportunity to visit divers meetings, as Burlington, the Falls of Delaware, Neshaminy, Wright's Town, and Philadelphia. In this city a concern was on my mind to declare to the people, that the Almighty had shewed me, that he had often visited them in Philadelphia and Pennsylvania, with his own hand, and with his own rod; but if that did not work the designed end, for which he visited them, of which they were told also before it came to pass, he then would chastise them with the rod of man, and this was plainly spoken to me in my own habitation, as though it had been the voice of a man, though it was not vocal.

The 12th of the Eleventh Month, being First-day, I was at Horsham meeting, and had a tender bowing time therein; and in my way home visited some Friends who were sick, it being a time of general visitation in those parts, and the next Seventh-day I was at the meeting of ministers and elders at Philadelphia, where we had a good meeting; here I was earnestly desired to be at the funeral of Edmund Orpwood, the eldest Friend belonging to Frankfort meeting; but was in a strait, this Friend being my neighbour, and I had before engaged to be at the burial of one with whom I had been acquainted near forty years, therefore I did my endeavour to be at both, being each of them buried in the afternoon, and five miles distant; the days being short also, divers told me it was impracticable; I told them they might be mistaken, as they were, for though we had a large meeting, and the company of Rowland Wilson, from Britain, who had large and good service therein, yet after meeting we mounted and got to Philadelphia about a quarter of an hour after the corpse was brought into the meeting-house, as I was informed; we had a large, and as I thought, a good meeting; after which I went home, being weary in my body but thankful in my heart, that the Almighty had been with us, and helped us to perform that day's service.

On the 20th of the Eleventh Month, and Second-day of the week, I went into a piece of ground, which I was clearing for meadow, in order to give directions to the workmen, and one of the trees fell, contrary to the kerf, and also to the wind, which was then at north-west, and when I saw it falling towards me, I ran from it, but before I could get out of the way, it fell upon me, across my back, from my shoulder to my hips, and struck me down to the earth, where for some time I lay speechless, and in all likelihood I should have been immediately killed, if I had not been providentially preserved by the body of the falling tree lying on a stump, which prevented its crushing me as I lay on the ground. A friend that was near me with the horse, desired the wood-cutters, when they were recovered from the surprise, and I to the use of my speech, to help me on his horse, and I rode home, but in extreme misery, and I was under great concern lest I should surprise my wife and children suddenly. We sent to Philadelphia for Dr. Griffith Owen, who came in about two hours, and let me blood, and ordered several things to be applied and taken, which through Divine favour proved very serviceable to me; notwithstanding which I was in great pain many days, and long and tedious nights, not being able either to feed myself, nor turn in my bed, for a great while. In this confinement I was at times favoured with a very comfortable sense of the presence of God, whose Providence is over all his works; and as his love to me was great, so the love of his people was also, many of whom, and of my neighbours came to see me, sympathizing with me in my distress; but among them I had one of Job's comforters, who wickedly abused me in this low state. I can scarce forbear mentioning his name, having example for it in holy writ, but through the Lord's help I will put on charity.

The 9th of the Twelfth Month, I got abroad the first time to our meeting at Frankfort, with which divers expressed their gladness to see me there again. In this meeting I exhorted them to think on eternity, and to prepare for it, by living to-day as though they were to die to-morrow; for I found it by experience to be needful, and then if sudden death comes, it will not surprise us.

CHAPTER VIII.

1728–1734.

MAKES, NOW AS MASTER OF A VESSEL, MANY VOYAGES BETWEEN PHILADELPHIA AND THE WEST INDIES — VARIOUS OCCURRENCES AND REMARKS DURING THESE VOYAGES, AND IN THE INTERVALS BETWEEN THEM—DEATH OF HIS SON GEORGE.

As I now found it continue my business to go to sea for a livelihood, I undertook the charge of the ship *New Bristol Hope*, as master, though it was a way of living to which I did not incline; I took care in our vessel that there should be no swearing in my hearing, nor drunkenness to my knowledge, without reproof, and if I could not be instrumental that way to break them from swearing and drinking to excess, my manner was to put them away, so that we generally had a pretty quiet ship. We left Philadelphia the 13th of the Twelfth Month, but storms and contrary winds detained us in the river and bay, so that we did not get out to sea till the 21st of the said month, when the pilot left us, by whom I wrote to my wife and family; and now I thought I felt the benefit of the good wishes of my beloved and dear friends I left behind, which did me a great deal of good, as it often hath done on the like occasion; for faithful friends, and good Christians, are as epistles written in one another's hearts. In our passage we took several dolphins, which were very welcome to us, we having a long passage, and our fresh provisions near spent. The 19th of the First Month we saw the island of Barbadoes, having had several meetings on board the ship on this voyage, the good effects I could see but little of, only for that day they would be a little more sober, and some of them addicted to swearing, did not swear so often as they did before. The day following we safely arrived at Speight's Town, where we had the next day a very comfortable meeting for the divine worship of God. The Fifth-day following I was at Bridge Town, at their week-day meeting; and next First-day, being the 30th of the month, I was at a meeting at Pumpkin Hill, where I was enlarged in the doctrine of faith.

After this I went to the Bridge, with a Friend from New England; we had two good meetings, it being the general meeting for the Friends of the island, and afterwards I with several Friends went again to Speight's Town, and on the 12th of the Second Month I was at the Thicket's Meeting at which were counsellor Weeks, colonel Charnock, and justice Sims; I dined with them at judge Weeks's, and they discoursed of what was said in the meeting about dancing, I quoting Luther's words, "That as many paces as the person takes in the dance, so many paces or steps they take towards hell:" and I told them, that I had heard several had used that vain exercise in our meeting-house, which was appointed for the worship of God, and I said, I hoped for the future it would be so no more; two of those persons who danced in our meeting-house, were then in the meeting, though I did not know it. This testimony so wrought on the colonel, that he said, He could scarcely feel his legs since I spoke it; and the justice said, If these words be true, he had taken many steps towards hell; and the counsellor and judge said, It was home doctrine to some that were there. Divers of them seemed to be touched with the testimony of truth, though not so solidly as I desired. Soon after I went with Joshua Byrch to visit the governor of the island, colonel Worsley, who treated us with much freedom and civility; he desired me to sit down by him, and then called for a decanter of wine, of which he kindly offered me a glass, but I told him I chiefly drank water; he said, water is certainly the best drink in the world, and told me I was a credit to my drink, as I looked as well, or better, than most who drank wine.

In the Second Month I was at a meeting on a First-day at Bridge Town, which was somewhat larger than usual; it was a good open time in the morning, but more so in the afternoon. At this meeting there was a merchant of the town, who sent to know if our Friends (he not being of our profession) would make a contribution for me, in consideration of my losses. He said he would contribute as much as any, although he had heard me only that one time; but he was informed that we received no money nor pay for our preaching; yet his good-will I acknowledged.

The 4th of the Third Month I was at a meeting at the Spring, where I met with Joseph Gamble, and John Oxley and his wife, and several others, not belonging to this particular meeting, and we were edified together in the love and life of Christ. I was concerned to speak of the divers visitations and speakings of God to the people since the world began, quoting the words of holy Writ, that God who spake to the fathers by the prophets, speaks now in these last days by his Son, whom he hath appointed heir of all things: and that this dispensation is the last and brightest dispensation of all, and is the greatest and most glorious manifestation of God's love to mankind; and that besides this vocal speaking of Christ, when in the body on earth, he now speaks spiritually, which spiritual speaking of Christ, in and to the true church, and true believers, will out-last time, and endure to all eternity; the great Lord of all, for his unspeakable benefit therein, was praised and glorified, as being alone worthy.

I had divers other meetings on the island, which I pass by, not being willing to be prolix. After a stay of about nine weeks, we proposed sailing. Judge Gray, a very noted man, and much esteemed among the people, took passage with us; also Joshua Byrch, of Bridge Town, for his health, and William Callender, and several others, as merchants. Though I came on account of trade, our Friends gave me a certificate that I had good service among them, and in my outward affairs had gained esteem among the people, as well as in my service in preaching Christ; all which I acknowledge to be the effects of Divine grace. Divers friends and acquaintance came to the sea-shore at Speight's Town, and in a great deal of tender Christian love, and good desires, we took leave, and committed one another to the protection of the Almighty. We had a comfortable passage, and arrived at Philadelphia, where I was lovingly received by my wife and friends.

In this voyage a great and weighty concern came on my mind, on account of the young and rising generation, desiring they might be happy in this world, and in that which is to come. And first, as to this world, I have taken notice, that divers of the youth are too apt to waste their outward substance, which often is given to them; (for when they get it themselves, they are for the most part more saving of it;) and this wasting and spending, those sparks call generosity, liberality, good-nature, gentility, fine breeding, and abundance of other fine names, not considering the labour and industry, frugality, care, and watchings of their parents or ancestors, to get what they have. May parents note this well, and not be anxiously concerned to get much wealth, which may be a means to ruin their posterity! and truly most of these spending, drinking, company-keeping, gaming, chatting, tippling youngsters, take a great deal more care, how they may get money from others, that they may spend it, than how to earn it, or faithfully labour for it themselves; they will beg or borrow, and run into debt, but take little or no solid thoughts to pay; by which means divers of those topping, beggarly beaus, and spenders, have brought both themselves and relations, parents and friends, to shame and disgrace, and sometimes to poverty, where their relations and parents have been too liberal. Let all indulgent parents note this also.

And if any concerned person should advise those inconsiderate youths of their evils, it is much if they gain not their lasting ill-will, and the epithets of niggards and covetous, ill-natured, censorious, sour, morose, &c. However, I shall venture to stand the shock of their displeasure, and in as moving terms as I can, consistent with the matter on my mind, entreat them to consider the end of their spending, slothful, idle life, which if continued in, must needs end in their ruin, and they may repent when it is too late, crying out, Oh! that I had hearkened to the advice of my father, and my indulgent mother! Oh! that I had taken the counsel of my good friends in time, then I had not been in this condition, nor in those straits I am now in. This, or worse, must at last inevitably be the condition of those unthinking, time-wasting, and money-spending, evil-company-keeping young people, of both sexes. Some of whom, if they can get it, will spend more in a few hours, than their parents can get in so many days, which is very unreasonable, as well as unthinking; for if the indulgent parents do not hold their hands, truly they must all sink together; and where the parents have been, what these sorts of youths call liberal, whole families have by such liberality been undone, which is a case to be lamented by all sober people.

I pray our spending youths to consider, how many brave, fine young men and women, whose parents have left them estates and handsome incomes, have by such extravagances soon spent all, and sometimes more than all, and disgrace and a gaol have been their portion; and how many, by living too fast, have died too soon, much sooner than might be expected, according to the course of nature.

Wherefore I would advise them to regard what the wise king Solomon said, "Go to the ant, thou sluggard; consider her ways and be wise; she provideth her meat in the summer," (*i. e.* she prepares against the winter.) Though this may be despicable in the eyes of our fine gentlemen, and learned spending wits, yet there appears more wisdom in these little industrious animals, than in those spenders, who, in the spring and summer of their years, take so little thought of saving what hath been with so much care gotten for them; or of getting more against their winter or old age, which, if they live, will certainly overtake them, when their youth or summer is gone.

But many youths object against this advice crying out, as I have often heard, "The aged give this advice when they are old, but did as we do when they were young as we are." Although this may be true in some, yet it will not hold good in the general, and if it do in some, is not that maxim good, Let others harms learn us to beware, before it be too late, that we fall not into the same snare, which hath entangled or caught thousands, to their great shame and reproach? Again, those who have been so overtaken in their youth, and are escaped out of the snare, are more fit to caution or advise how to escape it, or to show those parts which led them into that labyrinth of woe and misery.

The author of all evil useth his utmost skill and power to promote the practices of excessive drinking, &c., among mankind, it being a mighty support to his kingdom; for when the nobility of the understanding is clouded thereby, then oh! how many wicked oaths, oh! what corrupt language, what unhandsome, unbecoming words and actions, are brought forth! How are good manners corrupted! How is the sober, chaste soul offended, and above all other considerations, how is God dishonoured, and the end of our creation frustrated, and man condemned!

When people are in those excesses, how do they take the Sacred name in vain, and so bring themselves in guilty before God and man; for he has positively said, He will not hold them guiltless, who take his name in vain; so that let them plead never so many excuses, they are pronounced guilty by the Judge of heaven and earth: therefore let me persuade the youth to remember what the Lord by his servants said concerning drinking to excess, Woe to the drunkards; and that no drunkard shall inherit the kingdom. Again, "Woe unto them that are mighty to drink wine, and men of strength to mingle strong drink," &c. If it be objected, as it often is, when such poor souls are reproved, and their sins set in order before them, We trust in the mercy of God, and the merits of Christ: I say this is a good trust and hope, if upon a good foundation: but the wicked must forsake their ways, and the unrighteous their evil thoughts; but what forsaking is that, when strong conviction is upon the soul, to make covenants, vows, and promises, and break them from time to time? and though Christ hath satisfied the justice of the Almighty for sinners, it is for those who forsake their sins, not those who plead for the practice of them, and endeavour, by many vain excuses, to justify themselves in them.

Since then the salvation of the soul is precious, and hath cost the precious blood of the Lamb of God, and is much more precious than health or wealth, why should any be so cruel and hard-hearted to themselves, as, for a little vanity, froth and mirth, toys and trifles, vain sports, and evil pastime, to plunge and sink themselves into the eternal gulf of woe and misery; pray, O pray consider it, dear youths!

After my return from Barbadoes, in the Fourth Month, I visited Friends' meetings at Burlington, at the Falls of Delaware, Abington, German Town, and was divers times at Philadelphia and Frankfort meetings; which meetings were much to my satisfaction; the Lord being pleased to manifest his goodness to many, as also to my poor exercised soul; for which I was truly thankful unto him.

In the Sixth Month I was at the general meeting of Friends at Derby, in Chester county, which was a large good meeting, divers Friends appearing there in a lively ministry. About this time, some thousands of people came from Ireland, and also many Palatines from Holland; among whom, it is reported, were Romanists, or Papists, several of whom, it was said, gave out threatening speeches, which caused some consternation among the people.

At this large general meeting, I exhorted them to trust in the Lord, and not to distrust that Hand which had hitherto preserved us by his Providence without outward force; and that though the people who came among us were many in number, yet we, having the Lord on our side, were more than they, in a mystical sense; putting them in remembrance of the prophet, who when his servant was afraid, prayed to the Almighty, to open the eyes of his servant, and when they were mystically opened, he saw the mountains full of chariots of fire, and horses of fire, and that they were more than their enemies. I was also concerned to exhort Friends to be good examples to those strangers, who came among us in such great numbers; and that our lights, in our conversations might so shine, that those people, seeing our good works, might glorify our Father which is in heaven, according to the doctrine of Christ; and then we should do them good, and they would do us no hurt, but good also: but on the other hand, if we keep not our places, and do not live in the fear of God, nor according to our holy principles and profession, that then it might be just with the Lord God, to make them a scourge to us. Many were comforted in this meeting, and God was praised, who is worthy.

On the 15th of the Sixth Month, having loaded the ship *New Bristol Hope*, a second time, I sailed in her from Philadelphia, and having a concern to visit the meetings of Friends at Salem, I left the ship at Gloucester, under the care of the pilot, and went by land to the First-day meeting at Salem and from thence to Elsenborough, and staid till the ship came down; and on the 20th of the month we got to sea, and had a fair wind for several days, and lived very lovingly on board, being respectfully treated by my sailors.

In this voyage we had several meetings on board, the first of which was at the request of my second mate, to call the sailors together in the cabin; I not being forward to propose it to them, lest they should suspect me of some vanity, in desiring to preach to them; they not knowing the cross of Christ in that exercise.

On the 24th day of the Seventh Month, at noon, our ship, by observation, being exactly in the latitude of Barbadoes, we steered away west for the island, and on the 26th we saw it, after five weeks and one day leaving sight of Cape Henlopen; we having, after the first few days, light winds, calms, and head-winds, which made our passage long, and our sea-stores almost spent; but now the sight of land made the people forget all uneasiness, and for this favour, my heart was thankful to the great Preserver of men.

This time we came to a tolerable market with our provisions, which made our stay but short, yet I was divers times at the Bridge meeting of Friends, as also at Speight's Town, where my concerns chiefly lay, and once at Pumpkin Hill meeting, in which meeting it was observed to the people, that the salvation of the soul is precious, and that true religion is a solid thing, a thing of the greatest moment to both body and soul, and that people ought to be very serious and solidly concerned about it, taking special care to lay, or build, their religion on a sure foundation; it was shewed them, that Christ Jesus was the sure rock and foundation of all the righteous, in all ages; he was the Rock that followed Israel, which they drank of; any other foundation than him no man can lay; who is, in the truly religious, and the true believers, the hope of their glory. Many other precious truths were manifested to us in that meeting, for which we praised the Lord.

Soon after I went to Bridge Town, to clear out the vessel, and was at their week-day meeting: the subject matter I had to treat of in that meeting, was, that the Lord bringeth low, and he raiseth up again; and that in divers respects, as to kingdoms, families, and particular persons; and as to health, wealth, honour, &c., divers in that meeting were appealed to as witnesses of it. After this meeting I went to visit the governor, who was courteous to me, and took my visit kindly, and desired to be remembered to our governor, and several others, and wished me a prosperons voyage, and well back again, which he hoped would be in about three months. He said, whoever lived to see it, Pennsylvania would be the metropolis of America, in some hundreds of years. He said, he loved downright honest men; but he hated deceit and hypocrisy. A great man, and a great expression!

The 21st of the Eighth Month, 1729, we, having done our business, weighed anchor, and went to sea: and on the 26th, we had a good meeting with the ship's company, for the service and worship of God; in which the gospel of Christ was declared without partiality, and the reigning sins of sailors openly exposed according to the doctrine of the gospel, and the most high Lord entreated to carry on in the earth the great work of reformation. Hitherto we had fine pleasant weather.

The beginning of the Ninth Month we had a very blustering, stormy time, for many days, so that we could not carry sail, but sometimes lay by, and sometimes went with a reefed mainsail and foresail; the ship had such a violent motion, that it broke our glasses, and about a dozen bottles of wine, and our earthenware, and strained our hogsheads and casks, so that we pumped our molasses into the sea, and beat us back many leagues, and blew our sails out of the bolt-ropes.

After those storms we had a calm, and the wind sprung up westerly; our course being north-west, or thereabouts, we could barely lay our course; yet, it being moderate, we had cause to be thankful.

The 12th of the Ninth Month we found ourselves in the latitude of 36 deg. 17 min. north; but the wind was a-head, and our fresh stock of provisions almost expended, and winter coming on apace, the nights dark and long, made it seem tedious to our people; the which I was helped to bear with patience.

The 14th day, about eight o'clock at night, John Plasket, one of the best of our sailors, through the violent pitching of the ship, fell into the sea from off the bowsprit; one of the sailors, seeing him fall, nimbly threw a rope to him, which he caught hold of, and the people helped him into the ship; though in all probability, he had perished in the sea, if he had missed taking hold of the rope; I was thankful to the Almighty for this young man's life, and took it as a great favour from heaven. The next day, it was dreadfully stormy, the wind blew violently at south-west, with lightning, thunder, and much rain; the seas ran so high, and the ship had such a great motion, that the goods, or casks, shifted in the hold, and we lay by till next day; our sails also were much torn, and, in many places, blown out of the bolt-ropes, so that we were half-a-day mending them; and then proceeded on our voyage home, where we arrived the latter end of the month.

After I came home from this voyage, in the small stay I was on shore, I was divers times at meetings at Philadelphia and Frankfort, and was also at German Town, at the burial of our ancient friend Dennis Cunrad, who was one of the first settlers of this town (as I understood the first meeting of Friends, for worship, in it, was kept at his house). He was a man of an inoffensive life, much given to hospitality, and left a good report behind him: the meeting was large, and many of the first settlers of the country were there. I was also at the burial of Catherine, the daughter of Thomas Lightfoot, the wife of James Miller, a worthy woman, who died soon after their arrival from Ireland, and was buried from our great meeting-house in Philadelphia, in a decent and exemplary manner.

The latter end of the Tenth Month, Samuel Harrison, of New York, and Obadiah Lawrence, of Long Island, favoured me with their company all night at our house, where we called the family together, and had a seasonable time to take leave, they of me, and I of them, and my family also; and the next day divers very dear Friends came with me to the boat, to the river side, to take leave, and we parted with hearts full of love and good-will to each other.

So I went on board at Wiccacoe, and had a cold passage down the river and bay, and left the Capes the 1st of the Eleventh Month, being the third voyage, as master, and the 17th we passed the Tropic of Cancer. Hitherto we had a comfortable passage, and though we had a crowded ship, yet we had peace and quietness to a greater degree than I expected; for men that use the seas, are, too generally, inconstant as the wind and waters they wade through. We had several meetings on board the vessel in this voyage, and were at sea about four weeks, before we arrived at Barbadoes, and when we arrived, the markets were dull, which occasioned our stay so long as twelve weeks. During which time, I had divers religious and good opportunities with those of our own, and other Societies, I believe to general satisfaction; having the good wishes of people of all ranks, from the governor to the poor negroes: all of whom I profess love to for Christ's sake.

This voyage, in our return home, we had a full ship, and upwards of thirty passengers, and were on our passage home about a month, and had good comfortable weather therein.

Soon after I came home from Barbadoes, in the Third Month, 1730, I went to a meeting at Burlington, at which was married Thomas Evans; Margaret Preston was also there; it was a good meeting. I crossed the river Delaware twice, visited a sick person, and rode thirty miles that day. I also went to the Falls meeting, and, after the said meeting, appointed another at Neshaminy the same day; after which, I went with Joseph Kirkbride to William Paxton's, and lodged: next morning, Joseph Kirkbride rode with me home, and thence to Philadelphia. I was divers times at Philadelphia, Frankfort, and German Town, and at the general meeting at Frankfort, where our Friend John Cadwallader was married; Isaac Norris, Samuel Preston, and Margaret his wife, and John Oxley, were at this meeting, with many other Friends, a good share of whose company I got home with me, of which I was glad, ever loving and coveting the company of good men and women.

I was now preparing for the fourth voyage, as master of the *New Bristol Hope*, for Barbadoes; but it grew harder and harder for me to leave my family; which for many considerations, was very exercising; yet I was obliged to continue going to sea, upon an honourable account, *i. e.* that no person might suffer by me, if I could help it; and having got our vessel loaded, we sailed from Philadelphia the 9th of the Fifth Month. Next day came to an anchor at Chester, and visited my old friend David Lloyd, who, with his good spouse Grace, treated me with tender christian love; the judge and I being old acquaintance, and both of us in years, and he not well, we took leave as if we were not to see one another any more, which happened accordingly, for he died before I returned.

We weighed anchor at Chester, and got down to Elsenborough, and went to Salem meeting, it being First-day of the week, and 12th of the month, with some of our passengers and sailors. The meeting was pretty large, and I was earnestly concerned for their welfare, as I had often been when I was absent, and was glad I was with them that day.

After this meeting we proceeded on our voyage, and left the Capes the 15th of the aforesaid month; had small and contrary winds, and sometimes calms, until the 2nd of the Sixth Month, and First-day of the week, when the wind was at south and a hard gale, the sea high, and the ship having a great motion, therefore we had not a meeting as usual: many of the passengers were very sea-sick; as for my part, I thought, if the Almighty was but with me, that would make up for all difficulties; for in him was, and is my life and chiefest joy: and, as an answer of peace in my tossed condition, I sometimes had comfortable times; being inwardly refreshed with the love and presence of God, not only in the day but also in the night, in my sleep; out of which I was awakened one morning, in the morning watch, with these comfortable words, He took me to his "banqueting house, and his banner over me was love." These expressions were so fresh in my mind, for some days, that I could not forbear, but bless the holy name of the living Lord secretly in my soul.

The 16th of the Sixth Month we arrived at Barbadoes. The 17th there arose, about midnight, a hard gale of wind, which the Barbadians call a hurricane, or tornado, and blew more than ten vessels ashore, great and small, which were wholly lost; and our ship was very near the rocks, people looking every minute when she would come on shore; but through Divine favour, we escaped, with only the boat stove against the rocks. I would have got on board, but that was impracticable; but I got on the highest place I could, from which I could see them in the ship, and they me on shore; for we could not, for the violence of the wind, hear one another; yet they were so near the fort, where I stood, that I could discern them one from another, and they me from the multitude of people, many being in the fort with me. I seeing the chief mate look towards me, I waved my hat to him, and he, in answer, his to me; then I made a signal to him to go to sea, which they immediately did, letting slip their cables, and went to sea without either boat, anchor, or cables, and came in the next day, and got their cables and anchors again, to the great joy of many of the inhabitants, whose hearty prayers for our safety, as many of them told me. This, among many others, I put in my calendar of deliverances, and preservations from imminent dangers, by the hand of Divine Providence.

We staid this time in Barbadoes about five weeks, leaving the island the 27th of the Seventh Month; and there I met with Robert Jordan, my friend and brother in the work and fellowship of the gospel of Christ who took his passage with us for Philadelphia, whose company was pleasant and comfortable. One evening he was repeating some verses of the excellent Addison's, which I willingly transcribed, as well in memory of that great author, as also that they answered my state and condition in my watery travels, and in the extremes of heat and cold, and some poisonous airs I have often breathed in. They are as follow:

How are thy servants blest, O Lord!
How sure is their defence!
Eternal Wisdom is their guide,
Their help, Omnipotence.

In foreign realms, and lands remote,
  Supported by thy care ;
Through burning climes I pass'd unhurt,
  And breath'd in tainted air.

Thy mercy sweeten'd ev'ry soil,
  Made ev'ry region please,
The hoary Alpine hills it warm'd,
  And smooth'd the Tyrrhene seas.

Think, O my soul ! devoutly think,
  How with affrighted eyes,
Thou saw'st the wide extended deep,
  In all its horrors rise !

Confusion dwelt in ev'ry face,
  And fear in evr'y heart,
When waves on waves, and gulfs on gulfs,
  O'ercame the pilot's art.

Yet, then, from all my griefs, O Lord !
  Thy mercy set me free,
Whilst in the confidence of prayer,
  My soul took hold on thee.

For though in dreadful whirls we hung,
  High on the broken wave,
I knew thou wert not slow to hear,
  Nor impotent to save.

The storm was laid, the winds retir'd,
  Obedient to thy will ;
The sea, that roar'd at thy command,
  At thy command was still.

In midst of dangers, fears, and death,
  Thy goodness I'll adore ;
And praise thee for thy mercies past,
  And humbly hope for more.

My life, if thou preserv'st my life,
  Thy sacrifice shall be ;
And death, if death must be my doom,
  Shall join my soul to Thee.

The 4th of the Eighth Month, we met with a hard gale of wind, which broke the tiller of our rudder, and split our bowsprit and mainsail, and overset many of our chests. Robert Jordan narrowly missed his chest falling on him from one side of the ship to the other, which we looked on as a merciful providence, and spoke of it to one another, remembering Addison's verses, which the night before were repeated.

In this passage we saw three vessels only; it was a blustering time, but the shortest from land to land that ever I had, being but fourteen days and fourteen hours from the sight of Barbadoes to the sight of the main land: we arrived at Philadelphia the 16th of the Eighth Month.

In the Ninth Month I proceeded on a fifth voyage, as master, to Barbadoes, and went down the river Delaware on the Seventh-day, and on First-day was at Chester meeting, at which time there was a burial of a child, and a large meeting: our friends at Chester were glad to see me, and I them, and after meeting we set sail, and went down the river to Elsenborough, where we came to and landed Robert Worthington, whose son Ezra was on board, and went to Barbadoes for his health, being in a deep consumption.

This voyage we were on our passage about thirty-three days before we arrived at Barbadoes, when after doing my business, and visiting our Friends' meetings, in about five weeks, we put to sea the 10th of the Twelfth Month, and sailed along to leeward of divers islands, till we came to Anguilla, where we landed in expectation to get salt, but at this time there was not any to be had there. We came to an anchor here in the night, hoping to get to a harbour before it was dark; but it soon being very dark, and coming into shoal water, we saw a large rock, and came to by the side of it, in about five or six fathom water, taking it to be a ship, and when it was day we saw our mistake, and that instead of a vessel, we were too nigh a rock, and the wind coming about, tailed our ship towards it so near, that we were sensible of touching twice; I ordered the men to heave a little further a-head, and so we lay clear till morning. When morning came, of which we were glad, several boats, with a cable, came to us, and the people advised us to put a spring on our cable, and cut it, that she might cast the right way; which accordingly we did, and it had the desired effect; so that we soon got into a very fine harbour, it being about a mile off. Many thanks were given by many of the people for this deliverance to the Almighty. George Leonard, the governor of this island, heard in the morning, that a vessel was run on the rocks, and the people were running with saws and axes, in order to break her up, if she should not be got off: the governor seeing them, sent a lieutenant with orders, that let her belong to what nation soever, they should help to get her off, if it could be, and if she was likely to be made a wreck, he charged them at their peril not to meddle with her, nor anything belonging to her, until they had first come to terms with the master: which is worthy to be recorded.

We staid several days before we could get our anchor; for after we were in the harbour, it blew very hard for four or five days: so that with our four oars we could not row our boat a-head, but watching for a calm one night, our people went and got it, and then we went into the principal road and harbour in the island called Croaker's Bay; the name of that we came from was Rendezvous Bay, where lived a very kind friend of ours, named John Rumney, who, with his wife and family, treated us with great love, and courteously received us into their house, and he went with me to the governor's, who was my old acquaintance and friend, who with much love and tenderness, when he knew me, took me in his arms, and embraced me, and lovingly saluted me with a kiss of charity, and thanked God for our deliverance, and that he had lived to see me once more, (I having been there some years before); he was seventy odd years of age, as I remember, and had eighty odd who called him father: they living much on roots and pulse, are very healthy in this island. I was here nine days, and had seven meetings with the people; the longer I staid the larger the meetings were; so that I had some difficulty to leave them. Through the grace and gift of God I was helped to preach the gospel of Christ freely, and they received it both freely and thankfully, divers, if not all; for their and my heart were very open one to another, the Lord's holy name be praised for ever.

The 3rd of the First Month, Ezra Worthington died, and the 4th in the afternoon he was buried on the plantation of John Rumney, near his house; the governor and his son-in-law were at the burial, where I told them, that he was an inoffensive, innocent, sober young man, and that death was to be the end of us here, putting them in mind to remember their latter end. After I had done speaking, the governor said, that death was a debt due to nature, and that we must all pay it, and blessed is the man that in time truly prepares for it. This was a good expression for a man in his post, and worthy of my notice, as I thought.

I was at one meeting, where was the governor and his daughter, with divers of the best and soberest people of this island; it was a satisfactory meeting, which ended in prayer; and when I arose from my knees I found the governor on one side, and his daughter on the other side of me, both on their knees, a posture in which people are too seldom found in this degenerate age of the world.

On the 10th of the First Month, we departed from the island of Anguilla, with a pleasant gale; and had fair weather and winds for several days; I spent some time of this voyage in reading, and met with a passage of or concerning friendship; the comfort and beauty of it therein was notably set forth, yet most who treat upon that noble subject, place, too generally, the felicity thereof in humanity; whereas true and lasting friendship is of a Divine nature, and can never be firmly settled without Divine grace: Christ Jesus is the prime Friend of mankind, and from whom all true and lasting friendship springs and flows, as from a living fountain, himself being the head-spring thereof; out of which holy fountain hath sprung as followeth:—"Henceforth I call you not servants;" and "Ye are my friends, if ye do whatsoever I command you." And again, "By this shall all men know that ye are my disciples, if ye have love one to another." O holy expressions! much to be admired, and worthy every true and good man's and woman's imitation and practice. Observe, that when they had done whatsoever Christ had commanded them, then they were to be his friends, and they were not only to be his friends, but one another's friends, as he was theirs, and if occasion were, as he died, so they would die for one another. By this mark and truest seal of the truest friendship, all the world should know they belonged to Christ, that they were united to him, and in him united to one another. Nothing but disobedience and sin can ever separate this friendship.

Against this friendship, which is in Christ, and grounded and founded upon him, the gates of hell can never prevail; all friendship, upon any consideration, merely human, is brittle and uncertain, and subject to change, or mutability; as experience hath taught in all ages.

If any person hath a desire to have a particular friend, let that person be sure to make choice of Christ, and such as choose him, have a friend in whom all lasting peace, comfort and delight, joy and pleasure is, and in him alone is to be enjoyed for ever.

The 20th of the First Month, being the first of the week, we had a comfortable meeting for Divine worship, in which the goodness of God was extended to us as we were rolling on the mighty waters of the great deep, after which we had pleasant weather, and a fair wind for several days.

On the 26th the wind sprung up at east north-east, a hard gale, which lasted several days; and having but little sea-room for about thirty hours, it blew so hard, that we could dress no victuals; I then thought on the words of Job, when he spoke to his impatient wife, saying, "Shall we receive good at the hand of God, and shall we not receive evil?" or, that which is accounted or looks like evil in the eye of man. In this time of exercise, the love and heavenly life of God, in his beloved Son, filled my heart, and caused an overflowing of praises to his holy, glorious, and blessed name. Oh! it was exceeding precious to my soul at that time!

The 1st of the Second Month we saw land, being driven to the southward near two hundred and fifty miles in this last hard weather; but we soon after arrived at our desired port.

After which I visited the meetings of Friends at Philadelphia, Burlington, the Falls, Abington, German Town, Bristol, and Frankfort, and found the people had been under a general visitation of the small-pox, insomuch that many hundreds, especially of children, were taken off the stage of this life in the city of Philadelphia, and I was concerned to exhort Friends in that city to bring their children to meetings, and educate them, when young, in the way they should go, that they might not depart from it when old; and that he who had taken many away, could, if he pleased, take many more; for though he might have laid down his rod at present (the distemper in the city being much abated) he could soon take it up again. It is my belief that the Lord Almighty will still continue to visit the city and people, if there is not a reformation, with further, if not sorer, visitations, because he hath known them to do them good, and make them a blessing to many islands and people; giving them the fatness of the earth, and that which is far more, the dew of heaven;

so that he may justly say to us, as to Israel of old, you "have I known of all the families of the earth; I therefore will visit upon you for all your iniquities."

In the beginning of the Fourth Month, Robert Jordan was married to Mary, the widow of Richard Hill, all three worthy Friends. The meeting on this occasion was large, and the marriage solemnized in the fear of God. Divers Friends were concerned to speak to the people, and it was greatly desired that those present, who were then spoken to, might be married to Christ, the great lover of souls, who laid down his life, the most precious life that ever was on earth, and shed his precious blood for our salvation.

A few days after which I again took shipping for the island of Barbadoes, being the sixth voyage, in the *New Bristol Hope*, and left the Capes of Delaware the 8th day of the month. The 22nd of the said month, I being weary, laid me down to rest, and fell asleep, and was awakened out of my sleep with these words, Oh heart in heaven! it is an excellent thing to have an heart in heaven! Which words were comfortable to me, and left a sweetness on my mind all the day after, for which I was thankful, and greatly desired that my heart and mind might be set and fixed more and more on heaven and heavenly things, and that my treasure might be in heaven, that my heart might be there also, according to the doctrine of my Saviour, Matt. vi. 20, 21, "Lay up for yourselves treasures in heaven; for where your treasure is, there will your heart be also."

The 27th day, being the First-day of the week, we had a comfortable meeting, the weather being moderate; and on the 7th of the Fifth Month, we arrived at Bridge Town, in Barbadoes, where we unloaded part of our cargo, and from thence we went to Speight's Town, where, after a stay of about five weeks, we accomplished our affairs. I also visited all our Friends' meetings, and some several times, in which we were edified and comforted, and divers of us had occasion to bless the holy name of God for his mercy to us: before we left the island, there happened a great storm or hurricane, which did much damage to the ships, and to the island, blowing down many houses, and spoiling much provisions, destroying almost all the plantain trees on the island, which is a very wholesome and pleasant fruit, and much used by many instead of bread.

I was clearing out our vessel when this storm happened, and being twelve miles off, could not hear of or concerning her, but thought it altogether unlikely that she should ride out so great a storm, in so bad a harbour or road, it being open to the sea, and such a storm as had not been known for many years, and some said, never but one, to their knowledge; though much more damage hath at some other times been done to the shipping, by reason that the hardest of the wind was not that way which was most dangerous to them in Carlisle Bay, where they mostly lay; for they all got out to sea, except two or three that were lost by the violence of the weather. It was indeed a very dismal time, the vessels which rode it out were much damnified, and one being loaded, ready to sail, sunk right down, and was lost in the bay. When I had cleared our ship, I set forward in order to see what was become of her; but the floods were so out, and the ways were so bad, I could not without some danger get to her that night; but next morning I set out from Joseph Gamble's, and, to my admiration, from the top of a hill, on which a house in the storm was blown flat to the ground, I saw our ship at an anchor, having rode out the storm, with one sloop by her, for which cause my soul was humbly thankful.

On the 17th of the said month, with some more than ordinary fatigue, we got up our anchor, and took in our boat, and got our passengers and provisions on board, the sea breaking high on the shore, so that several of our people and our boat were in jeopardy of being lost; but at length being all on board, we set sail, and having sailed slowly about six or seven miles, we met with a sloop who had lost her mast in the storm, and next morning we met with two large London ships, who had put out to sea, not venturing to ride it out.

We had fine pleasant weather for several days after we left the island, and on the 22nd of the Sixth Month, being the First-day of the week, we had a meeting for the worship of God, which was comfortable and satisfactory to us. The 4th and 5th of the Seventh Month, we had very fresh gales from the north-east to the north, and were near a water-spout, about a stone's throw off, which surprised some on board, on which I came out of my cabin, and saw the water run up out of the sea into the cloud, as plain as ever I saw the water run into the river, till it filled the cloud with blackness, and then it would break in great quantities into the sea, which is dangerous, when falling on vessels. The 5th of the month, being the First-day of the week, we had a good religious meeting for Divine worship, wherein our people were earnestly exhorted to a holy life, and to be earnestly concerned for the true faith, which is in Christ; that faith which works by love, and is the evidence of things not visibly seen, being manifest by works of piety and virtue. In this voyage we were twenty-two days from the island of Barbadoes to the sight of Cape Henry, in Virginia, and had a pleasant passage in the main to Philadelphia, where, in the Seventh Month, was held our yearly-meeting, at which I had a desire to be, my watery employment having hindered my being at a yearly-meeting for several years : at this meeting I met with my old acquaintances, and dear friends, John Richardson of Yorkshire, and Paul Johnson of Dublin, both on a gospel visit to the brethren and Friends in America. The meeting was large, and attended with Divine grace and goodness, and ended with thanksgiving and praise to God and the Lamb.

While our ship was loading, I was at several meetings in the country, as at Abington, German Town, Fair Hill, and Frankfort, in Philadelphia county ; and at the falls of Delaware, Buckingham, Neshaminy and Bristol, in Bucks county. I was also at Burlington, at the marriage of William Calender, junior, of Barbadoes, with Katherine Smith, daughter of Daniel and Mary Smith, of Burlington.

On the 16th of the Ninth Month I proceeded on the seventh voyage to Barbadoes, in the ship *New Bristol Hope*, as master, having on board several passengers ; one of whom, Elizabeth Martindale, was on the passage convinced of the principles of truth, and afterwards suffered, in divers respects, for her making profession with us.

We had a long passage down the river, the wind being high and boisterous. On the 22nd of the Ninth Month, we left the Capes of Delaware, and saw the island of Barbadoes the 21st of the Tenth Month, before it was day, and in the afternoon came to an anchor in the bay of Speight's Town. In this voyage I met with an accident that was painful and troublesome to me, which happened in a hard gale of wind, I being to the windward, and the ship having a large motion, and missing my hold, was canted from my place to the other side of the vessel, against the edge of a chest, and so bruised my leg that I could not do my business as I usually did, which was a great hindrance and disappointment to me: but in about a month's time, with the assistance of some of my friends there, I got indifferently through it, and also rode to Bridge Town, and had several meetings there. I was also at several good and comfortable meetings at Speight's Town, where we had one the day we sailed, being the 21st of the Eleventh Month: and on the sea-shore parted with our friends in great love, and set sail, the wind being about north-east, so that we could not weather the island of Martinico; we therefore sailed along by the islands of Dominica and Guadaloupe, and had calms under the islands, and sometimes the eddy winds from off the mountains, or high lands, would take the sails, and carry the ship clear round, which made it sometimes tedious. The 23rd and 24th we passed the islands of Montserrat, Antigua, Rodondo, Christopher's, Nevis, Bartholomew, Eustatia, Saba, Barbuda, Martin's, and Anguilla, the winds and the weather being fair and pleasant. The 25th in the evening, it began to be hazy; and, in the night we split our main-top-sail, which cost us a great deal of labour, and loss of time, before we could get it mended and set again. We had pretty fair weather about twenty days, until we came on our coast, and into soundings; when a hard gale of wind springing up easterly, which setting on the shore, was dangerous, and we had a long night coming on; but, through the favour of the Almighty, we got off from the land. In the midst of the danger of this storm, my soul sang praises to the Lord.

The 12th of the Twelfth Month we met with another easterly storm, being in about thirty fathom water, it blew, and rained very hard, and was also exceeding cold, and our coming from a hot climate made it more hard to bear. In this storm we saw divers lights, which the sailors call corposants, one of them was exceeding bright, and sat, as near as I can compute it, about half an hour on our main-top-mast head, plain to the view of all the ship's company, divers of whom said they never saw the like, and I think I never heard of, or saw the like before.

This storm continued all night till day, when it abated, and it being the first of the week, we had a comfortable meeting, in which the people on board were advised to get divine and heavenly learning, and not to be fools in religion, or in the things of God, nor to hate his true knowledge; for if they had all the natural knowledge, and brightest natural parts in the world, they would be but fools without the true fear of God, which the wise king Solomon says, is the beginning of wisdom.

The 27th of the month we saw Cape Henlopen, having been twenty-seven days from the island of Barbadoes; this was a close, foggy day, we could see but very little before us, and had like to have been a-ground on the shoals, which they call the Hen and Chickens, but went between them and the Cape, in three fathom water; the wind blowing hard at south, we went up the bay by the lead, for we could not see the land ; and the gale being so fresh, we got to Bombay Hook, from our Capes, in about six hours, which is accounted twenty leagues, where we came to an anchor, and here met with abundance of ice. Merciful was the deliverance and preservation we met with from the hand of the Almighty, this voyage; may we ever gratefully remember it! About a league above Bombay Hook, when the fog broke up, we found ourselves close on the Jersey shore; and the wind sprung up at north-west, and obliged us to come to an anchor ; where the ice came down upon us, which surprised some of us much. The sudden coming out of so hot a climate, into one so severely cold, had a bad effect on most of our ship's company; and for my own part, I had a sore fit of the phthisic, and was at times, almost breathless, and thought I must die, for I could hardly breathe, or speak ; but yet I resolved, as long as I was capable of thoughts, I would think of God, and my beloved Jesus; in which thoughts and meditations I found some comfort and consolation. I sat up for divers nights, not being able to lie down for want of breath; and I could not drink any strong drink, as rum, wine, ale, or punch, such as the sailors drank ; but instead thereof, I drank sage tea, which was very helpful to me.

The next day, the ice came down more and more upon us, and we feared to put back, because, if we had gone aground in the bay, the ice might have demolished us ; so we took the most convenient time we could, and got up our anchor, with some difficulty, and stood for Reedy Island, one of the best harbours upon the Delaware; but the wind and tide failing us, we could not get in ; and the ebb brought down the ice mightily on us, so that it took away the head of our vessel, and cut her sides very much. The next tide we got into the harbour, and lay close to Reedy Island, making the ship fast on shore. While we lay here, several vessels came to us, and fastened on shore as we did. The ice drove one vessel on us, and broke our sprit-sail yard. Here I went on shore, where the people were very kind to us, particularly the sheriff of the county, John Gooding, and his wife and family. I went also to the house of John M'Cool, who, with his wife, were very tender in their care and love towards me; bathing my swelled and benumbed limbs until the frost was pretty well out of them. The good will, and tender love and care, I here met with, affect my mind in the noting of it: I pray the Most High, whom I love and serve, to be their rewarder.

I had two meetings at our meeting-house at George's Creek, where were people of divers persuasions, who gave good attention. For these meetings I was truly thankful; for though, through the extreme cold, I could hardly speak when on board, I now spoke freely, much to my admiration, and I believe the people's satisfaction, more than is proper for me to mention; wherefore I praise God. When the weather was a little more open, and the ice gone, we sailed up the river to Philadelphia, where I was joyfully received by my friends; and while the vessel was repairing and fitting for another voyage, I was not idle, but visited Friends' meetings at Philadelphia, Burlington, Abington, German Town, Biberry, Fair-hill, and Frankfort, being sometime at four or five meetings a week. I was also at Haddonfield and Evesham meetings in West Jersey; both good and comfortable meetings, and will not easily be forgotten;

for therein God was graciously pleased to visit us with his word ; blessed be his name !

The 4th of the Third Month, we again set sail for Speight's Town, in Barbadoes ; and the 6th of the month, about six in the morning, left the Capes of Delaware. From the time we left the sight of the Capes of Delaware, to the sight of Barbadoes, was twenty-five days, which was the quickest voyage that ever I had in this ship, in which time we had three meetings, for the public worship of Almighty God, and to me they were beneficial ; and for God's goodness, I could do no less than return praise to him, who alone is worthy for ever.

After I had done my business at Barbadoes, and visited Friends' meetings, on the 5th of the Fifth Month I sailed for South-Carolina, touched at the island of Christopher's, and landed some passengers there. From thence we went to sea, and the same night we had a storm, but suffered little, the wind being for us, that we went before it, and after it was over, we had a pleasant passage of about fourteen days to the coast of Carolina ; and when we saw the land, the wind came against us, which made some of our passengers very uneasy ; but in meditating on the Infinite Being, I was favoured with inward comfort and strong consolation, so that I was humbly thankful, and praised God.

We were prevented by contrary winds, and a strong current, from getting into Charleston, and while we were beating about the coast, we met with a vessel which came from thence, who gave us intelligence that many people died suddenly, and that they buried ten or twelve in a day. Hearing such news, and the wind being still against us, our passengers, who intended for Carolina, concluded to go for Philadelphia ; so we tacked about, and stood for Delaware-bay, and then we had a fresh gale a-head again for several days, and spending so much time on the coast, our water was far expended, and we agreed to come to an allowance of water, a quart a man for twenty-four hours, for several days before we got in. We were about five weeks in our passage from Barbadoes to Delaware river.

Soon after our arrival at Philadelphia, we got our ship on the ways, in order to refit and sheath her, in which time I travelled into several counties, and had many religious meetings in divers places, in which I had good satisfaction ; and my old acquaintance and friends said they rejoiced to see me again after my sea voyages. I was thankful in my heart for the good-will of my good Master, and of my friends, in those journeys, which was, and, I hope, ever will be better to me than choice silver and fine gold.

The winter setting in about a month sooner than usual, many vessels were detained from going to sea, being frozen up; also many vessels could not come from sea up the river, so that a great damp was put on trade, and the frost coming so suddenly, many people were taken with colds, and many died in both the provinces of New Jersey and Pennsylvania. My dear friend and kind landlord Paul Preston died about this time, who on his dying bed said he had no desire to live, but to do good, and that it had been his care to keep a conscience void of offence towards God and to all men, which now was his comfort. The hard weather continuing, I found an exercise and concern on my mind to visit Friends' meetings in the county of Bucks, in Pennsylvania, and the county of

Burlington, in West Jersey: in both which I was at above twenty meetings in about twenty days. In this journey I was favoured with the grace and goodness of the Divine hand, to a greater degree than I was worthy of, though I was exceeding poor in my spirit, and in my own judgment, very weak for service and labour, both in body and mind; our meetings, considering the severe season, were large, and, I hope, they were to general edification.

On the 25th of the Tenth Month, being the reputed birth day of our Lord Jesus Christ, at a little town near the Falls, called Borden Town, we had a meeting, where never any had been before of our Friends, in one of the houses newly built by Joseph Borden, the proprietor of the place. He entertained us lovingly at his house, when he was so generous as to offer ground for a grave-yard, and to build a meeting house on, and a handsome sum of money towards building it, though he did not make profession to be of our Society. Some that were at this meeting, who did not profess with us, came over the creek on the ice, to Isaac Horner's in the evening, where we had a satisfactory meeting, in which God, through Christ, was glorified. Daniel Stanton, my wife's sister's son, accompanied me in this journey, whose company and ministry was acceptable, both to me and Friends, and we had meetings at the Falls, Bristol, Middle-town, Wright's-town, Borden-town, Croswicks, Mansfield, Upper and Lower Springfield, Mount Holly, Rancocas, Evesham, and Chester, and divers evening meetings at several Friends' houses. It now being a sickly time, I was often sent for to visit the sick, in which visits we were comforted, and God's holy name was praised.

On the 18th of the Eleventh Month I was sent for to Bristol, to visit Ennion Williams, who was dangerously ill, and to Burlington, to the burial of Elizabeth, the wife of Jonathan Wright, who was buried from the great meeting-house at Burlington. The meeting was very large, she being well beloved by her neighbours and acquaintance, being a woman much given to hospitality, and indeed many of the Friends of Burlington have exceeded in that respect the most that ever I have observed in my travels; she was a pattern of piety, a loving, obliging wife, and tender and careful mother, a kind neighbour, a loving and faithful friend, and so continued to the end; for some of her dying words were, that she desired her love might be remembered to all her friends; which was done openly in the said meeting, and tenderly affected many.

After I came home, I was at the marriage of William Parker and Elizabeth Gilbert, at which marriage was our worthy, ancient friend, John Richardson, with divers other European Friends. The meeting was large and edifying.

The river still continuing frozen up, I had a desire to visit my friends and brethren in Chester county, whom I had not seen for some years; and in order thereto in the beginning of the Twelfth Month, I, with my kinsman, Daniel Stanton, set out from Philadelphia, and went to New-town, where we had a meeting next day, being the first of the week, and afterwards an evening-meeting at Evan Lewis's; from thence we went to the monthly-meeting at Providence, on Third-day to Middle-town, Fourth-day to Concord, Fifth-day to Birmingham, Sixth day to London Grove; after which we had an evening meeting at a widow's house; from thence we travelled on Seventh-day to Nottingham, and were at a large meeting there on First-day, and had an evening meeting at a Friend's house, where some persons came, who had never been at a meeting of Friends before; on Second-day we had a meeting at Susquehannah ferry, to which divers people came over the ice, and it was a good opportunity to many of them. Third-day we had a large meeting at West Nottingham, and in the evening at William Brown's; and next day we had a large meeting at New Garden; and at Michael Lightfoot's house we met with two Friends from Ireland, Mungo Bewley and Samuel Stephens, who were now proceeding on the course of their religious visit to Friends in Maryland, Virginia, and North Carolina. From thence I went to visit my old friend and acquaintance Ellis Lewis, who had a desire to see me: we had an evening-meeting in his chamber, to our mutual comfort and refreshment; and next day had a very large meeting in the meeting-house at Kennet; after which we went to Concord to the quarterly-meeting for the county of Chester, and were at three meetings there, and likewise had three evening-meetings at Friends' houses; at which meetings we had the company of my kinswoman, Alice Alderson, and her companion Margaret Coupland, who were lately come from the north of England, to visit Friends in this and the adjacent provinces.

We went on Third-day to the general-meeting at Providence, which was very large; Joshua Fielding and Ebenezer Large were there; and we had an evening-meeting at Rebecca Minshall's; and next went to Chichester, where we had a larger meeting than I expected, considering the season; we lodged at John

Salkeld's; and on Fifth-day we had a good, open meeting at Chester, and, in the evening, another at Grace Lloyd's; next day had a meeting at Springfield, which I believe will be remembered by some that were there, when we do not see one another; afterwards we travelled to Philadelphia.

In this year, 1732, arrived Thomas, Penn, one of the proprietors of Pennsylvania, and son of the truly honourable William Penn, governor and proprietor of this province, a wise man, a good Christian, and a mild governor, a great promoter of piety and virtue, and of good men. May this his son walk in his steps!

In the First Month was our general spring-meeting, at which were several public Friends from England, viz. John Richardson, Alice Alderson, and Margaret Coupland. The meeting was large and edifying, the said Friends having service therein to general satisfaction.

The 2nd of the Second Month, I proceeded on a voyage to Barbadoes, it being the first in the snow *Barbadoes Packet*, a vessel built on purpose for me. We got to the Capes the 20th of the Second Month, in the evening, where we were obliged to come to an anchor; and the 21st we put out to sea, but the wind being against us, and looking like windy weather, I concluded to come to under our Cape, and wait for a fair wind: as soon as our snow came to, we got our boat out, and went to Lewis Town; and next day, being First-day, we had a meeting in the court-house. In this town is an Episcopal, and a Presbyterian meeting-house; but neither of their teachers were that day in town, and divers of the people were glad of a meeting, and I had a good opportunity with them. After meeting I went on board, and weighed anchor, and had a fair wind for above a week after: in which time we overtook the ship *Amity*, —— Bowling, master, near the latitude of Bermudas, where we had smart gales of wind, which obliged us to carry our topsails double reefed; and, after having been at sea twenty-seven days and one night, in which time we had several meetings, we saw the island of Barbadoes; though, for the most part, we had contrary winds; but all was well, and God blessed, who is for ever worthy.

The 20th of the Fourth Month, havingdone my business, and also visited Friends' meetings, we sailed for Philadelphia; and on the 25th of the Fourth Month, being First-day, we had a seasonable and serviceable meeting, wherein the Almighty was worshipped and praised, and the people exhorted to sobriety and temperance. We were about twenty days from Barbadoes to Philadelphia.

After having staid at home about six weeks, and visited the meetings of Friends in divers places, to mine and their satisfaction, on the 28th of the Sixth Month, I proceeded on another voyage for the island of Barbadoes. We left sight of our Capes on the 31st of the said month. The winds were for the most part contrary, and, before we got into the trade wind, we met with two hard gales; the last of which was a kind of a hurricane, in which we could carry no sail at all, but let the vessel lie to the mercy of the seas, or rather to the mercy of Him that made the seas, and all that is therein, and in the earth also. In this storm we lost a spare top-mast, and divers other utensils belonging to the vessel: but all our people were well and safe. This voyage we had several comfortable religious meetings on board, in which we were exhorted to prepare for another and better world, this being so very uncertain and momentary, and full of various exercises, temptations, and afflictions.

I had on board three Whitehaven sailors, William Towerson, William Tremble, and William Atkinson, and I do not remember that I heard either of them swear an oath during the whole voyage, which I thought worthy to stand on record, because it is so rare in seafaring men. About the beginning of the Eighth Month, being in the latitude of Barbadoes, the thoughts of my leaving my family and habitation, and many of my loving relations, and near and dear friends, as at divers other times also, made me pensive and sorrowful; but it being on a principle of justice, and sometimes meeting with the presence and goodness of God, I was enabled to do my affairs and business, and forbore to appear sorrowful as much as possibly I could, or be of a sad countenance in the sight of men; but to Him, who knew all things, and sees in secret, I poured out my soul in all my afflictions, for he only is able to help me. I met with some who untruly censured me, as covetous of the things of this world, or to be rich; and that for the sake of these outward things, I might venture my life until I might lose it. Really, as to my life, it hath long been my desire to be ready to resign it, and is so still: and, as to those outward things, so far as I know, my heart is clear; food and raiment, and to be clear and even with the world, having rather to give than receive, is all the grandeur I desire, and if that be not granted, I hope to be contented without it, and to be thankful. I look upon crowns and sceptres, and all the fine things of this world, that are of the nature of it, but as trifles, and diminutive things, in comparison of a house and kingdom eternal in the heavens. In this voyage, as usual, I read in the holy Scriptures, and met with strong consolation therein, especially in the New Testament; I also read much in the works of that eminent judge and good Christian Matthew Hale.

The 7th of the Eighth Month, we arrived at Barbadoes, staid three weeks and one day, and had divers religious meetings. I hastened to accomplish my affairs before winter, it coming on, and the time of the year dangerous for sailing on our coasts. On the 30th of the Eighth Month we left the island of Barbadoes, bound for Philadelphia; and on the 11th of the Ninth Month, it pleased God to favour us with a gracious opportunity to worship him; wherein was declared to the ship's company, the nature and advantage of good, and the fountain from whence it flows, or springs; as also the nature and disadvantage of evil; the one being or springing from God, and the other proceeding from Satan, or the Devil, who is the root of all evil; and, that man might be left without excuse, God hath sent the Divine and supernatural light of his holy Spirit, to shew to mortals what is good, and what is evil; in order that they might embrace the good, and refuse the evil.

The 21st of the Ninth Month we had a very hard gale of wind at north-west, which blew so hard, that it put us by from sailing, so that we were obliged to lay the vessel to the wind; for, by the violence thereof, we could not carry any sail; and it was so dark, that we could neither see stars nor one another; nor hear one another without we were very near, the seas rising very high: indeed the long, stormy and dark nights were very dismal; and some of our goods got loose in the hold. In the beginning of the night, about the seventh hour, Philip Kearney, my apprentice, fell into the sea and was lost, which was a deep affliction to us in divers considerations.

The 25th we saw the land, and next day we came to an anchor in Delaware-bay. The loss of this lad was a cause that we were not so joyful as is usual for people to be when come to the shore.

The latter end of the Tenth Month I went the third voyage, commander of the *Barbadoes·Packet*, from Philadelphia, bound to Barbadoes: we were towed through the ice by two boats from Thomas Masters's wharf, and in two days got to Reedy Island; from whence we sailed down Delaware-bay, where we lay two nights, the wind being contrary, blowing hard, the nights being long, the days very short, and weather sharp; we left our Capes in the night, it being dangerous lying in the bay; and after being out several days, we had favourable winds, and pleasant weather; but when we got into the trade wind, it blew hard, and mostly against us, so that the first land we saw was the island of St. Christopher's, where we arrived in twenty days from our Capes; and the market for provisions being at that time better than at any other of those islands, and the property of the vessel mostly belonging to me, and the cargo generally consigned to me, I disposed of part of it. Here being no meeting of our Society on this island, I had meetings on board the vessel in the harbour, and divers from the shore, and several masters of vessels came to our meetings, the snow having large accommodations for such an occasion; and, so far as I could understand, the people were generally satisfied, and spoke well of our meetings.

Of late times, and also in this voyage, meeting with

many losses and crosses, and much afflictions, and various exercises, I was ready to say in my heart, Lord, why am I thus afflicted now in my declining years, since thou knowest I love thee above all things, and that I would not willingly or knowingly offend thee, my great and dear Lord: It was answered, as though vocally spoken, My only begotten and beloved Son, who never offended me, suffered much more. This word being such an evident truth, I begged patience to go through all my sufferings and afflictions, so that at last I might live with Christ in the glorious kingdom of God for ever, where I might always bless and praise his holy name.

Five or six days after our arrival at this island, a vessel, that came out five or six days before us, arrived, she meeting with the same boisterous weather as we did, yet we made our passage ten or eleven days sooner. Divers other vessels, bound to Barbadoes, put in here, through these contrary winds; and when I saw others in the like circumstances with us, I was the more thankful for being preserved safe, and so soon to this place; yet it was a considerable loss and sore trial not to get to Barbadoes, the island I was bound to, and a great disappointment to me and many more.

At this island a person whose name was ——— Galloway, a man of a great estate, hearing that I kept meetings on board the vessel, kindly invited me to have a meeting at his house, and said he would give notice of it to divers of the gentlemen, as he called them, of the island, telling me that I should be welcome to his house, which was much more convenient than the vessel; but I was not very forward to accept of my friend Galloway's kind offer, being sensible of my own weakness and inward poverty, so that I made several excuses to evade it; bu he obviated them all. First, I asked him if he could bear the reproach of having a Quakers' meeting at his house: he answered, yes, there is good and bad of all Societies. Secondly, I asked if his wife would like it, or be willing that a meeting should be in the house; he said she desired it, and would be very willing. Thirdly, I asked if he thought he could sit in silence; he told me he believed he could. I then told him, I was obliged to him for his kind and friendly offer, and, God willing, I intended to come, and tell my people of the ship's company to come also, and desired him to give notice of it; the which he did, and there was a large satisfactory meeting: Oh may the Almighty sanctify it to some souls, is my desire!

He and his wife were both very courteous to me, and invited many of his rich friends and relations: his wife's father was a judge in this island, of good repute. Divers people, of several professions, were at this meeting, and many expressed their being glad of it. An attorney at law said he was thankful for the words he had heard that day, and if I would stay with them he would always come to our meetings. One judge Mills was at this meeting, and very kindly invited me to his house. Some meeting me next day, said they were sorry they were not there. The mistress of the house told divers of the people, who were persons of note, that they should remember what they had heard; and spoke it with a religious concern, as it seemed to me. When I went to this meeting, I was very poor, and in much fear, speaking with a great concern on my mind for the people's salvation; and that God, through Christ, might be glorified.

After this meeting, it was (as though a voice) said unto me, How dost thou know but for this cause, and for this meeting thou art brought here to this island, though against thy will? The people told me, that they did not remember that there ever was a meeting of our Friends before on this island. The meeting had this effect, that the people had a better opinion of our Society than they had before. The subject in this meeting was the excellency of the gospel dispensation above that of the law, in that it brought us to the law, went through the law, and was above the law, and far from destroying the law, but fulfilled it; for proof of which they were referred to Christ's most excellent sermon which he preached on the mount, Matt. v.

From the island of Christopher's, I proposed, God willing, for Barbadoes; the which I apprehended would be a troublesome voyage, it being about one hundred leagues to windward, and a strong current against us. On the 19th of the Twelfth Month we sailed towards Barbadoes; and the wind being a-head, and blowing hard, we tarried two nights at the island of Lucia, where we took in wood and water. The people here were mostly French, and were very civil to us.

The 21st we put out again to sea; but the wind and current being against us, obliged us to go into the harbour from whence we came, and tarry for an opportunity more favourable. While we were in this harbour, which is a very good one, several vessels came in on the like occasion; and a vessel that came from Christopher's about three hours after us, came here three days since we did.

We went out again, in order to proceed to Barbadoes; but, as before, the current was so strong against us, and the wind also, that we could not get forward on our way; wherefore we put back again to Christopher's, and, by the way, called at Antigua, where I had an open, satisfactory meeting, for which I was truly thankful, and so were some, not of our Society, of whom there were divers, and some who had not been at our meetings before.

The next day we arrived again at Christopher's, and there unloaded the remainder of our cargo, though much against my mind. After having sold the most of our cargo at Basseterre, we went to Sandy Point, and there sold the remainder, and took in our loading for Philadelphia.

In loading our vessel, judge Brown was my very good friend, and helpful to me therein, for which I think myself much obliged to him.

While we lay here, I had a meeting on board our vessel, to which came five masters of vessels. It was a good meeting, though I spoke to them in much misery and pain, having very angry painful sores on my legs, occasioned by a fall in getting out of the boat, the seas running high, and through the violence of the waves, I fell across the boat, and broke both my shins very grievously.

The 31st of the First Month, 1734, we had another meeting on board our vessel, to which came several from other vessels, and some from the shore, among whom was a young baronet, and his host (a tavern keeper) with him, who at first behaved airily, but after some time he was more sober, and seemed respectful at parting.

I was invited to have a meeting next First-day on board the ship *King George*, a large vessel; the master told me his cabin was large, and would accommodate many more than mine : but we did not stay so long as till the First-day.

After this meeting was over, the master of the large ship came on board, and said he was sorry he had not come sooner, so as to have had the opportunity to have been at the meeting.

From Christopher's, we set sail for the island of Anguilla, and had a meeting at the governor's house on a First-day. We staid at Anguilla three days, and there took on board some bags of cotton on freight, and sailed from thence the 10th of the Second Month. The governor of this island, whose name was George Leonard, told me that he should live and die in our principles, saving that he must defend his people. But he did not consider, that his defence might destroy both him and them, and that such defence was directly contrary to Christ's doctrine and practice. A remarkable and dismal passage he related to me, that some days before, a vessel came from the island of Saltitudas (which went there to take in salt) the people going on shore, the master told him, that there lay at the landing the heads of above twenty men on one side the path, and the quarters of them on the other ; which so surprised them, that they made the best of their way to Anguilla, where they related this dismal story, and supposed the slain to be Britons by their appearances, and that they were destroyed by the Spaniards, who are known to be cruel to them. This action being far from the spirit of Christianity, is a reproach to the actors thereof.

Not far from Anguilla is an island they call St. John's, the inhabitants of which are Dutch. The negroes there lately rose and took the island, killed the people, spoiled their plantations, and burnt their houses. I lodged at the house of a person, who went to subdue those negroes, who were too strong for him and his company, and the negroes killed divers of them, and among them, killed this man's two sons, for which their mother and sisters were in bitter mourning when I was at their house. The thoughts of the bloodshed and vast destruction, which war makes in the world, caused me to cry in my heart, How long, O Lord, thou holy, just, and true God, will it be till nation, lift up the sword no more against nation, nor the people learn war any more!

When I came home from this voyage, which was the 30th of the Second Month, I met with the sorrowful news of the death of my only son George, a beloved, dear youth, who was taken sick the 5th of the Eighth Month, 1733, and departed this life at my house in Frankfort, the 13th of the said month, about the ninth hour, in the evening of the Sixth-day of the week, and was carried to the Bank meeting-house of Friends in Philadelphia, and buried from thence on the First-day following, being accompanied by many Friends, and others. He was ten years and seven days old when he died, and as he was much beloved for the sweetness of his nature and disposition, so he was greatly lamented by many who were acquainted with him. I have this account to leave concerning him, not so much that he was my son, as to excite other youths to serve and fear the Lord, and to love him above all; and that they might remember their Creator in their youthful days, that it might be well with them in this world, and when time here to them shall be no more:—

He was a lad much inclined to read the holy Scriptures, and other good books, especially religious ones; and was always obliging, obedient, and loving to his parents, and ready and willing to do any service he could do to his friends: any little services in his power he cheerfully performed, and took delight in. He was very diligent, and ready to go to religious meetings, and an entire lover of religious people. In his sickness he behaved himself more like a wise man, than a youth of that age, bearing his pain and sickness with a great deal of patience. I being in another part of the world, he would gladly have seen me, but said he should never see me any more, and therefore desired his mother to remember his dear love to his father, and tell him that he was gone to his Heavenly Father. He was very fervent in prayer in the time of his sickness, and prayed that God would preserve his people all the world over. One time, when in great misery and pain, he prayed to Christ, saying, "Sweet Jesus! blessed Jesus! give me patience to bear my misery and pain, for my misery is greater than I can well bear! O come, sweet Jesus, why art thou so long a coming? I had rather be with thee than in the finest place in all the world." Many religious expressions he spoke on his dying bed, greatly to the satisfaction and melting of his friends and relations who came to see him in his illness. One day he said, "My misery and pain is very great, but what would it be if the wrath of God was in my soul?" He believing in the love of God in Christ, made him desirous of being with him; and seeing the joy that was set before him, thought the time long to be with Jesus, as knowing that then he would be out of all misery and pain. His heart was full of love to his relations, acquaintance, and friends, who came to see him in his illness; and full of tender sweetness and Divine love, he took his last leave of them, which greatly affected many. This was one of the most pinching exercises I ever met with in all my days; but as he said in his illness, so I now write, "The wisdom of the Lord is wonderful!" One time in this dear child's sickness, he said, "Oh! the good hand of Thee, the Lord, help me, give me ease, and conduct me safe," *i. e.* to God's kingdom, uttering this verse;

> "Sweet Jesus, give me ease, for mercy I do crave;
> And if thou'lt give me ease, then mercy I shall have."

Although this was a great and sore exercise, and deep affliction to me, in losing this promising youth, and my only son; yet, considering that he went off the stage of life like a solid good Christian, it was made tolerably easy to me; for he departed this life in much brightness and sweetness, and more like an old Christian than a youth of ten years of age.

It was usual for me to advise his mother not to set her affections too much upon him, thinking he was too good to live long in this world, and too ripe for heaven, to stay long here on earth, or in this world of sorrow and misery. This dear and tender youth, when reading (to which he was much inclined) if he met with any thing that affected him, either in the sacred writings or other good authors, he would write it down, and get it by heart. He was, more than common, affectionately concerned for his mother, doing whatever he could freely and cheerfully to serve her, and told her not to do divers things which he thought too much for her, saying "Mother, let me do it; if I were a man thou should not do any thing at all," (meaning as to labour,) my dear wife being very industrious, and apt to overdo herself at times, and she being affected with his filial love and care for and towards her in his father's absence, it caused her sometimes to turn about and weep, in consideration of his great care for and love to her. I thought a little memorandum of the life and death of this religious lad was worthy recording, in order to stir up other youths to obedience and love to their parents, who begat them, and carefully and tenderly nourished and brought them up; and also to love and obey God, from whom they have their life, breath, and being, and to believe in Christ, who died for them; who is the glorious Light of all the nations of them that are saved, and walk therein, according to sacred writ.

As noted above, he got several pieces by heart out of the Bible, and other religious writings, first writing them with his pen. The short ones I may recite, of which nature were divers others, which peradventure may be edifying to some, who may cast their eye thereon.

One place, which much affected my mind, that he wrote down, and got by heart, was the fifteenth verse of the fifty-seventh chapter of that evangelical prophet Isaiah: "For thus saith the high and lofty One that inhabiteth eternity, whose name is Holy; I dwell in the high and holy place, with him also that is of a contrite and humble spirit, to revive the spirit of the humble, and to revive the heart of the contrite ones."

Another little piece was five verses, which among others he wrote, and got by heart, viz.

As one day goes another comes,
And sometimes shews us dismal dooms,
As time rolls on, new things we see,
Which seldom to us do agree:
Though now and then's a pleasant day,
'Tis long a coming, soon away:
Wherefore the everlasting Truth
Is good for aged and for youth,
For them to set their hearts upon,
For that will last till time is done.

I have now but one only daughter, Rebecca, left me out of twelve children, (except my wife's son and daughter.)

CHAPTER IX.

1734–1736.

VOYAGE TO DUBLIN AND BACK—THEN TO BARBADOES, AND THENCE TO LONDON—SETTLES HIS AFFAIRS SATISFACTORILY — VISITS FRIENDS IN SEVERAL PARTS OF ENGLAND; AND RETURNS HOME.

AFTER this long and tedious voyage, which ended in the Second Month, I staid but a few weeks at home, and loaded with wheat and flour for Dublin, in Ireland; had Alice Alderson, my kinswoman, and Margaret Coupland, passengers. We had a very comfortable, pleasant passage, fair winds and weather, and good religious meetings. I think it was the most pleasant time that ever I crossed the seas; about Nantucket we saw several sloops a whaling, and spoke with one, by which opportunity we inquired of the welfare of our Friends on that island and sent our loves to them. Not many miles from the sloops we saw a shoal of whales: I counted eight in a row lying side by side in the water.

We were four weeks and six days from our Capes to Cape Clear in Ireland; coming near the land we met with fishing-boats, and got plenty of choice fresh fish: in the evening we got into Kinsale, took in a pilot for Dublin, and sailed next day from Kinsale, and were out one night at sea; got next day to Dublin Bay, where we went ashore, and were kindly entertained by our friends. We were at divers large meetings in that great city, which some of us, while we live, at times I believe shall remember. My stay in Ireland was about seven weeks, in which time I visited several meetings in the country, and at Edenderry, the Moate of Grenogue, Carlow, Ballytore, &c.

We set sail from Dublin with a fair wind in company with the ship *Neptune*, and our friends sent many prayers and good wishes after us. We were about forty persons, sailors, passengers, and servants, on board, and had a good passage, all things considered.

We had divers religious meetings on board, and were on our passage, from the sight of Ireland, to the sight of our land, five weeks and six days: it was the quickest voyage I ever made to Europe and back again to Philadelphia.

When I came home, finding all well, I was thankful to God, in the name of Christ, for all his mercies, and the many preservations wherewithal he had favoured me.

After being a little at home, and at several meetings, and not being clear of the world, in order to it, I undertook another voyage to Barbadoes, and from thence intending for London, in order to settle my affairs there, which I intended some years before, but losses and disappointments hindered me. Wherefore, the 7th of the Tenth Month, I proceeded on a fifth voyage in the *Barbadoes Packet*, and left Philadelphia, and was at a meeting the next day at Chester, (being First-day,) and in the evening we had a large meeting at Grace Lloyd's, where I met with my dear friend Joseph Gill, who had good service in the said meeting: we rejoiced in Christ to see each other. We left Chester the 9th, and got that tide down the river to Newcastle, and, after visiting those few Friends there, we set sail the 12th in the morning; the wind being high and the weather very sharp, freezing hard; our sails were so froze, that we had hard work to get the vessel under sail. The 13th day weighed anchor, and sailed down the bay, and the 14th we were clear of the Capes. The First-day following we had a good seasonable meeting, for the worship and service of God, and, in the said meeting, as I was treating of disobedience to parents, and disobedience to Almighty God our great Parent and heavenly Father, a youth, who was a passenger in the vessel, went out hastily and abruptly, as I was shewing the ungratefulness of the first, much more of the last. When I asked the reason of his going out, he said it was because he could not forbear crying; and thinking I spoke so because of him, he said he could not hear me any more. Afterwards I understood that he was a youth who was very ungrateful and disobedient to his parents; the which I knew not of, for his mother told me, and himself also, that he went to sea on account of his health. I thought his going out so hastily was occasioned by some indisposition of body; but it was, as he gave us to understand, through resenting what was spoken, and by his taking of it to himself. I have in like manner sometimes observed, that divers people have shewn a restlessness and uneasiness in public assemblies of worship and devotion, and sometimes going out, &c. so that they have thereby exposed themselves to the notice of the people, as persons guilty of the matter publicly reprehended, or spoken against; just as though they were the only persons in the assembly, who were guilty of the evil then taken notice of. Such public restlessness is a great folly and weakness, besides so openly and publicly exposing themselves.

After we left our Capes, we had divers hard gales of wind, which lasted several days. The 28th being a First-day, we had a meeting for Divine worship, in which God was praised, and his holy name exalted, for his unspeakable grace in sending his only begotten Son, a Divine Light, to enlighten the inhabitants of the world. After which we had stormy weather and contrary winds for some weeks, so that our passage was tedious; and of fifteen times going to Barbadoes, I found this the most difficult; and the prospect was very discouraging of making a losing voyage, by the great expense I expected for repairing and refitting the vessel, &c. so that I began to despair of accomplishing my design of discharging my debts in Great Britain, and the thoughts and consideration of losing so much of the company and conversation of my wife, relations, and friends, and spending so much precious time, which cannot be recalled, to so little purpose, lay heavy on my mind; yet by the grace of God, my mind was supported, and my resolutions confirmed to praise the Almighty for every dispensation of his Providence.

The 23rd of the Eleventh Month, we saw the island of Barbadoes, at the breaking of the day, having been from the Capes of Delaware forty days and one night; and [I] was truly thankful, that at last, we, through Divine favour, got well to our desired port, where we were lovingly received by our friends at Speight's Town, who were joyful at our arrival. From thence I went to Bridge Town, and so on to the governor's, in order to enter our vessel; but, staying a little too late, the governor, who was the Lord Howe, was come from his house on his way to Bridge Town, with his coach and six, and his attendants; but he, seeing me, courteously stopped his coach, and did my business as he sat therein; and though I made an essay towards an excuse, he would not admit of it, saying there was no need of any excuse. He was indeed an extraordinarily courteous man: he died soon after, much lamented, as he was much beloved.

My stay at Barbadoes this time was the longest I ever staid, believing it to be the last time I should go there, and that I should see them no more. My so saying troubled some of them; but growing in years, being then turned of three-score, I thought it would be too hard for me to undertake such another voyage; therefore I was at all the meetings of our Friends on the island.

Here I met with Moses Aldridge, a Friend from New England, who came on a religious visit to Friends of this island, with whom he had divers good meetings, his service in preaching the gospel being edifying and acceptable; we were together at the marriage of Andrew Drury and Mary Lewis, after which meeting and marriage I was ill of a fever several days, which distemper was very much among the people, of which near twenty masters of vessels, and some hundreds of people died; and though I had been at Barbadoes many times, I never had so much illness there before; Moses Aldridge, and several Friends of us, had a large meeting at John Gibson's, where were many people, not of our persuasion, who generally were sober; but as I was recommending charity to the people, according to the doctrine of the apostle Paul, as the most excellent gift, I advised them to shew it forth to all people of all professions, and also to their negroes, telling them that some of the gentry of this island had observed to me, that the more kind they were to their slaves, they had their business the better done for it: though I observed also, that I had been at some places, where I had watched to hear some expressions that might look like charity; but in divers houses, and some of note, I could not hear any Christian-like expressions to their slaves or negroes, and that with sorrow I had seen a great deal of tyranny and cruelty, the which I dissuaded them from: this doctrine so exasperated some that were there, that they made a disturbance in the meeting; one of which persons meeting me on the king's highway, shot off his fowling-piece at me, being loaded with small shot, ten of which made marks on me, and several drew blood; by which unfriendly action, the man got a great deal of disgrace, it being highly resented by all who were acquainted with me; the president of the island looked on it as a very base action, as did also divers of the justices and the gentry, also the vestry, and several clergymen and lawyers; one of the lawyers told me I should not be just to the country, myself, nor the man, if I did not prosecute him; another, professing the law, said he ought to be abandoned by all mankind, if he shot at me with design; many were for prosecuting him, for the people generally took notice of it with abhorrence; but he sending for me, and signifying he would not do so again, I forgave him; and I pray it may not be laid to his charge in the great day, and that he may be forgiven, he being ignorant of the love I had and have for him and all men, even them whom I know to be mine enemies. It would be too great a scandal and reproach to expose his name and station in the world. Some thought I did well in forgiving him, and some thought I did ill in it; but I spoke my mind to him alone freely, in which I had satisfaction and peace.

Intending my vessel for London, I made my chief mate, Ralph Loftus, master of her, not knowing whether I might proceed the voyage, it being a very sickly time; afterwards my mate had the distemper also, but I bless God we both recovered a good state of health.

It was this voyage that my friends in Barbadoes published a little piece I wrote at sea, which I called "Free Thoughts communicated to Free Thinkers," done in order to promote thinking on the name and works of God; which had, as far as I understood, a good acceptance among the people; the principal clergyman on the island thanked me for it, and said there was need enough for it: but I could be glad another, or a better hand, had done something of that nature, and more large. If this may be of any service, I shall be thankful.

I had also a meeting at John Lewis's, in Joseph's parish, at which were divers not of our profession, and some who were never at any of our religious meetings before; who said they were glad they were there that day; it being a satisfactory open meeting.

After I had visited my friends, and settled my affairs as well as I could, and loaded our vessel with sugars, for London, being willing, once more, to see my native land, and to settle my affairs there, and see my relations and friends, on the 6th of the Third Month we set sail from Barbadoes to London, and had pleasant weather. The 16th, being the First-day of the week, we had a religious meeting for the worship of God, in which I was concerned to speak on the government of the tongue, having on board several hands, who did not sail with us before that voyage, that were much used to swearing. After that meeting, we had not so many bad words and oaths as before. I was thankful in my soul to the Lord, and blessed his holy name, for his goodness to us that day; and, in the night, my sleep was very sweet and comfortable, being sensible of the love of God in the visions of the night; so that I witnessed the fulfilling of the prophecy of Joel, chap. ii. 28.

The 23rd, being the First-day of the week, we had a meeting, in which the grace of God, that comes by Jesus Christ, was magnified, and a blessing begged for all who love and serve God, throughout the world, by sea and land; also a tender petition was put up to Almighty God, that, as he was graciously pleased to look down on these eight persons in Noah's ark, so he would please to look upon us in our vessel; and that, as by his Divine Providence, they safely landed on the earth, so we, if it were his will, might safely land at our desired port; yet not that our wills, but his will might be done: which supplication was put up with great submission. Both day and night I often sought the Lord, and was much alone in this voyage. I read the Old and New Testament almost through, and much of it divers times over; my time being mostly taken up in reading, writing, and meditating, in which at times, my heart would be broken into tenderness; and I was humbly thankful to God, that my heart was not hard, he having promised to visit the contrite ones; the which he sometimes fulfilled, to my unspeakable satisfaction: glory to his holy name for ever. My heart was also thankful, that God was pleased to visit me in my watery travels and troubles, and in my separation from my family and friends, which are much nearer, and more valuable to me, than all riches, and a great cross to my natural inclination to part with.

The 8th of the Fourth Month, being the First-day of the week, we had a meeting, in which acquaintance with God was exhorted to, shewing the benefit of it, and of loving him above all things, and delighting in his law, and meditating therein day and night. The 19th, in the morning, a strong northerly wind came up, and blew so hard, that we could not carry sail, but lay to the wind under our mizen, which was split or torn with the violence of the wind, and the sea rose high, so that it came into the windows of our great cabin: it was very rugged for the time, and though it was midsummer, it was so cold, that we were obliged to clothe ourselves, as in winter. The 22nd, being First-day, we had a comfortable meeting after the storm, wherein the great benefit of true religion was a little opened to our small company, and the Lord, most High, was praised for our deliverance and preservation. The 26th we sounded, and found about seventy fathom depth of water. The 29th, we were a-breast of the Isle of Wight. From the time we left the island of Barbadoes, to the time we found ground, was seven weeks. Thus, through many perils and dangers, we came to Great Britain; for all which mercies and providences, let my soul bless and praise the holy name and mighty power of the Most High. It was now a time of very great pressing for seamen, and several men-of-war's boats came on board to press our sailors; but they had prepared a place in the vessel to hide themselves, and the men-of-war's people could not find them: one lieutenant, with his men, came on board, and seeing us weakly handed, the best of our hands being hid, he asked me if I had any more hands on board; I made him very little answer; he then said he was sure I could not bring the ship from Barbadoes without hands: I told him sailors were hard to be got in Barbadoes, either for love or money, to go for London, for fear of being pressed, and I was obliged to take any I could get: he said it was in vain to talk much, but if I would say I had no more hands on board, he would be satisfied; he having a belief that I would speak the truth, though he never saw me before; and he said if I would say there were no more men on board, he would go away, for then he had no more business there: but I made him no answer, not daring to tell a lie. "Now I know that there is men on board," said he; so he commanded his men to search the ship to her keel; so they stripped, and made a narrow search, and sweated and fretted, but could not find them. He being civil, I made him, when he went away, a small present; he wished me well; and so I carried my people safe up to London.

In the beginning of the Fifth Month, I came to London, and lodged at the house of Simeon Warner, in Southwark, and at divers kind friends and relations in and about London; the tender and brotherly respect which I received from divers, in some of those families, in my sickness, will not, I believe, ever be forgotten while I am in this world, at times, by me; and, I hope, that He, whom I serve with my might and strength, will be their reward. When in the country about London, my residence was mostly at

Edmonton, at my dear brother George Chalkley's, who with my sister and cousins, were a comfort to me, both in health and sickness; for I was often in London sorely afflicted with the phthisic and asthma, which sometimes made me very uneasy; and, though my affairs required me to be often at the city, yet I was obliged to return into the country for air, and, both in health and sickness, was kindly and very affectionately received and tended by my dear brother, sister, and all my loving cousins; the memory thereof is cordial to me in penning these lines: it may be truly said, we were very joyful in meeting one another, and our sorrow in parting not easy to be expressed.

In London I sold my vessel, the *Barbadoes Packet*, and settled all my affairs to general satisfaction, so far as I know, on which account I had laboured for several years, and was joyful that Providence had favoured me so far as to see it accomplished; so that I now wholly intended to leave trading by sea, the which I never inclined to, only on a principle of justice; for I was fully resolved in my mind, that my creditors should be paid their just debts, though I might lose my life in the pursuit of it, about which I had no anxious guilt, because I never was extravagant nor indolent, but met with divers casualties by fire and water: by the latter I lost many hundreds of pounds for several years together. And I would persuade all in their undertaking for a livelihood in this world, to be sure to have an eye to Divine Providence, who will not suffer us (if we do well) nor so much as a sparrow to fall to the ground, without he think it best for us, he knowing what is for our good better than we know ourselves. Thus when I had paid my debts, and in a good degree settled my affairs, I visited several of my relations, as at Kingsworth, Staines, Guildford, &c., had a meeting at Market-street, and one at Guildford, another at Staines, and one at Longford; in all which I had some service, and my relations were joyful to see me once more, having never expected to see me again; and when I had visited meetings in and about London, I went towards the north, in order to visit some places where I had never been, and some that I had been at. The number of meetings, and the names of the places where I had meetings, while I was this time in England, are as follow. While I was in and about London, I was at eighteen meetings in that great city, at two of which, I was with May Drummond, a virtuous young woman, who had a good gift in the ministry, and had a gracious opportunity of declaring her convincement to our noble Queen Caroline, our great King George's royal consort. The kind treatment, and good reception, she had with the Queen, spread so in the city and country, that many thousands flocked to hear her, and more of the gentry and nobility, than ever was known before, to our meetings. I had some private conversation with her, which put me in mind of the apostle's exhortation, where he adviseth the primitive Christians, that their words be few and savoury, and that they should be seasoned with grace, for this great reason, that they might administer grace to the hearers; and truly I thought there was the influence of grace in her conduct and conversation, whom I pray God to preserve in Christ to the end.

I had a meeting at the house of my brother, with his scholars at Edmonton, and also with his family and divers of our relations, which some of us may have occasion to remember. We had seven meetings at Tottenham, at sundry times, and four at Hertford; I travelled to Hitchin, from thence to Baldock, and then to Stadtfold and Ashwell. The 7th of the Eighth Month, being the Third-day of the week, to Royston; Fourth, to Ives; Fifth, to Huntingdon; Sixth, to Ramsey. First-day, being the 12th of the Month, we had a meeting at a small town named Finedon, and the same day, in the evening, had a large meeting at Wellingborough, in Northamptonshire. The 14th, being the Third-day of the week, we had a meeting at Northampton, Fourth-day at Braybrook, Fifth-day at Oakham, the county town of Rutland, Sixth-day at Long-Clackson; and First-day, being the 19th of the month, I was at a large and open meeting at Nottingham, where were many people, not of our Society, who were very sober; Third-day had a meeting at Farnesfield, Fourth-day at Mansfield, Fifth at Chesterfield, in Derbyshire; from whence we went over the moors and mountains, Benjamin Bangs, the younger, accompanying me, who came on purpose from Stockport, to be my companion and guide thither: his company was both pleasant and profitable to me in that hill country, through which we travelled to Stockport, where we had three meetings, and where I met with my dear worthy old friend, Benjamin Bangs. When we met, we embraced each other in arms of Christian love, having not seen one another for many years, with whom I staid four days. This worthy Friend, though upwards of fourscore years of age, went with me to Manchester, where we had two meetings, and then I went back with him to his house. He was a man of extraordinary character, and well beloved, he being a pillar in the church of Christ.

When at Manchester, I went to visit a Friend newly cut for the stone, who had a stone taken out of him, the measure of which I saw, and had the stone in my hand; it was nine inches about, and three inches over. Before I went out of those parts, he was well enough to ride home, which was near a hundred miles; he was cheerful as well as thankful.

From Stockport I went to Macclesfield, to Joseph Hobson's, where I met with Joshua Toft, and his brother, two choice ministers of Jesus Christ, of whose company I was glad, though at that time I was very low and poor in my spirit. We had two meetings here; on the 2nd of the Ninth Month, being First-day, I was at a large meeting at Morley, and, in the evening, at the meeting at John Leigh's; at both which meetings there were many people, not of our Society, who were very still, and some were broken into tenderness. From Morley I went to Penketh, where we had a large, solid meeting, and had an evening-meeting at Warrington, where I met with many brethren and sisters, who sincerely love our Lord Jesus Christ, with whom I was refreshed, particularly at Gilbert Thompson's, and Lawrence Calen's. From Warrington I went to Langtree, Preston, and Clifton, where I had meetings, and so went on to Lancaster. I went to Wray, in order to visit my old shipmate, Elizabeth Rawlinson, whose son, Hutton Rawlinson, went with me. When I came to Wray, they desired me to have a meeting with them; and though there was little notice, yet we had a large meeting, divers neighbours coming in, and Christ was preached to them freely; this was the 10th, in the evening, and Second-day of the week. Third-day I went to Kendal, and, in the evening, with very little notice, we met with several hundreds of people, Friends and others; it was a surprise to me, I expected but a few, because of the shortness of time; but I acknowledge it was a pleasant surprise, to see the willingness and readiness of the people to hear the gospel preached. Friends here are a great people, and well beloved and esteemed by their neighbours, and live in much love and unity. The Fourth-day many Friends came to see me from divers parts, I giving them some notice that I designed no further northward, and hastening to get ready to go to America betimes in the spring, having been from home near two years; wherefore divers of my friends, some of whom had been at sea with me, met me here. We rejoiced to see one another, and, after a large and good meeting, we took a solemn farewell, divers of us never expecting to see each other any more.

In this journey and travel I endeavoured to be, as much as I well could, at such meetings as I had never been at before, and because I was short in this visit to my friends, some were not so well pleased; but my call was most to the American shore, where I thought my service mostly lay, and in order to return I set my face towards London, and expected to meet with my friend and brother in Christ, Isaac Pickerell, in Cheshire, who designed to accompany me towards the south; wherefore I went from Kendal to Lancaster, and was at Penketh on a First-day, being the 16th of the Ninth Month, which meeting was large and solid; after this meeting we went to

Sutton, were I met with Isaac Pickerell; also with our ancient friend, James Dickinson, and Christopher Wilson, a choice young man, his fellow-labourer. We had meetings at Sutton, New Town, Chester, and Shrewsbury: James Dickinson was about four-score years of age, and yet held out in travels to admiration, and was lively in preaching the gospel: he is a worthy elder, of whose company I was joyful. At Shrewsbury we parted, and Isaac and I went to Colebrook, where, on a First-day, we had a solid, good meeting; from thence we went to Stourbridge, and after having a meeting there, we had another at Broomsgrove, and so went on to Worcester, where we had divers large and solemn meetings; we lodged at John Corbyn's, who was very kind to us, as also were his hopeful children, and in great love and unity we both met and parted. From Worcester we went to Evesham, where we had two meetings, and from thence to Oddington, and had a large evening-meeting; the people, who were mostly of other societies, were very sober, and gave good attention; this was the Fourth-day of the week; Fifth-day we had a meeting at Charlbury, and a tender time with a Friend very weak at Wallingford, who expressed his satisfaction and thankfulness for the visit; his children were very tenderly affected also. The good Lord, the great Physician of value, was with us, and his balsamic grace was at that time shed abroad in our hearts. From Wallingford we went to Reading, where my good companion and fellow-traveller Isaac Pickerell dwelt; we were lovingly received by our friends; I staid here and rested several days and had several satisfactory meetings with Friends, they being a large people, living much in love and good will;

here Samuel Thornton, of Edmonton, my kinsman, and Isaac Brown, my wife's son, came to see me from London. From Reading, Isaac Pickerell accompanied me to Maidenhead, and to Jordans, at both which places we had meetings. The house and burying-ground at Jordans, are kept in the neatest order I ever saw, in which ground lie the bones of divers worthy Friends, Isaac Penington, William Penn, Thomas Ellwood, George Bowles, and their wives, as I remember. This meeting is often, if not mostly kept in silence, yet several have been convinced there through the grace of God, and the power of the Holy Ghost, which Christ said he would send to the true believers, and that should abide with the church for ever. Here my beloved friend Isaac and I parted in much love, having good desires for each other's welfare. From Jordans I went with my kinsman to my brother's at Edmonton, where I staid and rested a few days from travelling.

Then a concern came upon me to visit Friends' meetings in the county of Essex, and I went from my brother's to Hertford, and had several meetings there; and one I had also at Ware, which was very large. After which I went to Hertford again, I having divers relations there: from thence I went to Bishop's Stortford, where I had a meeting, and so on to Stebbing, where I had a large meeting; and had a meeting at Braintree, Coggeshall, and a large meeting on a First-day at Halstead, and there was abundance of people at Colne, at an evening-meeting we had there, where I met with our worthy friend Joshua Toft, and his fellow-traveller, Joseph Hobson, we rejoicing to see each other. From Colne, I went to Cockfield, which was a very small meeting; from thence I went to Colchester, where I staid several days, and went to several meetings, as at Rockstead and Manningtree, and then back again to Colchester, where, on the First-day I had a large meeting in the afternoon, and after meeting, divers of the Friends came to see me, and were for appointing meetings for me to be at, in the ensuing week, and desired to know my mind therein. After a little pause I told them, I found a full stop in my mind from going to any more meetings at present, and that I would wait some days with them in the city [town,] till I saw further. While we were sitting together, a letter came to me from London, that a Friend, Stephen Payton, had set up my name on the Exchange in London, as master of the *Barbadoes Packet*, which was the vessel bought of me by John Agar, who sold her to the said Stephen Payton, who intended her for Philadelphia, and next morning a messenger was sent for me from London. Thus having such a favourable opportunity of returning home, I embraced it, and went on Second-day to Witham, where I again met with Joshua Toft, and Joshua Hobson, at a meeting; from thence we went to Plaistow, where we had a meeting; and then [I] went to Bromley, near Bow, and was at Joseph Ollive's; had a meeting with his people and servants, which were many; several scores of people belonging to his family. I thought it was a good meeting, a Divine hand of love was reached out to the young people, and they were advised to give up their hearts to their Creator in their youthful days; after this meeting I went to London, and prepared for the voyage. When our vessel was loaded, which was chiefly by Israel Pemberton the younger, who went with us, as did our owner,

Stephen Payton, and Isaac Brown, and four of my kinsfolks, whose names are Freeman, with divers other passengers; in the latter end of the Twelfth Month, my brother, and his eldest daughter, Rebecca, with her husband, Samuel Thornton, accompanied me to Gravesend, where our parting with them was, as at Edmonton, very solemn and sorrowful, we never expecting to see one another more. From Gravesend we sailed the 3rd of the First Month to the Downs, and from thence down the British Channel to the sea, and were at sea above nine weeks, which we thought long, having many contrary winds; but, after we came on shore, we understood, that there were divers vessels that were much longer. At sea we had divers meetings, which were some of them to my satisfaction. I came very unwell on board, but, when at sea I mended; for which favour I am truly thankful. We landed all well and in health at Philadelphia, in the Third Month, 1736, where we were received with joy by our relations, friends, and acquaintance; it was much more so, because they had heard I was like to die, having at London, had a sore fit of the asthma or phthisic, three persons sitting up with me for three nights, who, I thought, would see my end: but the time was not yet come that I must die; though indeed death was no terror to me, hoping my change would be much for the better; for then I hoped I should be for ever with Him whom I love better than life.

CHAPTER X.

1736–1738.

AFTER SOME SHORTER JOURNEYS, HE ENTERS ON A VISIT TO FRIENDS IN NEW ENGLAND—ON RETURNING, IS ENGAGED IN A FAMILY VISIT IN PHILADELPHIA, AND IN OTHER RELIGIOUS SERVICE—JOURNEY INTO THE SOUTHERN PROVINCES.

AFTER I had been at home some time, I went to Salem, and from thence to Cohansy, and, in my return, was at Woodberry Creek, and had meetings at each place: and, soon after, I visited the meetings of Friends at Bristol, Burlington, Trenton, and Borden's Town, and, in my return home, at Middle Town; by the way, calling to see my ancient Friend, Joseph Kirkbridge, and the widow Warder; she was ninety-two years of age, and perfect in her understanding; she said, she did not know for what end the Almighty should prolong her days to that age; but she was satisfied in His will.

In the Fifth Month, I visited the meetings of Friends at Haddonfield, in West-Jersey, and at Newton, Hartford, German Town, Abington, North Wales, and Plymouth, and was divers times at Philadelphia and Frankfort.

After many exercises and large travels by sea and land, my brethren, and divers others, not of our

Society, expressed their gladness to see me, rejoicing that I was like to spend my time more on the land, hoping that I would go no more to sea; the which (God willing) I determined, having so settled my affairs, that I could stay on shore; and am truly and humbly thankful to the Almighty, that He, by His good hand of Providence, in His due time, had favoured and helped me so to do.

In the Sixth and Seventh Months, I again visited the meetings of Friends at Bristol, Burlington, Byberry, Abington, Horsham, German Town, Fairhill, and divers times at Frankfort and Philadelphia.

In the Eighth Month, I went to Cohansy and Salem, and was at two meetings at Cohansy, and one at Alloway's Creek, where I met with Edward Tyler, a Friend on a religious visit from Europe, and John Sykes, a Friend living near Croswicks, in the Jerseys; here we had an open, satisfactory meeting: from whence I went to Salem, it being their week-day meeting, which was large, and to the edification of many. I was also at Piles Grove on Fifth-day, and at Woodberry Creek Sixth-day; in which last meeting the obedient son was encouraged, and the disobedient earnestly called home to his heavenly Father's house. In this journey I had John Bringhurst, the younger, for my fellow-traveller; his father being unwilling that I should go the journey alone.

After I had been at home some time, I, with some others, went to the yearly-meeting at Shrewsbury, in East Jersey, which was on the 23rd of the Eighth Month: it was exceeding large, and the quietest and most settled meeting that ever I was at there; and many Divine truths were delivered therein. From thence I went to Manesquan, and had a meeting, and then back to Shrewsbury, and so to Middle Town, where we had a meeting in the Baptist meeting-house, divers of whom were there, and glad of the meeting ; thence came back to Shrewsbury, and had a meeting on the First-day, being the 30th of the month : from whence, on my return home, had meetings at Moses Robin's, Allen's Town, at Croswicks (where I met with divers of my old friends) Borden Town, and Mansfield ; some of which were large, open, and satisfactory meetings. After the last meeting, we went to Burlington, and next day came home, accompanied by Richard Smith, jun. After being a few days at home, I was sent for to Chester, to the marriage of John Lee, who had sailed several voyages with me. Next day I went to the week-day meeting at Providence, and on First-day was at Springfield, from whence I returned home. The 23rd of the Ninth Month, I left home again, and went to Philadelphia, and from thence with Daniel Stanton, John Easton, and John Proud, jun., (the two latter of Rhode Island) to Radnor meeting, and from thence to Goshen meeting ; and by the coldness of the weather, and crossing several creeks, I got a cold, which settled on my lungs, so that, in conversation, I was hoarse ; but I was helped in meetings to admiration, for which I was truly thankful to the Almighty, the great helper of his servants and children. We had an evening-meeting with an ancient Friend, who said she had above two hundred who called her mother, being her children by blood and marriage to the fourth generation : we took our leave of her, as never expecting to see each other more, and parted in tenderness of heart. One of this Friend's grandsons went with us to Concord, where, on a First-day, we had a very large meeting, and an evening-meeting at Moses Mendenhall's ; and the remainder of the week we had meetings at Birmingham, Kennet, New Garden, Marlborough, and the monthly meeting at Center, on the Seventh-day following, at which were many young people, for whose sakes I was drawn and moved, in my exercise of ministry, to shew the rise and design of our meetings of discipline :—

First, That the same power that gathered us to be a people, inclined our elders to establish those meetings, and settled them in most parts where we were gathered, and had meetings for the worship of God.

Secondly, They were advised to do their business, and speak to their affairs, in the sense of the same power, spirit, and wisdom of Christ, which, as it had raised us, would, as we kept to it, preserve us to be a people to the praise of God's holy name.

Thirdly, They were advised, in doing their business, not to run out into many unnecessary words, which might lead to contention, and spending much time to little purpose : religious affairs being done best in a meek and quiet spirit, that being of great price with the Lord ; great evils having been known in many ages, through hot and long contentions about religion. It is also good to avoid, in matters of difference, respect of persons, on account of being acquainted or related ; so as to be swayed thereby from justice.

Fourthly, They were advised to be very careful of giving any just occasion of offence to any, to Jew or Gentile, to Indian or Negro ; for, Woe to them, says our Saviour, by whom offences come ; and if any will take offence when none is justly given, it is the best way to be patient, and to take our Saviour for our example, who got the victory through suffering; a safe way, and glorious in the end. And, as to few words, ——— Let your words be few and savoury, seasoned with grace, that they may administer grace to the hearers.

Fifthly, I was engaged, for the sakes of the youth of both sexes, to shew them, that a material part of the service of these meetings, is, that care be taken therein to see that persons are clear of prior engagements or entanglements, in relation to marriage, and that they had the consent of parents, or parties concerned as guardians, &c.; and also, that they, and all that belong to our Society, walk orderly in conversation; otherwise they could not be in unity with us, or owned by us, as a Society of religious people. We do not own scandalous persons, nor admit them to be married amongst us, without acknowledging their faults, and promising amendment for the future, through Divine grace and assistance. Also, in those meetings, the widows and fatherless are taken care of, that they may be supported and visited, and youths put apprentices to learn trades, &c.

This meeting concluded with supplication for the rising generation, and for the king, and all his subjects, and with thanksgiving and praises to the sacred name of Him who lives for ever.

After the abovesaid meeting, we went to Wilmingtou, a new settled town on Christiana Creek, which I believe will be a flourishing place, if the inhabitants take care to live in the fear of God, and seek his glory, and the riches of his kingdom, preferring it to any thing or things of this world. We had a pretty large meeting here, considering the season (for it was very cold) which was held in a large house of William Shipley's ; but they are making provision for a meeting-house. From this town we went to Newark, and had a comfortable meeting at George Robinson's in the evening, and next morning set out for Philadelphia.

As it was now the winter season, and having been divers times at this season of the year in the warm climates, the cold was become harder for me to bear than usual, so that I staid in and about home pretty much, being divers times at Philadelphia, Frankfort, German Town, and Abington meetings.

The latter end of the Tenth Month, on a First-day of the week, I was at a large open meeting at Derby, in Chester county. After meeting I rode home about fourteen miles; but it was so cold, that my limbs were much benumbed, and were not fully recovered in more than a week. Coming home between Schuylkill river and Philadelphia, we saw the largest meteor that I ever saw, though I had seen many by sea and land; this was in sight almost a minute, as near as I could guess; it was a mighty stream, like a flame of fire, leaving, as it were, sparks of fire behind it, as it went along, and then settled like a star, and disappeared. A few days after this meteor, there appeared in the sky an uncommon redness, with streams like fire.

About this time was buried at Frankfort, John Hurford, who was about ninety years of age; at whose burial, the coldness of the season considered, were a pretty many Friends, neighbours, and relations, of the deceased; as also divers from Philadelphia. I was concerned to advise those present, to prepare for their final change, that being certain, though the time is uncertain, which generally none know but the Almighty; therefore we ought always to be preparing for our dissolution, and always watching and praying, lest we enter into temptation; as said our dear Lord, "If the good man of the house had known what hour the thief would come, he would have watched," Luke xii. 39. And we not knowing whether death would come in our youth, or middle, or old age, therefore, were earnestly desired to prepare our hearts to meet death, so that we might dwell with God and Christ in his kingdom for ever. It was also observed, that though this Friend had lived to a great age, yet that few lived so long, no, not one in a thousand, and many die very young; therefore they were earnestly entreated, in the love of God, through Christ, to prepare for their latter end, and not to set their hearts and affections on things below; for, by how much they set their hearts and affections on natural or outward things and objects, by so much the harder it would be to part with them, when death should come. This meeting ended with prayer for reformation, and preservation to the end of life; and praises, yea, high praises, were given to Him, who had given to all present our life, our breath, and our being.

It being exceeding severe weather, with much rain, wind, and snow, there were great floods, so that we could not get over Frankfort Creek to meeting; wherefore the Friends on the west side met together at my house, and we had a satisfactory, good meeting, in which we were exhorted to build our religion on the sure foundation, that storms, rain, or winds, might not be able to shake us from this foundation, which is Christ, the Rock of ages.

This winter we were visited at Frankfort with the small-pox, of which many died at Philadelphia, and several in our neighbourhood.

The latter part of this winter, staying much at home, I spent my time much in reading and writing, often being sensible of the love and goodness of God, my exceeding great reward; he, by the Spirit of his Son, comforting me, and sometimes melting my heart into tenderness, in consideration of his many mercies, which caused me to praise his holy name, who is thereof worthy, beyond expression, for ever.

In the First Month, I went with my friend John Oxley, of Barbadoes, to Bristol, where we had a large meeting; thence went over the river Delaware to Burlington quarterly-meeting; we were obliged to get to the Jersey shore on the ice, laying boards thereon for about a hundred yards together, and being long on the ice, and poorly as to health, I took such a cold that I could not get to meeting next day; but was at the youths' meeting Third-day following. Fourth-day I went to Ancocas meeting, thence to a large meeting at Mount Holly, where was a marriage; afterwards at Evesham and Upper Springfield, or Hanover, and then returned to Burlington, and next day was at the monthly-meeting there, which, to me, was a good, open meeting; wherein church discipline was somewhat treated of, and Friends advised to wait for that Spirit which leads into all truth, to guide them in their discipline.

In the Second Month, 1737, I went to Cohansy, in order to negotiate some affairs there, and, while there, had three meetings at Greenwich, and one at Alloway's Creek; and on the 9th of the said month, being First-day, was at Salem meeting, which was large and open; and in the evening, we had a heavenly meeting at Bartholomew Wyat's.

After my return from Salem, on the 1st of the Third Month, I took a journey to the eastward, having a desire to see Friends in those parts, whom I had divers times visited, in the service of the gospel, in my young years; and though now upwards of threescore years of age, was willing to visit them once more before I died: who, in some places, where I had formerly travelled, were now grown very numerous. I set out with Joseph Gilbert, and several other Friends, and we travelled together to Long Island, where we parted, and I went to Newtown, where I met with John Fothergill and Samuel Browne; at which place we had a meeting, which was appointed on John's account, and his service therein was to the satisfaction and edification of Friends. From thence, John went to West Chester, on the Main, and I went to Flushing, where we had a large open meeting; it was a solid, good time, and the sacred name of Him who lives for ever, was praised.

From Flushing I went with my old friend and school-fellow, Joseph Latham, to his house; our conversation was pleasant and comfortable to each other, wherein we remembered our walking to and from school, in the suburbs of that great and populous city, London; when we were beaten, stoned, and abused, only for being the children of those called Quakers: the priests, who had money for preaching, had preached, and printed so many lies against our Friends, that the common people were almost ready to make a sacrifice of us; they telling us, (when we pleaded our innocency, by telling them, we went quietly along the streets to school,) that it was no more sin to kill us, than to kill a dog. But now, through the grace and favour of the Almighty, we enjoy the exercise of our religion, according to our consciences, free from gaols and prisons, in which our primitive Friends suffered much : for which we ought to be truly thankful to the God and Father of our Lord Jesus Christ.

From Joseph Latham's we went to Westbury and Matinicock, after a meeting at Cowneck, and afterward to New York; where I had also religious service, and a meeting; and from New York I took my passage in Robert Browne's sloop for Newport, on Rhode Island, was two days and nights on the water, and on my arrival at Rhode Island, the brethren lovingly received me, and we were joyful to see each other.

After having had divers good meetings on Rhode Island, I went to Dartmouth, where we had a large, serviceable meeting, at a place called Ponyganset; many hundreds being added to the church since I first visited those parts. From this place I went to Holder Slocum's, and he lent us his shallop to go over to Nantucket, but the wind not favouring, we had a satisfactory meeting at a large farm of his on an island bearing his own name, and after meeting set sail for Nantucket, had several large meetings there, and I rejoiced to see the growth and increase of Friends on this island; where God hath greatly multiplied his people, and made them honourable: glory to his name for ever.

The priests, who have money for preaching; the lawyers, who have it for pleading; and the physicians, who have money for giving receipts for health, are poor trades here on this island.

At Nantucket I had been about thirty-nine years before, at which time there were only two men and one woman who joined with our Friends in profession, and now it was computed there were above one thousand who went to our meetings, they being a sober, religious people; and there is a great increase of Friends in divers other places in New England: and whereas formerly we were greatly persecuted for our religion, now we are treated with more civility and respect in those parts.

From Nantucket, Nathaniel Starbuck and Elijah Collins went with me, with several other Friends, to the yearly-meeting at Rhode Island; which was so very large, that it was difficult to speak so as to be heard all over the meeting; but the last day of the meeting, our friend John Fothergill, who had a high voice, being attended with the Divine Power, gave good satisfaction to the meeting, and it ended well. After this meeting was over, I went with Benjamin Bagnal to Boston, and from thence to Lynn and Salem, had several satisfactory meetings, which tended to the uniting our hearts together in the love of Christ, and the fellowship of his gospel. From Salem I went with Zaccheus Collins and his wife to their house, and lodged there three nights, and was lovingly entertained, as I was also at many other Friends' houses. From Lynn, Zaccheus Collins accompanied me to Boston, where we had a meeting on a Fourth-day of the week, and the next day there was a very large meeting, (the greatest gathering of people which had been seen there at Friends' meeting-house for a long time,) occasioned by the marriage of John Miffin, of Philadelphia, to Benjamin Bagnal's eldest daughter.

From Boston I returned to Rhode Island, and had divers meetings at Newport and Portsmouth, wherein our hearts were made glad in Christ, and we were strengthened in our faith in him; blessed be his holy Name for ever.

From Rhode Island I went to Conanicut, and from thence over to Kingston, in the Narraganset country, and had meetings, and then back to Rhode Island again, and thence by water in company with divers Friends to Greenwich, where I was at two large meetings: at this place they shewed me the trees, under which, about forty years since, I had a meeting; but now they have a pleasant meeting-house.

The next First-day, I was at a large, solid, edifying meeting, in a new meeting-house at Tiverton. From thence I went to visit Joseph Wanton's wife, who had been long sick; and in her chamber, with several of her friends and relations, I had divers religious seasons, with which she expressed much satisfaction: she died of the sickness, and I was at her burial, which was large, she being well known and well beloved. The next day was at an appointed meeting at Portsmouth, which was large, and to satisfaction, for which we blessed the holy name of God. I had divers good opportunities at Rhode Island, in private families, and was at several meetings over the beach at John Easton's, who was about ninety years of age: he had formerly travelled with me, when I was a young man. We took leave of each other, never expecting to meet more in this world.

Now, after divers meetings on Rhode Island, I took my passage for Long Island, in my return homeward, and, after a boisterous passage, and being four nights on the water, I got well again to my loving friend Joseph Latham's, where I had left my horse, and on Fifth-day had a meeting at Cowneck, where I met with Elijah Collins, Rose Tibbets, and Patience Barker, we rejoicing to see each other, after their long journey by land, and mine by water, they being likewise going for Pennsylvania. These Friends went to Flushing First-day meeting, and I went to Westbury, where was a large meeting, in which there was a drunken school-master who disturbed the meeting, though at last it ended quietly, and I hope well also. The next Fourth-day was at the monthly-meeting at Westbury, where many Friends met from divers quarters, and it was a solid good time. We had a meeting at Thomas Rodman's who was unwell, and had not been at a meeting for some months; he took our visit kindly, expressing his love to us: we had also a meeting at Jeremiah Williams's, to good satisfaction. Fifth-day we had a large gathering at Matinicock, and in the evening a tender broken meeting at Samuel Underhill's, and Sixth-day a good meeting at Newton, wherein primitive Christianity was opened, and experimentally declared to the people, and in the evening we had a good opportunity to declare the truth of Christ at the house of Richard Hallet, among several of his sober neighbours; next morning, being the seventh of the week, we went to West Chester, to a yearly-meeting, which was much crowded, and the people very unsettled, so that it was not so satisfactory as could have been desired. After meeting we went over again to Long Island, and then to New York, where we had a large quiet meeting in the evening. At New York, Third-day in the morning, divers dear and loving Friends accompanied us to the water-side, where we solemnly took leave of one another in the love of Christ, and in the fellowship of his gospel, some of us not expecting to see each other any more, and from thence passing over Long and Staten Islands, to Elizabeth Town, we travelled to Raway, and had a meeting at Friend —— Shotwell's, on a Fourth-day in the evening, where many neighbours came in, and after meeting a certain person was dissatisfied about women's public speaking in religious meetings, (Rose Tibbets having publicly exhorted them in this meeting to be religious and to fear God, and having prayed to God for us all, and praised his holy name,) which said person desired we would endeavour to satisfy him about it, inasmuch as the apostle Paul forbad it, as he apprehended. To which it was answered, that the apostle Paul only forbad, or did not permit, forward or overbusy women to speak or ask questions in the church; but advised them to ask their husbands at home, and that doubtless he never intended to debar such godly women, who had a real necessity laid on them, and were concerned, by the Almighty, to speak unto, or pray for the people, else he would not have shewed them, how they ought to behave themselves in their speaking unto, or praying for the people or church; for if he had any design to hinder such, whom the Almighty should concern, then he must have contradicted himself (where he shews how they must behave themselves in their duty of speaking or praying) and he would likewise thereby have opposed the apostle Peter, who said, Now is fulfilled the prophecy of the prophet Joel, that in the latter days sons and daughters should prophecy. So that it is clear and plain, they who would limit or silence those who have a gift from God to preach or pray in public, from the words of the apostle Paul, oppose him to himself, and to the apostle Peter, and also to the prophet Joel.

From Raway we went to Woodbridge, where we had a meeting, and there I parted with my fellow-travellers, having a concern, though much in the cross to my own will, to go back in the woods, to a meeting about eight or nine miles off; which meeting was much to mine and their satisfaction, as divers of them expressed. From this place I went to Stony-brook, had a pretty large meeting, considering it was rainy in the time of the meeting's gathering. At this place my son-in-law, Isaac Brown, with several Friends, came to meet me, whom I was glad to see, and went after meeting with them to Trenton, and next day to Bristol, it being their Third-day meeting, which was large, and after meeting went home to Frankfort, and there was lovingly received by my wife and family. In this journey I was from home three months and nine days, had fifty-five meetings, and travelled by land and water above a thousand miles; and I may truly say, that therein I was favoured with the Divine presence and grace of God by Christ in a good degree, and also with the fellowship of many sincere believers in him; which in my return caused my soul to bless his holy name, who lives for ever.

In the Sixth Month, after having had divers meetings at and about home, I went to Derby, Chester, and Newcastle, having meetings at each place; which was to the tendering of some mournful souls, and to the comforting and strengthening them. From Newcastle I ferried over Delaware river to Pennsneck, where I had a meeting, at which were several that had never been at any of our meetings before, who went away well satisfied. From thence I went to Salem monthly-meeting, which was very large, and thence to Cohansy, to the Third-day meeting, and staid till next First-day meeting, which, though small, by reason of rainy, stormy weather, was a very precious meeting. After I negotiated some affairs at Cohansy, I returned to Salem, where I met with my fellow-traveller, Elijah Collins, of Boston, with whom I went on to Philadelphia, and from thence home, having much satisfaction in this journey, in which I had nine meetings, and travelled about one hundred and fifty miles. I cannot be clear in my mind without saying, that I did not, nor do study what I preach to the people, nor did I, or do I receive any pay or natural consideration for preaching; it being, as I really believe, contrary to the doctrine of Christ, and his apostles and disciples.

This fall I visited several of the meetings of Friends in Bucks county, and the meetings in and about home, as at Frankfort, Philadelphia, Abington, Byberry, and German Town. In the Ninth Month I was appointed, with several other Friends, by our monthly-meeting, to visit the families of Friends in Philadelphia; my lot was to visit the upper part of the city, in company with Phœbe Morris, Hannah Parrock, and Daniel Stanton; in which service we were of one heart and mind, and we performed the said service in pure self-denial, and in the cross of our holy Lord Jesus Christ; and wonderful it was, how the presence and goodness of God went with us from house to house, and opened the states and conditions of the families to us; to the tendering of many hearts, both of parents, and of their children. We visited about forty families of our Friends, and the winter setting in, and I being but weakly, having had a sharp spell of the fever, we, by consent, were willing to defer the conclusion of this work, until longer days, and warmer weather.

In this month I was sent to, in order to be at the burial of the wife of Richard Smith, junior; she was a virtuous woman, and well beloved, at whose funeral were many of her neighbours and friends; it was a very solemn time, in which meeting, it was desired that those who had lost their parents would live so, that they might not be a dishonour to them; for it was observed of some children, after their parents were dead, they grew worse than when they were alive, taking undue liberties, which their fathers and mothers could not have allowed of, which was a sore grief, and trouble to their friends, and such as wished them well; wherefore they were exhorted not to do that now, when their parents were dead, which they would not have done, if they were living, which would be heavy on them, and tend to bring a blast on them in this world; and they were desired to consider, how they would answer it in the world to come. It was also observed, that sometimes the death of parents had a good effect on divers sober young people, they being thereby led more seriously to think on their own mortality, and to consider the great loss of their careful and religious fathers and mothers, and the good example and counsel they gave them. This meeting concluded with a solid weighty frame of mind, in many. From Burlington I went to Mount Holly, had a large meeting at the meeting-house, and another in the evening at Mount

Holly town, at the house of Thomas Shinn; both which were open meetings, and divers people, not of our profession, were there, who were well satisfied therewith. From Mount Holly I went to Evesham and Chester, as also to Haddonfield, at all which places I had large meetings, and then I went back again to Burlington, and was at their Fifth-day meeting. From Burlington I went with Richard Smith, Caleb Raper, and Jonathan Wright, to visit a Friend who was sick, after which the said Friends accompanied me to the ferry; after I was over the ferry, I rode home, where I found my family well, for which I was thankful.

In the fore part of the Tenth Month our worthy friend, John Fothergill, sailed in the brigantine *Joseph*, Ralph Loftus, master, for Barbadoes, he having made a third visit to America from Europe, on a religious account. His visit was acceptable and serviceable, and we parted in great love and tenderness; the night before, about the eleventh hour, was an earthquake, which was the greatest known in this province, the whole city of Philadelphia being shaken, and most part of the adjacent provinces, though little or no damage done thereby, which shews the abundant mercy of a merciful God; as also, if it were the pleasure of his will, how soon he can lay cities and countries waste and desolate, and bury thousands in a moment. But notwithstanding the mighty power of the eternal Jehovah, oh, how hard are the people's hearts, and how they hate to be reformed, and how unconcerned are the inhabitants of the land about their eternal peace and well-being! This is really lamentable: oh! how do earthly-mindedness, pride, covetousness, and drunkenness, abound; with many other evils, which were scarcely known amongst the first settlers of this peaceful, and now plentiful land of Pennsylvania.

The 26th of the Twelfth Month, being the First-day of the week, was buried at Merion, Edward Jones, aged about ninety-two years: he was one of the first settlers of Pennsylvania, and was a man much given to hospitality, a lover of good and virtuons people, and was likewise beloved by them. There were many hundreds of people at his funeral. I had a concern to be at this meeting before I left my place at Frankfort, and before I heard of this Friend's decease.

The beginning of the First Month, being the fifth of the week, I was sent to, in order to be at the burial of Hannah, the wife of John Mickle, at New Town, in West Jersey. My kinsman, Daniel Stanton, was with me at this burial: it was a solid, heart-melting time, my heart was broken into tenderness, with many others. This deceased Friend was much beloved by her friends and neighbours, and there was much mourning among her relations at her grave, among whom she will be greatly missed. The people were desired earnestly to prepare for their latter end and final change, and that, as we had all reason to hope it was well with our deceased Friend, we might likewise have a well-grounded hope, that it would be well with ourselves, when we came to put off our mortality, and put on immortality. The meeting ended with fervent supplication for our future well-doing and well-being, both here and hereafter, and praise to the most High, who is alone worthy for evermore.

As soon as I returned to Philadelphia, on the

Sixth-day of the week, I heard of the death of Joseph Kirkbridge, at Israel Pemberton's, who told me I was desired to be at his burial. He, his son, and William Logan, accompanied me as far as Samuel Bunting's that afternoon, with which journey I was exceedingly tired, so that I could hardly stand or go when I alighted off my horse, but being refreshed with a good night's rest, I went in the morning to the house of my deceased friend. There was a multitude of people at the burial, among whom we had a good opportunity to invite them to lay hold of truth and righteousness, and prepare for another world. They were reminded that neither natural wisdom, nor riches, youth nor strength, crowns nor sceptres, would, nor could secure them from the stroke of death. Robert Jordan was at this meeting, and had good service therein; it concluded in supplication for the widow and fatherless, and for mankind universally. First-day being the 4th of the First Month, I was at Middleton meeting, in company with Thomas Brown, wherein the Divinity of Christ, and his being made flesh, born of a virgin, crucified, dead and buried, and his being raised from the dead by the Divine power, was largely opened to the people, and that the same power must be witnessed to reform our lives, and give us the true saving faith and knowledge of God the Father, and Christ the Son, and of the Holy Ghost.

This month, at our general spring-meeting, I acquainted Friends, that I had a desire once more to see my Friends in Virginia, Maryland, and North Carolina, if health and strength did permit, and Divine Providence favoured, I not having yet fully recovered my former health and strength, to which the meeting consented.

The latter end of the First Month, I was at the burial of Robert Evan, of North Wales; he was upwards of fourscore years of age, and one of the first settlers there. A man who lived and died in the love of God and his neighbours, of whom, I believe it might be truly said, as our Saviour said of Nathanael; "Behold an Israelite indeed, in whom is no guile." He was a minister of Christ, full of Divine and religious matter. In this month I was at Fair-hill, at a meeting appointed for Ruth Courtney, and Susannah Hudson, who were on a religious visit from Ireland, to Friends in this and the adjacent provinces; it was a good meeting, the Friends speaking to the state thereof.

The beginning of the Second Month, I went over Delaware and so to Cohansy, intending home before I set out for my journey to the southward; but my affairs not answering to come home, and afterwards to reach the yearly-meeting of Friends at West River, the which I proposed to our general-meeting; I now wrote to my wife and family, that I intended to procecd to West River meeting, it saving me much time and riding, and after having been at several meetings at Cohansy, and at the yearly-meeting at Salem, and at a meeting at Piles Grove; being accompanied by a Friend at Salem, I proceeded and went over Delaware river, and first had a meeting at George's Creek, and from thence to the head of Sassafras River, where we had a meeting, but by reason of the wet weather, it was but small; thence we travelled to Cecil meeting, and so on to Chester, where we had a meeting on First-day, then to Queen Ann's county, and back from thence to New Town, on Chester River, at which town we had a large satisfactory meeting, in which it was shewn, that no good Christian might or could break the moral part of the law, for it, saith the apostle, is a schoolmaster to bring to Christ, and that those who come to the gospel of Christ, can in no wise break the least commandment of God. As for example, the law saith, "Thou shalt not forswear thyself;" but if a man, according to Christ's gospel, swears not at all, then that man cannot forswear himself. Again, the law saith, "Thou shalt love thy neighbour and hate thine enemy;" but Christ saith, "Love your enemies;" the which if ye do, there is no doubt but we shall love our neighbours. Again, the law says, "Thou shalt not commit adultery;" but if, according to the doctrine and gospel of Christ, a man doth not look on a woman with a lustful eye, there is no danger of committing adultery with her, &c. Those things were largely spoke to, and opened in the meeting, and the people, there being many not of our Society, were very attentive and sober, and the good hand of the Almighty was amongst us in this meeting. From Chester River we crossed Chesapeak Bay, to the yearly-meeting at West River, with Chester Friends, in William Thomas's boat, and sent our horses over by Kent Island, to West River, where we met with our Friends, Michael Lightfoot, Elizabeth Wyat, and Grace Mason, with divers others, (Elizabeth and Grace being on their return from a religious visit to North Carolina and Virginia:) we all being far from home, and well acquainted, were glad to see one another, being thankful to the Almighty, who had been pleased to preserve us so far on our way. After the meeting was ended at West River, taking leave in the love of Christ of divers Friends, with hearts full of love, and eyes full of tears, as never expecting to see one another again, I, with my companion, and Armiger Trotter, who came up with the Friends from Virginia to West River, set out for Virginia, and having passed over Patuxent River, had a meeting among the family of the Plummers, one of whom, with another Friend, accompanied us to the River Potomack; we rode, as near as we could compute it, sixty miles that day; I being heavy and aged, and the weather hot, was very much tired, and laid down in my clothes all night, and the next morning ferried over the River Potomack, computed about three miles over, and parted with our guides. When over this river, we travelled about fifteen miles to William Duff's, had a meeting there, and from thence to a meeting of Friends at John Cheagle's, and so on to Black Creek, had a meeting there, and then went to the monthly-meeting of Friends on the west-side of James River, and so to William Lad's, after which we went to the monthly-meeting of Friends at Nansemond River, and from thence to Carolina, and on a First-day had a large meeting at a new meeting-house built to accommodate the yearly-meeting; it was a good solid meeting, and there the Friends appointed for us the meetings following: Third-day of the week, being the 13th of the Fourth Month, at Joseph Barrow's, Fourth-day at Jacob Butler's, Fifth-day at Samuel Newby's, Sixth-day and First-day at the upper meeting-house at Little River, Third-day at the lower meeting-house on the said river, and Fourth-day at Pospotanck, and Fifth-day at Amos Trueblood's, up Pospotanck River, and then we went to the quarterly-meeting for Friends in North Carolina, which was very large; the people were exhorted to overcome sin, as Christ overcame, that they might sit with him in his kingdom, as he overcame, and is sat down in the kingdom of God his Father; that subject was largely spoken to that day, and we had a good opportunity with the people, and the great name of God was exalted over all. After this quarterly-meeting, we had a meeting at James Wilson's, in the Barrens, which was a large, good, and open meeting; in the conclusion thereof, I told them, that I came among them in great love, (though in a cross to my own will, with respect to my age, and the heat of weather,) being willing to see them, in that province, once more before I left the world; and, as I came in love, so I parted with them; desiring them to dwell in love and peace, and then the God of love would be with them.

From Carolina we travelled into Virginia, Zachariah Nickson accompanying us, and had a meeting at the widow Newby's, and from thence had a meeting at Nansimund, and so to the Branch, where we had a very large meeting; many people were there not of our Society, and were very attentive and sober; and next day, being the Second-day of the week, we had a satisfactory meeting at Bennet's Creek, and thence to Chuckatuck, and so on to Rasper Neck, and then to Pagan Creek, thence into Surrey county, to Samuel Sebrell's, and thence to Robert Honicut's, had a meeting there, then to Curl's, up James River, to Thomas and John Pleasant's, had a meeting there on a First-day, and then to the Swamp and Cedar Creek, and so on to John Cheagle's. We came to John Cheagle's the 20th of the Fifth Month, being the Fifth of the week, and being unwilling to be idle on Sixth and Seventh-days, intending to have a meeting at his house on First-day, I asked John if he could tell where we could have a meeting on Sixth and Seventh-days; and he said, yes, he could. And he appointed one about three miles off his house, and another six miles off; at which places we had good service; and then had a very large meeting at his house on First-day, which was, I hope, to pretty general satisfaction, to the religious part of the people. From thence we travelled to William Duff's, John, and another Friend going with us, and had a meeting at their meeting-house, and afterwards William went with us over Potomack River, as far as Piscataway, in Maryland. This river is computed to be near four miles over, and when about the middle, there was a large swell in the river, so that our horses could not stand, and the motion of the boat made them fall down, and the boat having much water in it, being very leaky, she was near oversetting; they in the boat were in some concern and consternation, saying, when we came to the shore, that they did not remember they were ever before in the like danger; and I apprehended we were in danger, and if the boat had overset, in all likelihood, we might all have been drowned; and I then thought I was in the service of Christ, my great Master; and I also knew I must die, and I thought I might as well die in his service as my own; so I gave up my life for Christ's sake, and he gave it to me again. Oh! may I, with all those who sincerely love him, serve him truly all our days, is my desire!

From Piscataway we travelled to Patuxent, to the family of the Plummers, who were ten sons of one father and mother, who were convinced about the time I first had meetings in those parts, and, so far as I know, they were all sober men. After this meeting we went to Gerad Hopkins's, and from thence to Patapsco, had a large meeting, the house being full before the Friends came, so that they were hard set to get in; to me it was a good seasonable opportunity, as was our next in the Forest of Gunpowder River, where Friends have built a new meeting-house, which at this time, could not contain the people: from Gunpowder River we went to Bush River, had a good open meeting, and one at Deer Creek, and so over Susquehannah, to Elihu Hall's.

At West Nottingham I parted with my companion, he having about a day's travel home. I had two meetings on First-day at the great meeting-house at West Nottingham, which were very large, and Friends glad to see me once more: and after having meetings at Christine Bridge, Wilmington, Center, and Kennet, went to the quarterly meeting of ministers at Concord, and was there First and Second-day, and Third-day at Derby, all which were very large meetings, and Friends were satisfied and comforted, and I was encouraged in the work and service of the gospel of Christ. From Derby I went home, having been abroad about four months, and rode, by computation about eleven hundred miles, and at about seventy meetings.

While I was on this journey, I had an account of the death of my dear and only brother, George Chalkley, a religious, prudent man; he died the 24th of the Ninth Month, 1737, near the seventieth year of his age, and left behind him a mournful widow and four daughters, all virtuous women.

When in Virginia, I wrote to those of our Society at Opeckon, Shannadore, &c., (many of whom went out of our province, to settle in the government of Virginia,) to the following effect:

"Virginia, at John Cheagle's, 21*st of Fifth Month*, 1738.

"*To Friends of the Monthly-Meeting at Opeckon*,

"Dear Friends who inhabit Shannadore and Opeckon.

"Having a concern for your welfare and prosperity, both now and hereafter, and also the prosperity of your children, I had a desire to see you; but being in years, and heavy, and much spent and fatigued with my long journeys in Virginia and Carolina, makes it seem too hard for me to perform a visit in person to you; wherefore I take this way of writing to discharge my mind of what lies weightily thereon: and,

"First, I desire that you be very careful, being farand back inhabitants, to keep a friendly correspondence with the native Indians, giving them no occasion of offence: they being a cruel and merciless enemy, where they think they are wronged or defrauded of their right, as woeful experience hath taught, in Carolina, Virginia, and Maryland, and especially in New England, &c.; and,

"Secondly, As nature hath given them, and their forefathers, the possession of this continent of America, or this wilderness, they have a natural right thereto in justice and equity; and no people, according to the law of nature and justice, and our own principle, which is according to the glorious gospel of our dear and holy Lord Jesus Christ, ought to take away or settle on, other men's lands or rights, without consent, or purchasing the same, by agreement of the parties concerned; which, I suppose, in your case is not yet done.

"Thirdly, Therefore my counsel and Christian

advice to you is, my dear Friends, That the most reputable among you, do, with speed, endeavour to agree with and purchase your lands of the native Indians or inhabitants: take example of our worthy and honourable late proprietor, William Penn; who, by his wise and religious care, in that relation, hath settled a lasting peace and commerce with the natives, and, through his prudent management therein, hath been instrumental to plant in peace, one of the most flourishing provinces in the world.

"Fourthly, And who would run the risk of the lives of their wives and children, for the sparing a little cost and pains? I am concerned to lay those things before you, under an uncommon exercise of mind, that your new and flourishing little settlement, might not be laid waste, and, if the Providence of the Almighty doth not intervene, some of the blood of yourselves, wives, or children, be shed and spilt on the ground.

"Fifthly, Consider, you are in the province of Virginia, holding what rights you have under that government; and the Virginians have made an agreement with the natives, to go as far as the mountains, but no further; and you are over and beyond the mountains, therefore out of that agreement; by which you lie open to the insults and incursions of the southern Indians, who have destroyed many of the inhabitants of Carolina and Virginia, and even now have destroyed more on the like occasion.*

"Sixthly, If you believe yourselves to be within the bounds of William Penn's patent from king

* The English going beyond the bounds of their agreement, eleven of them were killed by the Indians while we were travelling in Virginia.

Charles the Second, which will be hard for you to prove, you being far to the southward of his line; yet, if done, that is of no consideration with the Indians, without a purchase of them; except you will go about to convince them by fire and sword, contrary to our principles; and if that were done, they would ever be implacable enemies, and the land would never be enjoyed in peace.

"Seventhly, Please to note, that in Pennsylvania no new settlements are made, without an agreement with the natives; as witness, Lancaster county, lately settled; though that is far within the grant of William Penn's patent from king Charles the Second; wherefore you lie open to insurrections of the northern, as well as southern Indians.

"And, lastly, Thus having shewn my good-will to you, and to your new little settlement, that you might sit every one under your own shady tree, where none might make you afraid, and that you might prosper naturally and spiritually, you and your children; and having a little eased my mind of that weight and concern, in some measure, that lay upon me, I, at present, desist, and subscribe, in the love of our holy Lord Jesus Christ,

"Your real friend,

"T. CHALKLEY."

After my return from this journey, I staid much at home that winter, travelling now being hard for me, so that I could not perform long journeys as formerly, being more broken in the long and hard travelling in this journey, than in divers years before.

CHAPTER XI.

1739-1741.

AT SEVERAL MEETINGS IN WEST JERSEY, &c.—VISIT TO FRIENDS IN THE THREE LOWER COUNTIES ON THE DELAWARE, AND IN OTHER PARTS—EMBARKS IN THE SERVICE OF THE GOSPEL FOR TORTOLA—ARRIVAL—AFTER A SHORT TIME SATISFACTORILY SPENT ON THE ISLAND, IS SEIZED WITH A FEVER—DECEASE AND INTERMENT.

In the year 1739, I took several short or lesser journeys, and had many meetings in divers places, as in Salem and Burlington counties, in West Jersey and Philadelphia, Chester, and Bucks counties in Pennsylvania; having many large and comfortable meetings, and some satisfactory service in divers of them.

This year the war broke out between Great Britian and Spain, the Spaniards giving great occasion of offence to the British nation; notwithstanding which, king George the Second sought to accommodate matters peaceably: but the crown of Spain not complying with the terms agreed on for an accommodation, therefore war was proclaimed; which occasioned much disturbance and distraction in our little peaceable province and government; war being destructive to life, health, and trade, the peace and prosperity of the people, and absolutely against the doctrine and practice of the Prince of life and peace, our Lord and Saviour Jesus Christ. A great concern came on my mind to promote his doctrine; in order to which, I was largely concerned to treat thereof in or at the general spring-meeting at Philadelphia; with which service divers wise and pious people were well satisfied, though some were offended.

When the meeting was over, I having a desire and concern once more to visit Friends in the three lower counties, Newcastle, Kent, and Sussex, among whom I had not travelled for near twenty years, and being now a little better in health than I had been, I set out from my home, and went to Chester, and from thence to Wilmington, and had a meeting there; and then to Newcastle, where we had another; William Hammond being with me, he and I went from Newcastle to George's Creek, had a meeting there; and then went to Duck Creek; after having two meetings at Duck Creek, I went to Little Creek meeting, and so proceeded to the Mother Kills, where I had a large, open time in preaching the gospel to the people, which divers of them received with gladness; and there were many, not of our Society, who were very sober and attentive, a door being open among them. Yet notwithstanding there may be much openness both in speakers and hearers, I have observed with sorrow, that there are but few who retain the truth so as to be really converted; many are convinced, but few converted and come to be regenerated or born again, as our Saviour taught.

From Mother Kills I went back to Little Creek, to Timothy Hanson's he accompanying me, and from Timothy's I went to Duck Creek, and from thence to Appoquinamy, to the burial of a Friend's son, who died of the small-pox; on which occasion we had a solid meeting, the mournful relations being thankful for our company. From Appoquinamy I went to John M'Cooll's, and from thence to Newcastle, where we had a large open meeting, to the satisfaction of divers; though I was very weakly and poorly, as to my health, so that it was hard for me to stoop to take any thing from the ground, and with difficulty I walked from the Friend's house to the meeting; but being helped by grace, and carried through the service of the meeting beyond my expectation, was, with divers others, truly thankful to God the Father, and Christ, my Lord and Saviour.

From Newcastle I went to Wilmington, had a meeting there, and from thence to Newark, to the marriage of Alexander Seaton; the meeting was uncommonly large, and to general satisfaction.

From Newark I went back to Wilmington, and from thence to the Center monthly-meeting, and so on to Kennet, where was a very large meeting: here divers who had professed among us, refrained coming to the public meeting for Divine worship; with whom, next day, we had a meeting, wherein the evil consequence of forsaking the assembling ourselves together was spoken to, and that it would be a great hurt to the young and rising generation, and themselves also; being a bad example to them, and contrary to the advice and counsel of the holy apostle, not to forsake "the assembling ourselves together, as the manner of some is."

From Kennet I went to Concord, to the burial of Benjamin Mendinhall, where we had a large and solid meeting, several lively testimonies being borne therein. This friend was a worthy elder, and a serviceable man in our Society, and one of the first or early settlers in Pennsylvania; a man given to hospitality, and a good example to his family, and hath left divers hopeful children surviving him.

The night before this meeting I lodged at the widow Gilpin's, whose husband, Joseph Gilpin, was lately deceased; there was true Christian love and friendship between us for above fifty years. When first I saw Joseph in Pennsylvania, he lived in a cave in the earth, where we enjoyed each other's company in the love and fear of God. This Friend had fifteen children, whom he lived to see brought up to the states of men and women, and all but two married well, and to his mind.

From Concord I went Wilmington, and from thence after meeting to Newcastle, where I, with George Hogg, went over the river Delaware into Penn's Neck, and had a meeting at James Wilson's; from Penn's Neck we went to Salem, and thence to Cohansy, where I had several meetings at Greenwich, and at the head of Alloway's Creek, also at David Davis's, where the people kindly lent us the benches of their meeting-house, and many of them came themselves, and were very attentive; after which I went to Piles Grove and had a meeting there, and from thence to Woodberry Creek, and so to Gloucester, where I ferried over Delaware to Philadelphia, and from thence came home, having travelled about five hundred miles in this journey, after which I staid at and about home for some time.

I was at the yearly-meeting at Burlington, in the Seventh Month; going to this meeting, my horse started, and threw me, which hurt my shoulder and hip badly, of which hurt I did not recover for above half a-year.

This meeting was very large, and though I was

outwardly in misery and pain, yet in the sense of the love and goodness of God, and grace of our Lord Jesus Christ, I was, with many others, much comforted in spirit.

From Burlington I travelled to Shrewsbury, having several meetings by the way, as at Borden Town, Croswicks, Trenton, &c. This journey I rode in much pain, but the satisfaction I had in meetings through the Spirit and power of the Most High, made amends for all the labour and pain I underwent. I bless the sacred name of God, and may I do it for ever! I made what haste I could home, being in pain with my fall, and tarried at home most of the winter, which was one of the longest and hardest known in these parts, by some of the oldest livers here; divers people being frozen to death in several places, and many sheep and cattle perishing, and much of the winter grain killed with the frost, so that there was some apprehension of a want of bread; all which I took to be warnings of the just and righteous judgments of God, for the ingratitude, pride, and other sins and iniquities of the people, the which I was divers times, and at divers places, concerned to put them in mind of. How well would it be, if the people would lay the judgments of the Most High to heart; and when his judgments are abroad in the earth, that the inhabitants would learn righteousness!

After this winter I was at a general-meeting at German Town, and at meetings at North Wales, Horsham, and Byberry, and from thence, with Joseph Gilbert, went to Burlington, and was at a marriage there, and then returned home.

In the Second Month I was under an inward

and religious engagement in my mind to visit the meetings of Friends in Gloucester and Salem counties, in West Jersey; and the 19th of the said month I went over Delaware River, and was at Haddonfield on a First-day, and Third-day at Chester, Fourth-day had a meeting at the house of Josiah Foster, and Fifth-day at Evesham; from which meeting I went to John Estaugh's, Ebenezer Large, and Samuel Jordan being with me. In the morning we went to Woodberry Creek meeting and next day down to Salem, in order for the yearly-meeting, which began on the 26th of the Second Month, and was an extraordinary solid meeting, the Divine presence and glory being richly manifested amongst us.

From Salem I went, in company with John Evans and Elizabeth Stevens, to Alloway's Creek, and Cohansy, where we had meetings, I believe, to the satisfaction of many; here I parted with the said Friends, and not being well, I staid at Greenwich, and they went to David Davis's, in order for Piles Grove meeting.

The 3rd of the Third Month, being the first of the week, I was at Cohansy meeting, which was solid and weighty; in which the mighty works of God and his wonderful power, was set forth to the people in divers respects:—

First, As to the work of the creation of the heavens and the earth, and of man to govern in the earth, reserving to himself the government of man; to whom he gave a law, for the breach of which he was turned out of Paradise, and brought death into the world.

Secondly, Notwithstanding man's fall, God had love, mercy and compassion towards him, and promised the seed of the woman should bruise the head of the serpent, who led them astray, which seed was Christ; whom all are commanded to hear, believe and follow, in the practice of his holy doctrine, which is contained in his words spoken to his immediate disciples and apostles, and likewise made known and revealed in our hearts.

Thirdly, That now in our day his righteous judgments are abroad in the earth, as the sword, and a threatening of famine, or want of bread. All which was spoken in the tender love and fear of God, and faith of Christ, and all were entreated to lay these things to heart, and turn to the Lord, and he will have mercy, and to our God, and he will abundantly pardon. In this meeting God was glorified, and His name magnified, through the assistance of the Spirit of His dear Son our Lord.

From Cohansy I went to Salem, and thence to David Davis's, where we had a meeting, at which were several people of divers professions, who were satisfied and edified therein: and thence we went to Piles Grove Meeting, afterwards into Penn's Neck, and had a good open meeting at the widow Hughs's, and so to Woodberry Creek meeting, which I hope was serviceable; after which I went home with my friend James Lord's widow, who, with her sister Ann Cooper, and Joseph Clews, went with me to Gloucester gaol, where we visited one under sentence of death for stealing. I asked him, if he truly repented of that sin of stealing, of which he had been so often guilty. He told me he hoped he had, and was willing to die. He was recommended to the grace of God, and to keep in an humble frame of mind, and beg mercy of the Almighty, for the sake of Christ, for all his sins. While a friend was praying by him, he was broken into tenderness.

Here the aforesaid Friends parted with me; I crossing the river Delaware to Philadelphia, and so home to Frankfort. I was at ten meetings in this journey, besides the yearly-meeting at Salem, and travelled about one hundred and fifty miles; but travelling was painful to my body; for I now more and more felt the effects of many old falls and bruises, which much disabled and hurt me in riding.

In the Fourth Month I was at divers meetings about or near home, as at Fair Hill, German Town, and a meeting at Thomas Roberts's; also was at Philadelphia meeting. In the beginning of the Fifth Month, I visited Friends' meetings at Derby, Merion, and Haverford; at the last place the meeting was large, and very open, wherein the mighty power of God was exalted over all, and it was plainly manifested, that if there was any virtue, or any good gift or genius in the creature, it derived its excellency from the Creator; and that man, in his best capacity, in either natural or spiritual attainments, hath no cause to boast or glory in any thing or things, which he, as an instrument in the Divine hand, might help to do or perform; wherefore we ought to humble ourselves under the mighty hand of God, attributing no glory to self, or the creature, but all glory and praise to the Creator, who is in and over all, blessed for ever.

The 20th of the Fifth Month, I set forward on a journey, in order to visit Friends at and near Burlington, and was next day at a meeting at Bristol, which was large, considering the heat of the weather, and the shortness of the notice; next day, being the

Fourth-day of the week, and the 22nd of the month, I was at Mount Holly, at the burial of our ancient friend, Restored Lippincoat: he was, as I understood, near an hundred years of age, and had upwards of two hundred children, grandchildren, and great grand-children, many of whom were at his funeral; the meeting was large, and thought to be a serviceable meeting by divers. After this meeting I went with a few choice friends to visit Susannah Fearon, who had been long ill, in which visit we were favoured with the Divine presence and goodness of the Most High, for which we returned him thanks and praise. After which we went to Burlington, and next day had a meeting, which was an acceptable opportunity to many.

Next First-day being the 27th of the month, we had a good solid meeting at Trenton; from thence I went with divers Friends to Bristol, and so home to Frankfort, and was thankful to the Almighty for the grace which he was pleased to bestow upon me, a poor worm; and that, considering the extreme heat, I had my health better than usual. After coming home, I visited divers meetings at Philadelphia, Haddonfield, Frankfort, &c.

In the Sixth Month there was a great mortality in Philadelphia, and many were taken away; on a Fifth-day, I was concerned to put the people in mind of it, and of their own mortality, and exhorted them to prepare for it, they not knowing whose turn it might be next, nor the hour when death might come to their own habitations; and was concerned, in the same nature, at several large burials. In the meeting at Philadelphia, they were told, it was better to fall into the hands of the Lord, than into the hands of men; and that since we had been settled in this province of Pennsylvania, we were preserved from the hands of men; there having never been an enemy in it, in a war-like way; our dependence being on Providence, and our principle against war, and against spilling of human blood by wars and fighting, according to the doctrine of Christ, the peaceable Saviour; wherefore I believe the hand of God was manifested in preserving us in peace: yet I would not be understood to be against the magistrates exercising the power committed to them, according to just law; but national wars, woeful experience teacheth, are destructive to the peaceable religion of Jesus, to trade, wealth, health, and happiness. Our dear Lord preached peace to the people, and against wars; telling his followers, that they must love and pray for their enemies, and rather take a stroke or a blow, than give one; and that they should not resist evil; which peaceable doctrine of Christ, the Jews could not away with; no, no, by no means: Oh, said they, If we let this man alone, the Romans will come and take away our place and nation; just as the people now say in this province, among and to those peaceable men, who for the sake of Christ and his doctrine, cannot use the sword: The Romans will come and take our country, if we do not build forts and castles, and have military preparations. And I wish it were not true, that some who profess this peaceable principle, too much endeavour to smother, stifle and keep under, this peaceable doctrine, through a slavish fear, and too much distrusting of the Divine Providence; which may cause the Divine Hand to deliver us to the Romans indeed; at which I should not wonder, since we distrust that Divine Hand that hath hitherto preserved us, without our preparing for war, above these fifty years. To which I know that it is objected, But now there are abundance of people who are not of that principle. I answer, Then why did they come among us, if they could not trust themselves with our principles, which they knew, or might have known, if they would? The king gave the province, and the government of it, to our worthy proprietor, William Penn, who was a man of this peaceable principle, for which the Heathens loved him, and honour his name and memory to this day, and those of his Society and principles, whereof I am a living witness. The sense of the sweetness and social life that the first settlers of the province of Pennsylvania and the city of Philadelphia lived in, makes me express myself in this manner. Oh! that the inhabitants of the city and country, did but live and dwell in that first love, and hold it fast; and then I believe that the Almighty would not suffer any to take our crown; which crown is righteousness, peace, and love, through true faith; which true faith works by love in Christ Jesus.

On the last day of the Fifth Month, I acquainted my friends of the monthly-meeting of Philadelphia, with a concern I had been some time under, to visit the people in the Virgin Islands, and more particularly in Anguilla and Tortola, in order to preach the gospel of our Lord Jesus Christ freely, to those who might have a desire to hear, as the Lord should be pleased to open my way; and my friends having unity with me therein, at their next meeting gave me a certificate of their concurrence. Soon after which, having settled my affairs, and taken leave of my dear wife and daughter, and the rest of my family and friends, on the 19th day of the Seventh

Month, I embarked at Philadelphia, in the sloop *John*, Peter Blunder, master, bound for the island of Tortola.

We sailed down the river, and came to an anchor near Christine Creek that night, in which there was a violent storm, which drove several vessels on the marshes, so that when the tide ebbed, one might walk round them. Next day we sailed to Reedy Island, where we waited for a fair wind. We sailed down the bay, in company with two sloops, one bound for Bermudas, the other for the island of Christopher's, and left the Capes on the 23rd day of the month, and in eighteen days from that time, fell in with the island of Thomas, and in one day more turned up to Tortola.

In this voyage we saw nine sail of vessels, but spoke with none of them: had a rough passage, the wind being high and contrary above a week, and much rain; yet, through the mercy and grace of God, I was preserved above all fear, except the holy fear of the living Lord, in which I blessed his holy name.

On the 12th day of the Eighth Month, John Pickering, the owner of the sloop, who was likewise governor of the island, with his spouse, met me at the waterside, and lovingly embraced me, and led me up to their house, and the same evening, had a meeting at his house; and on the 15th of the month, being the Fifth-day of the week, we had a large satisfactory meeting, at which were many people, divers of them not of our profession, and I think, the good hand of the Lord was with us. I was concerned in this meeting to shew, that the last dispensation of God to mankind, in and through his dear Son, was a spiritual dispensation; a dispensation of pure Divine love, which is to last and be with the true believers in Christ for ever, according to his own doctrine in the New Testament.

On the First-day of the week, and the 18th of the month, we had another meeting, larger than the former, (and the governor told me he had never seen so large a gathering on the island on any occasion.) My spirit was much set at liberty in this meeting, and great openness and brokenness was among the people, so that the gospel was freely and largely declared to them. The case of Cornelius, and of the apostle Peter going to his house, was treated of, with divers other matters, tending to edification. I was so affected with the power, spirit, and grace of our Lord Jesus Christ, that, when the meeting was over, I withdrew, and, in private, poured out my soul before the Lord, and begged that he would be pleased to manifest his power and glorious gospel more and more. At this meeting there was a woman who had suffered much for her going to meetings; her husband being a proud, haughty man, had beat her to the drawing of blood; he also drew his sword, and presented his pistol, with threatenings to kill her; but she thanked God, that she was resigned to lose her life for Christ's sake: this woman expressed some words in supplication in this meeting, in a broken manner. There was also another, a beautiful young woman, whose father had turned her out of doors for coming to Friends' meetings.

I went, with the governor and his wife, to visit a few families up the mountains, and had a meeting, in which was great brokenness and tenderness in the time of prayer.

On Second-day, we visited several families in the division called the Road, to which we went by water in a cobble, somewhat like our canoes; there were four of these in company, five persons in two of them, and seven in the other two. In this visiting of families, the people came and filled the rooms, and we had seasonable meetings, in which the people were so loving, and well affected, that we could seldom go in a friendly way to visit our Friends, but they would presently fill their little rooms, and we scarcely could depart, without having a time of worship.

Next day we went to visit a young man's habitation, who had not yet finished his house, and the neighbours coming in, as usual, we had a good meeting.

I cannot but note, that the hand of the Lord God was with us, and I felt his visitation as fresh and lively as ever, for which I was truly thankful, and thought, if I never saw my habitation again, I was satisfied in this gospel call, and religious visit; though, being in years, it was sometimes a little troublesome to the flesh, being in the 66th [*qu. 67th*] year of my age, and stiff in my limbs from hurts with many falls and bruises; but, as to my health, I had it better now, than for several years past; for which I am humbly thankful to Him in whom we live and have our being: glory to his name, through his dear Son.

Third-day and Fourth-day, visited several families, and had divers good opportunities; in one of those meetings, a young man, named Jeremiah Martin, spoke a few words in prayer; in which season, we were, I think, all broken into tenderness, so that in truth we might say, that the power and Spirit of

Christ was with and among us, and his great name was praised.

Fifth-day, being the week-day-meeting, it was larger than was ever known of a week-day at that place, there being divers Friends who came from an island called Jos. Vandike's, and many neighbours and sober people, who were very attentive.

Sixth-day, was at several people's houses, and had religions meetings, which we could not well avoid, the people were so loving and desirous to hear what might be spoken to them; they being many of them like thirsty ground, wanting rain, and our good and gracious Lord gave us celestial showers, which were refreshing to us, and thankfully received.

Seventh-day, I went, with several Friends, to the house of one, who, with his wife, had been at our meeting on Fifth-day; he kindly invited me to his house; his name was Blake, he and his wife were loving; though he had formerly written against Friends; he was now better informed. From his house I went to Townsend Bishop's, and there being many Friends there from another island, we had a most comfortable, tender evening-meeting; in which we offered up an evening sacrifice of high praises and thanksgiving to the holy name of the living eternal God, and his dear Son our Lord and Saviour Jesus Christ, through the influence of the Holy Spirit, one God over all, blessed for ever. And,

On the First-day of the week, being the 25th of the month, we had a larger meeting than ordinary; and, in expectation of larger meetings than usual, the governor, John Pickering, had made several new forms to accommodate the people at his own house, which he sent six miles on men's heads, the roads not being passable for carriage by carts, &c. This I think worth noting, that their zeal may be had in remembrance, and that others may be stirred up to a more religious concern, who will scarce go six steps to a religious meeting, or will not go at all. In this meeting I was concerned to speak of, and set forth the doctrine of Christ, which he preached on the Mount, contained in the fifth, sixth, and seventh chapters of Matthew; and to press the people to come to the practice of what is there commanded by the great Author of the Christian religion; and to shew that the despised Quakers had learned out of that excellent sermon, much of their religion, which displeases many people, and divers of the great men of the world; and to urge them to regard the grace of God, which bringeth salvation, and hath appeared to all men. In this meeting Dorcas, the wife of John Pickering, spoke to the people in public testimony, to which they gave good attention.

After meeting we returned by water from the Road harbour, to Fat Hog Bay, where John Pickering lives, being upwards of twenty of us in company, in three cobbles.

These two weeks I spent in the island of Tortola, to my great satisfaction.

[*Here the Journal terminates. The Supplement which follows was collected from some Notes transmitted from Tortola, by a Friend resident in that Island*]

THE SUPPLEMENT.

On the Second-day of the third week of his being among us, he visited some Friends in the neighbourhood, and likewise the man who had treated his wife so cruelly for coming to Friends' meetings.

On Third-day, he was employed chiefly in writing to his family and friends in Philadelphia.

On Fourth-day some Friends from the Road came to see him, which prevented his going out to visit the neighbours as usual.

On Fifth-day morning, being the 29th of the Eighth Month, he found himself much indisposed; yet he went to our week-day meeting, about a quarter of a mile. When the meeting broke up, he had a hot fever on him. Doctor Turnbull, the chief physician in our island, thought it proper to take some blood from him, and he being very willing, it was done that afternoon, and the fever abated some time that night, and the next day he walked about, and made no complaint until about eight o'clock in the evening, about which time the fever returned, and continued very severe until First-day morning; when the doctor advised him to take a vomit, which he declined that day, being desirous of attending the meeting, which was held at my house, and was a large, sweet, and tender meeting; in which he spoke to us first concerning temptations, and how Christ was tempted, and how to withstand them; and afterwards on the parable of the great supper, and other subjects; ending his testimony with the words of the apostle Paul, "I have fought a good fight, I have finished my course, I have kept the faith; henceforth there is laid up for me a crown of righteousness:" which words, and most part of this last sermon, were delivered in great brokenness; from whence I judged that he was sensible that he had not long to live, though, I believe, he was not afraid to die.

On Second-day morning the fever abated a little, and he complied with the doctor's prescription of taking a vomit, which seemed to have its proper effect; but that night the fever returned, and continued on him until he died; which was between two and three o'clock on fourth-day morning, the fourth day of the Ninth Month, being speechless about seven hours before.

A general invitation was given to Friends and others, to his funeral, where three testimonies were borne, all in great brokenness, under a just sense of our great loss. After which he was decently interred on the evening of the same day, in a piece of ground which is since given to Friends for a burial place, and on which a meeting-house is built, by John Pickering, the governor of the island at that time.

It is said in the Scriptures, That the righteous are taken away, and no man layeth it to heart; but, I hope, it may be truly said, this was not the case at this time, for Friends in general, much lamented their great loss, in being so soon deprived of so instructive a Friend and Elder, whose care over us was very great; and who, by his loving and exemplary life, and tenderness to people of all ranks and professions, engaged the love and respect of most of the people in the island. We are fully assured, that his labour among us was not in vain, and that many have felt the good effects of it; so that we believe some of the last words he expressed in public, may justly be applied to him, and that he now enjoys a crown of righteousness.

THE END.

THE foregoing JOURNAL *of the* LIFE *of* THOMAS CHALKLEY *forms the first Part of his* WORKS; *of which the earliest edition appears to have been one printed at Philadelphia in the year* 1749. *The second and only remaining Part consists of several Epistles and other Writings, the titles of which it may be acceptable to the Reader to be made acquainted with. They are therefore here subjoined, with their respective dates as given in the above-mentioned edition:—*

1. GOD's great love unto mankind through JESUS CHRIST our LORD 1697

2. Fruits of Divine Meditation, at Sea, in the year 1699 1699

3. An Exhortation to Youth and others, to follow; being part of a Letter from Thomas Chalkley to a Friend in Dublin 1707

4. A loving Invitation to young and old, in Holland and elsewhere, to seek and love Almighty God, and to prepare in time for their eternal welfare 1709

5. Forcing a maintenance not warrantable, from the Holy Scripture, for a Minister of the Gospel. Being an answer to some false and erroneous pages, written by Joseph Metcalfe, tending to stir up Persecution 1713

6. Some truly tender scruples of Conscience about that form of Prayer called the Common Prayer, as used by the members of the Church of England . . . 1717

7. Some Observations on CHRIST's Sermon on the Mount 1718

8. A Letter to a Friend in Ireland; containing a relation of some sorrowful instances of the sad effects of intemperance, as a warning to young people . . . 1718

9. A Letter to Aquila Paca, high Sheriff of Baltimore County, in the Province of Maryland, and to other Friends there . 1718

10. CHRIST's Kingdom exalted; being a short Essay, in order to promote truth and righteousness in the Earth, and to discourage unholiness, ungodliness, and unbelief 1719

11. Some Considerations on the call, work, and wages, of the ministers of CHRIST 1720

12. Concerning Personal Election and Reprobation . . . . [no date]

13. A Letter to Cotton Mather, in New England 1726

14. Youth persuaded to obedience, gratitude, and honour to God, and their Parents. Also, Some Touches upon the Life of Man, from the cradle to the grave . . 1730

15. Free Thoughts communicated to Free Thinkers, in order to promote thinking on the name and works of God; with a relation of a remarkable providence which fell out at Port Royal, in Jamaica, suitable to the subject: written at sea. [The Preface and Postscript by another hand.] 1735

_ *The Treatises Nos.* 1 *and* 7 *in the preceding List have been adopted by the* London Tract Association *of the* Society of Friends, *as two of its publications; and the same* Association *has also printed, as another of its Tracts, a* Memoir *of the Life of the* Author, *taken from the foregoing Journal. These Tracts are sold by* Edward Marsh, 84, *Houndsditch, London.*

Richard Barrett, Jun., Printer, 13, Mark Lane.

CPSIA information can be obtained
at www.ICGtesting.com
Printed in the USA
BVHW04*1017300818
526054BV00005B/62/P

9 780265 206508